For Alfred Dunst

Long time supporte

With best wishes

Alan Tyler

July 2007

# CHEERFUL AND CONTENTED

*'A cheerful and contented boy...'*

Dartmouth House Officer's report

# CHEERFUL AND CONTENTED

Alan Tyler

The Book Guild Ltd
Sussex, England

The Book Guild Ltd,
25 High Street,
Lewes, Sussex

First published 2000
© Alan Tyler 2000

Set in Times
Typesetting by IML Typographers, Chester, Cheshire
Printed in Great Britain by
Antony Rowe Ltd, Chippenham, Wiltshire

A catalogue record for this book is
available from the British Library

ISBN 1 85776 423 4

# CONTENTS

vi

# FOREWORD

*Sir John Harvey-Jones, MBE*

I am delighted and honoured to have been invited by Alan to write a foreword to his autobiography. The system at Dartmouth ensured that, in a service with a strong sense of unity and shared values, the bonds were especially strong between term mates who were of the same age at joining and whose careers proceeded in synchronisation. Perhaps this is the reason that, even though our naval and subsequent careers followed very different paths, I have always kept in touch with Alan and admired him enormously. The Royal Navy's determination to impose itself on its officers could all too easily produce a degree of conformity and the suppression of individualism. Not so with Alan. He was, and is, his own man and a very fine one too. Most naval officers were called upon to show physical courage – indeed this was expected and almost invariably delivered. It was in the area of moral courage – the rarest of virtues – that the differences between us all showed most clearly. The price of being different in pre-war Britain was high and clinging to your beliefs if they were not the same as the others demanded integrity and a willingness to go one's own way. Alan's faith, as well as his character, forced upon him more need to be different, and yet 'cheerful and contented' than most of us. None of us who knew him and served with him doubted at any time his total patriotism and commitment to the service of his country, but equally none of us doubted his quiet faith and beliefs in his Jewish background, which he represented with dignity and courage.

It says a great deal for him, and also for the Navy's belief in him, that he should have been so closely involved in the struggles of the handover of power in Palestine and the creation of Israel.

Alan taught me a great deal as a human being. He was and is a splendid representative of his faith. Never aggressive, always tolerant and always living up to the highest moral standards. I greatly enjoyed sharing his reminiscences. As one gets older the vividness of one's early experience dims and it was great to be returned once again to an age when we accepted unquestioningly the 'Great' in 'Great Britain'.

# 1

## *Not an Alien*

I was born on 2nd April 1924 into a well-established family of British Jews. Jews had been expelled from England by King Edward I, and began returning under Cromwell when the majority settled in London. Scotland never had many Jews, but nor did it expel them, and my maternal great-grandmother's family – refugees from the Spanish Inquisition – settled there when Jews were still banned from England. Later they moved to London, and were fruit wholesalers in Covent Garden when my great-grandmother Elizabeth Garcia married Lawrence Engel. His father Jonas – an umbrella manufacturer in the City of London – stated in his application to become a Freeman of the City that he was 'not an alien' and that his father was 'Pernart Engel late of Bavaria'.

Elizabeth died only a few weeks before I was born, having celebrated her eightieth birthday the previous year. A photograph of that event shows her sitting among her children and family – almost every one overweight by modern standards. On her right sat her eldest child Sarah Engel, who married my maternal grandfather Joseph Hart in 1891. He was the son of Isaac Hart of Stockton-on-Tees, son of another Joseph Hart of Canterbury, cousin of the Lemon Hart who gave his name to the rum he imported. Isaac married Louisa Levy of Stratford, after whom my mother was named.

My paternal grandparents Charles Lawrence Cohen and Amelia Levinsohn were married in 1883 in Merthyr Tydfil by the local minister assisted by Rev. Manasseh Cohen, father of the groom. My great-grandfather Manasseh had been brought over from

1

Poland as a boy by his father Eleazer Cohen, who settled in Cornwall. He was probably a pedlar, as his son's marriage certificate gave his profession as 'Clothes Shop'. Manasseh was the 24-year-old minister of Cardiff synagogue when he married Harriette, the daughter of Moses Moses of Swansea. Later he was for many years the minister of Wolverhampton synagogue, in which town my grandfather was educated. Manasseh, his twin brother Ephraim and another brother were all ministers, which was a poorly paid vocation traditionally supplemented by part-time trading.

My fourth great-grandfather was Benjamin Levinsohn of East London, a tailor who married Rachel Rubinstein and also became a minister. He served first the Merthyr Tydfil community and then that at Middlesbrough, where he died aged 38, leaving a penniless widow and seven young children. His community paid for his burial and contributed to an appeal, supported by the Chief Rabbi and published in the *Jewish Chronicle*, which raised about £50 for his family. With that nest egg and by keeping house for her brothers, the pauper widow raised all seven children to a healthy adult life. She died in her eighties, survived by her children, of whom two, including my grandmother, lived into their nineties.

My Cohen grandparents moved to London, and there my father was born in 1886. As the eldest son he was given the Hebrew name Manasseh ben Eleazer after his late grandfather in accordance with Jewish custom, and the English names Bertram Maurice. My grandfather was involved in a number of small businesses, and eventually took over a little company called Charles Tyler and England. Charles Cohen was so frequently called Charles Tyler by his customers, who assumed it was his name, that in 1912 he changed his name by deed poll, followed by his three sons. Partly this was to end the confusion, but probably also because the name Cohen – the Hebrew for priest – attracted much anti-Semitism due to the recently stemmed flood of impoverished Jewish refugees fleeing the Czarist Russian pogroms. They were seen as stealing good Englishmen's jobs, in the same way as recent coloured immigrants have been regarded.

My father's first job was as a travelling salesman for Raphael Tuck, who were a leading printer of popular picture postcards. He used to go off in a hansom cab smartly dressed in morning coat and top hat to call on local stores and wholesalers. It sounded excessively formal, even for Edwardian London, but so he always told us. From there he moved on to obtain agencies, mostly clothing and textiles, and adventurously travelled to China in the days of the last Emperor. His big break came when the Republic was proclaimed and millions of Chinese cut off their pigtails, a sign of servitude to the Manchu regime. They bought Western hats and caps to complete their emancipation, and his share of these orders established him in business.

Soon after the Boer War he joined the Militia as a volunteer, before the Territorial Army replaced it, but resigned in June 1914 prior to another Far Eastern journey. Out there after war broke out he joined the 5th Indian Cavalry, with whom he went to France as a second lieutenant. The cavalry were not much use in trench warfare, so he was soon moved to the Supply and Transport Corps to work in the port of Marseilles, where he picked up some very effective argot which he used in later life. He was then transferred to Egypt to join Allenby's army driving the Turks back through Palestine into Syria, and spent 1919 there as Military Governor of Homs and an acting major. I recently presented to the Armenian Bishop in London the embroidered handkerchief given to him by the Homs Armenian refugees in appreciation of his care for them.

His younger brothers Bill and Douglas had already been demobilised when he returned home, and in 1920 together with their father they formed Tyler Brothers (Eastern) Ltd to export textiles and clothing to the Far East. The three brothers went out in turn over a two-year period to cover the whole of eastern Asia. One covered the Indian subcontinent, one South-East Asia, and one China and Japan. They travelled out and home in comfortable P&O liners with cabin trunks full of samples, and by rail and sea from city to city, cooled by punkah wallahs wafting punkah hangings across their hotel room ceilings by hand-held cords. Gradually electric fans took their place, and my father did not wake up bathed in sweat to find that the punkah wallah had fallen asleep.

Meanwhile my mother Louisa Hart had been born in 1893 as the eldest child of Joseph and Sarah Hart of Canonbury in North

3

London. Joseph was a glass and china merchant, but the whole family went up in the world when Sarah's bachelor uncle Samuel Engel – a money-lender or 'financial adviser' to King Edward VII when Prince of Wales – died in 1907 and left over £60,000 to her and each of his brother Lawrence's other children. It was the equivalent of several million pounds today, and like winning the National Lottery. The family moved to a mansion in Eton Avenue in Hampstead and my mother was sent to finishing school in Brussels. She came back to the pleasant life of a rich young woman in the servanted world before the Great War, which is what everyone called the First World War when we were young. During the war she worked in hospitals, and her fiancé, like so many other young men, was killed in the trenches.

She met my father soon after his return from the war, became engaged, and they were married on 1st November 1921 at the West London Synagogue. He then took her round the world by combining their honeymoon with his Far Eastern journey. They returned with plenty of oriental souvenirs and mah-jong counters, and for pin money taught mah-jong to the bright young things for whom this Chinese game and the Charleston were the latest crazes.

My mother had received a £5,000 marriage settlement, a form of dowry administered by trustees to ensure that a dastardly husband could not make off with his wife's money. With half of this sum they bought a six-bedroomed house at 63 Exeter Road in Brondesbury, which was their home for the next 30 years. Homes were not then a profitable investment, and when they sold it in 1952 the proceeds had nowhere near kept up with inflation.

Brondesbury in Willesden, now part of the London Borough of Brent, was at that time the pre-Golders Green centre for middle-class London Jewry. My father's parents and unmarried brothers lived less than a mile away in Christchurch Avenue, where the family business was conducted on the second floor My mother's widowed mother and one uncle were even closer in Mapesbury Road, and a few years later both my mother's brother and sister and my father's married brother all lived with their families within half a mile of us.

4

# 2

## *A Willesden Childhood*

My first memory is of being taken into my mother's bedroom when I was nearly three – almost all births were at home in those days – to see my new brother Michael. I was not very enthusiastic, and suspect that I was old enough to feel that I would now have to share my parents' attention.

My mother's father had died the year she married and her mother when I was six months old, of cancer like her husband, so I only knew one set of grandparents, but all the great-uncles and aunts were on her side. Both my father's parents had come from Wales, leaving all their siblings and relatives behind, so the only ones we knew were my grandmother's niece Sairlie and her husband Barney Abelson in Kilburn. They had no children, and treated us as their family. Their warm lilting voices always made us welcome, and permanently coloured my feelings for Wales.

We rarely saw the Hart family members, except for my mother's Aunt Molly, who had never married and was helped out financially by her relatives. As against this, there seemed to be unlimited Engel great-uncles and aunts. It was many years before I discovered how they all fitted in, and realised that they were rather like members of *The Forsyte Saga*. They ranged from Uncle George, the brains of the family and a big man in Shell, to fat Uncle Leon, who had to have the turnstiles opened for him at the Zoo, and kindly Uncle Frank the stockbroker. His twin daughters Nellie and Anna were my mother's bridesmaids and are now the last survivors of their generation. They were named after

5

their childless aunts, Aunt Anna being the widow of the family solicitor and my rather formidable godmother.

Exeter Road was developed about the turn of the century and ran uphill from Kilburn and Brondesbury Underground station, which was actually in the open as the Bakerloo line came up for air at Finchley Road and continued north on the surface. They were all large houses by modern standards, with five to seven bedrooms and long rear gardens, but no garages as cars were an upper class luxury in 1906 – the date set in the brickwork of a nearby house.

I was five when my father bought his first car. It was an Austin with a kind of artificial leather exterior which gave off a smell in the summer and soon made me feel sick. It was kept half a mile away at a petrol station in Shoot Up Hill which possessed a long row of garages, and my father found nothing unusual in walking that distance before every journey.

We never considered anything but walking for distances of a mile or less, and I doubt if it would have been different if we had our own garage, since fresh air and exercise were unquestioned as the best treatment for children. A garage to us meant a place where cars were repaired, not where they parked. Cars were for holidays, excursions and my parents' golf club and evening visits. My grandparents also had a car, though neither could drive, and Russell their chauffeur was another figure of my childhood. Part of my mechanical limitations may have been due to my assumption that such matters were a technical mystery handled by others, since Russell maintained their car as well as driving it. It was a hangover from carriages, in which a coachman drove the gentry, and only the young tearaways drove their own carriages. Chauffeurs faded out during the Second World War, when most went on military service and people with a petrol ration had to drive themselves. Aunt Anna died of a broken neck during the war when her chauffeur braked too suddenly.

In memory our house was decidedly dark, with deep brown paint carried over from Victorian taste, and the dining room was the darkest and most depressing room I knew. Its dark brown panelling was hung with dull steel-engraved pictures, received as wedding presents, around a heavy dark oak table and scrolled chairs with wicker ovals in their high backs. The drawing room would have been better but for a conservatory beyond it which reduced the light. The room was decorated in oriental style with Japanese and Chinese wall hangings and paintings, tables, decorations and carpets. I was put off oriental art for years by a surfeit of it when young, from Burmese Buddhas guarding my father's pipe rack to Indian elephants progressing along the mantelpiece. Of the three living rooms only the small morning room, where we later on breakfasted and where my parents spent the evening if not out or entertaining, was comfortable and homely but even then not too bright due to heavy lace curtains.

Upstairs there were six bedrooms, one of which, opening off their bedroom, my father used as his dressing room and study. My brother and I shared another, while adjoining it was our nursery and playroom with the cook and housemaid's bedroom opposite ours. The sixth bedroom was at the side of the house, used by our nanny, and I never remember us having visitors to stay as there was nowhere for them to sleep. It was a sign perhaps of post-Victorian enlightenment that the servants lived almost cheek by jowl with the family, but there was only one, family, bathroom and the staff used a little adjacent pantry for their ablutions. I assume that they used the public baths on their day off, but, as bathrooms were only a nineteenth-century innovation for the rich, I don't suppose they felt too deprived.

We did however have no less than three lavatories, one upstairs next to the bathroom, one downstairs off the hall and one beyond the scullery for the servants. They were all long, narrow and unheated, and one did not dally there in winter. My brother Michael aged about two somehow locked himself in the upstairs lavatory by pushing the little bolt into its socket and did not know how to push it back. I remember him howling, people shouting through the door, and eventually the gardener climbing a ladder and getting in through the window to release him. The bolt was then moved higher.

We had electric light, though we could see when the walls were repapered the marks where the gas lights had been, gas fires upstairs in the bedrooms and coal fires in the three downstairs living rooms. There were also portable electric fires to take off the chill if it wasn't worth lighting a coal fire, and anyone our age will recall the pop as gas fires lit when one put a match to the white clay columns over the jets after turning on the gas tap. The gas fire used to putter and purr as it absorbed bubbles of air, and I remember that soothing noise as one went to sleep when ill, since otherwise it went off with the lights.

We also had a telephone. Gladstone 2097 was the number, taking its name from Gladstone Park, where we used to be taken for our walks. It had been the estate of friends of Victorian Prime Minister Gladstone, who visited them there. Telephone exchanges did not change names for numbers until the late 1960s, and it was only in the 1930s that dialling started to become automatic and you ceased giving the number you required to the lady operator when she asked 'What number are you ringing, Caller?' The old stand up and beg telephone of those days, with a mouthpiece on a column and a receiver attached to it by a cord, is now copied as a modern gimmick phone.

Nanny was Miss Florence Hawkins, a middle-aged Dorset lady who had been nanny to a number of naval families. She somehow instilled in me by a sort of osmosis a desire to join the Royal Navy, which was hardly a normal career for a Jewish boy in those days. By the time she left us, when I was about eight to my brother's five, the seed was sown. We always kept in touch and nearly 30 years later, when she had retired to Bournemouth and I was stationed at Portland, she visited the family several times.

Nanny used to take us for our regular walks to the local parks, and there I remember her reading to me the first political event I can recall – the abdication of King Alfonso of Spain when I was seven. It so impressed me because I thought that kings were permanent, and could not understand how a kingdom could overnight become a republic.

Other things also changed, apart from Alfonso with his Salvador Dali-like moustache. We used to enjoy watching for the lamplighter at dusk in the winter. With his pole over his shoulder, he would bicycle up to the big triple streetlight opposite us and trip the gas switches to make the lamps flare up. They were converted to electric at about this time, and the lamplighter came no more.

The jolly coalmen in their heavy horse-drawn wagon called regularly, with peaked sack headdresses like Armenian priests and

8

faces black with coal dust as they humped the hundredweight sacks into the coal shed. With them and all the itinerant street traders, the road was full of interest. There was the call of 'Any old iron' from the rag-and-bone man with his horse-drawn cart weighed down with household junk, the knife-grinder who set his wheel up on the pavement to sharpen knives and garden tools, and the chair-mender who would reseat a cane-bottomed chair while you waited. There were ice carts delivering the blocks of ice for the iceboxes we used before refrigerators became common, errand boys on bicycles delivering from the local shops, and of course the daily baker with his bread and cakes. The only one remaining is the milkman, who now glides by in his electric van instead of with his horse-drawn milk cart.

Like all children we loved feeding lumps of sugar on our flat palms to the soft muzzles of the tradesmen's horses. At intervals near street corners stood the granite horse troughs of The Metropolitan Drinking Fountain and Cattle Trough Association. Most local tradesmen still found it more economical to deliver by horse and cart than buy a motor van, and regularly paused for water at these charitably provided troughs. Most have gone now, or been turned into council flower displays.

The second Industrial Revolution of the last 60 years has mechanised or modernised so many of those jobs away – the telephone girls, the lamplighters, the coalmen and icemen, the knife-grinders and chair-menders and errand boys, let alone the millions of household servants employed by even the lower middle classes, and the millions of factory workers made redundant by faster and more automated machines. Locked into those changes was the Great Depression sparked off by the Wall Street crash of 1929, which I was too young to remember. It was only when I joined the family company and read the old minute books that I discovered how the family salaries had been cut by one third as early as 1930, and the reserves built up in the good years were almost exhausted when a gradual recovery began. It must have been a time of great worry for my father as the company faced bankruptcy, but I had no idea that anything was wrong with the business or the world.

I certainly remember the ex-servicemen wearing their medals standing on the pavement selling boxes of matches for a penny. It was a dignified form of begging, and people usually put in three-pence for a box or a penny in the tray and left the matches. Now sadly we have mothers with babies begging on the Underground and the homeless sleeping in doorways. Instead of buskers there were the ex-servicemen's bands, shabby bemedalled men walking the shopping streets in all weathers.

Surprisingly there was little crime or fear, and I used to be sent off to Potters the barbers in Cricklewood Broadway on my own, clutching my shilling, for an eightpenny boy's haircut and the other fourpence as a tip for the assistant. The barbers was old-fashioned even for those days, with shiny stainless steel towel heaters which belched steam as they were opened for the hot towels to be applied after the men had been shaved with cut-throat razors. A man's haircut was a shilling, 5p, about 1% of what it costs today, so a barber's wages must have been low even relatively, yet they were glad not to be unemployed and food and lodgings were low enough for them somehow to support a family.

Advertising like everything else was much slower moving than today, the same advertisements appearing in the newspaper for weeks, and in the case of the hoardings for months or years, so they had to be good. Among those which I still remember was the 'Bovril prevents that sinking feeling' picture of a jolly man in his pyjamas riding a Bovril bottle in rough seas, which seemed to decorate a bridge in Kilburn for years, and the poetic jingle that appeared on a board behind the driver in many of the buses:

> They come as a boon and a blessing to men –
> The Pickwick, the Owl and the Waverley Pen.

I was too young to have ridden on the old open-top buses, but they still had an open spiral staircase leading from the lower to the upper floor until covered ones came in during the 1930s. Destinations were on rollers, and the conductor used to turn a little handle to reverse the route, when they reached their destination at the Crown in Cricklewood, to show that they were heading back down Edgware Road to Marble Arch and the West End.

One big invention came into our lives at this time, the wireless. The BBC had been established in the early Twenties, and within a few years factory-made radios or 'wirelesses' became common, as radio became a mass taste instead of the preserve of enthusiastic amateurs with their self-built 'cat's whisker' sets. I remember a peculiar brown box suddenly appearing in the nursery, and being switched on at teatime for the *Children's Hour* programme. 'Uncles' and 'Aunts', as they were called, told us stories and sang us songs. Absolutely magic entertainment.

We were not a very cultured family. My mother had learnt to play the piano well as a girl, and there was a grand piano in a corner of our drawing room, but she rarely played it. This disappointed my father and us, but she was a perfectionist and gradually gave up playing, since she was not prepared to practise enough to maintain the high standard she wanted. They had no interest in opera or ballet, and going to the theatre was the limit of their activities except for the pleasure of dinner and dancing 'Up West' as the fashionable West End was known. That was all very formal, dinner jacket or tails for the men and long dresses for the ladies even to attend a theatre or restaurant in the evening. Our live entertainment was limited to a pantomime or two in the winter, and one disastrous visit to Bertram Mills Circus with my grandmother when I was about five and found it so frightening for some reason that I kept sobbing until I was removed and taken home. It was still the era of silent films in black and white, cartoons were just beginning, and the cinema was not regarded as a suitable entertainment for young children.

Nanny practically ran our lives except for the annual summer holiday, when we went down to the Beresford Hotel at Birchington in Kent for a fortnight. We used to enjoy beach games on the sands with my father, and shrimping in the rock pools and the shallows. We had been taught to swim at the Hampstead Baths near Finchley Road station, and I don't remember the sea as cold, although facing north near Westgate it can't have been a very warm spot, but there were plenty of children to play with, and lots of good food. The journey there by car, which we dreaded, took quite a time, broken by unsynchronised halts for Michael and me in turn to be sick by the roadside, even when my father changed the Austin for a more modern Rover. Still, there was the reward of meals — except supper — with our parents, instead of just Sunday

11

lunch when my father carved the roast beef joint and we were allowed the treat of a piece of bread soaked in the gravy. The rest of our meals we had with Nanny in the nursery upstairs.

Like most boys, my hero was my father, who was very much our role model. He was quite a short man at about 5 foot 4 inches, roughly the same height as my mother. At 5 foot 7 I eventually overtook them, but had only reached 4 foot 9 by age 13½ and was getting anxious. He was sturdy and bald, with a round face, small ears and a small military moustache, thick eyebrows and a hairy body. My mother's pet name for him was 'Monk', short for Monkey, and his for her was 'Monque'. Most of his characteristics have been passed on to his grandsons, and he himself was very like his own father, so the Cohen-Tyler genes must have been very strong.

He was a great extrovert and raconteur, which sadly skipped a generation before reaching his grandsons, but I inherited his short temper, which with both of us burnt out as quickly as it came. He was a great charmer with a wide circle of friends, and a stickler for honesty and good business practices. This paid off over the years, and Michael and I were proud to inherit and maintain the high moral standards of the company.

He was not a deeply religious man, but grew to love the West London Synagogue and its services. He served on its council for decades and eventually became a life member. He was Senior Warden, the equivalent of Senior Churchwarden, throughout the Second World War and its bombing worries, though the synagogue – an ornate Moorish-type building – was fortunate to escape with only minor firebomb damage. He passed on to me his delight in the humorous side of religion, and he and the philanthropist Leonard Montefiore used to pass each other *bon mots* across the council table when discussions became boring. I also inherited his love of Judaism and his refusal to take its restrictions too seriously. Jews in Britain were and are mostly Orthodox or traditional, in some ways equivalent to Roman Catholics in being strictly regulated. Reform, of which we were members, followed a reformed and relaxed traditionalism, rather like Anglicans compared to Catholics, originating in developments in Germany after the French Revolution and the release of the Jews from their ghettos. Finally there were the Liberals, who separated from Reform early this century to further scale down the ritual, and prayed mostly in English. Orthodox services were all in Hebrew except the sermon and the prayer for the Royal Family, but with Reform about half was in English. Reform and Liberal placed special emphasis on the prophetic messages of justice and loving one's neighbour, and tended to regard the dietary laws against eating pork and shellfish as sensible hygienic rules in the Middle East but a needless distraction in modern Europe, so bacon and eggs presented no problem at school.

My mother was born with an inherent dress sense, and was always beautifully groomed and turned out. We as boys failed to appreciate this, but my father was tremendously proud of his smart good-looking wife, and elderly friends immediately recall her smartness first of all. She was slim and handsome, rather than pretty, which fades with age, slim mainly thanks to my grandfather Hart, as my grandmother's Engel family all ran to stoutness and her lively younger sister Lizzie inherited that side of the genes. I think she always regretted that we weren't girls whom she could teach how to dress and groom themselves, and later tried to influence my wife – who had her own ideas. She was undoubtedly self-indulgent, as most girls would be whose family came into money and could suddenly let her have any luxury she wanted, within reason. Her personal interests and pleasures tended to come first; she was never very involved in children, her own or her grandchildren, and she could barely boil an egg. She did have a good brain though, headed a household fairly effortlessly, and in the Second World War ran the Women's Voluntary Service for the Borough of Willesden through the Blitz and the V bombings, efficiently and fearlessly. Like many others in similar positions she never received any official recognition of her services, nor expected any. She was generous, humorous and cheerful, with a wide circle of friends.

The closest of these in every sense was Sybil Snapper, who lived next door with her husband Ernest and children Vera and Leonard. Sybil was one of several sisters, with a younger brother Monty Birn, whose sons Lawrence and Stuart were later among our schoolmates. Sybil and my mother were bosom friends, who used to chat through open bedroom windows from one house to the next, and were both slim, good-looking and well dressed. Auntie Sybil was as close as any of our real aunts and took a great interest in us, but her children were just that few years older which made us out of kilter. Three doors further along the road lived Solly and Iris Davis with their three boys John, Peter and Victor, who were very much our age and more our playmates until they moved to Hampstead. When I married, I discovered that Solly was my wife's grandmother Davis's second cousin. Peter and I kept meeting when he was in the Marines and I the Navy, and we still see them all quite frequently. Across the road lived the Sussmans, with whom we used to go to tea. Decades later I met Ruth again, married to Lieutenant Commander Stanley Brilliant, one of the leaders of the Association of Jewish Ex-Servicemen and Women, and marshal of our annual parade at the Cenotaph.

We were closest of course to our real family, especially my Tyler grandparents, to whom we used to go for tea most Saturday afternoons when they kept open house. They were doting grandparents, showering us with love and sweets. They were both little people about 5 foot high – generations of living in ghettos on insufficient food kept most Jews small – but bubbling with Welsh enthusiasm and Jewish family pride. They had both come up in the world, and enjoyed having servants and amenities which they had lacked when young. They were really friends with their staff, especially Cassy the Welsh cook, whom as a treat we might visit in the kitchen for further spoiling. My father's youngest and unmarried brother Douglas still lived with them, and delighted us in summer by throwing tennis balls over the house.

As we grew older we used to go to my grandparents for Friday night supper, when the Sabbath candles were lit and the grace after meals chanted in Hebrew by the grown-ups. We also of course went there for Seder, the eve of Passover, for the traditional reading of the Haggadah and the festive meal with matzah – an evening that seemed to go on forever for a young boy. There I first read the Mah Nishtanah, the four questions about the Seder asked by the youngest present who can read. By the time my grandfather died I was 11, and Michael had inherited that chore in their long dark dining room with brass light fittings like great wheels skirted

14

with dark red curtains – a very odd and rather gloomy kind of lighting.

Down the street facing us, Saint Gabriel's Road with his church at the far end, lived my mother's sister Auntie Lizzie. We often went to tea there with our cousins Anne and Brian, who were a couple of years younger than us, and to watch Uncle Sidney Capper building a cabin cruiser for the Broads in his garage. He was a real craftsman and engineer, who had run the first motor buses in Kuala Lumpur before the Great War, but thanks to Lizzie's income could now indulge his hobbies. He smoked like a chimney, and reckoned to fit out his boat with the exchangeable coupons from his innumerable cigarette packets. In the mid 1930s they moved to Rapallo, where my aunt's income went further, and then to the South of France, so they temporarily went out of our lives until the war brought them home. Anne was my friend, the sister I did not have, and we still remain close though physically she could hardly be further away now, in Fiji.

I was page at the marriage of my father's younger brother Bill, and he followed my father's example by taking Aunt Phyllis round the world on her honeymoon before settling close to us and Lizzie in Walm Lane. He was a keen early cine-photographer, whose honeymoon film my cousin Bill has turned into a fascinating video of the world on the eve of the Great Depression. He used to delight us with his films of the family and his travels, even before we were old enough to be taken to the cinema, but died of acute appendicitis in Marseilles in 1934 on his way home from an eastern journey. He left a widow of 27, with a girl of two, my cousin Rosemary, and about to give birth to my cousin Bill. I was allowed to go round sometimes to help bath this adorable little girl, but fond as I am of Bill I never recall the urge to rush round and help bath him! He was named William Bertram after his father and uncle, and was lucky soon to outgrow the nickname Billbert which my father gave him, to my aunt's annoyance. Nanny Hawkins had moved on from us to them after Rosemary was born, and stayed on to look after Bill.

Opposite these Tyler cousins lived the other Snappers, Ernest's brother Albert and his beautiful blonde wife Gladys. Their children Babs and Royston were too old to play or come to tea, but the parents were all in the same bridge and partygoing circle of yet more honorary uncles and aunts whom it took years to sort out from the real ones. Our only other real uncle was my mother's brother Lawrence, who lived in a flat near us with his raven-haired wife Marie, whom he had met and married during a business stay in Latvia, and our cousin Denis. We rarely went there as the marriage was unhappy and broke up fairly soon. He went off to live with another woman as Marie refused to divorce him and remained 'faithful', hoping for him to return. We didn't see much of Denis until we stayed with his father in Suffolk during teenage holidays.

We did not see all that much of our parents, since my father was at work all week and just saw us before we went to bed, while my mother always seemed to be out shopping or visiting or holding her afternoon bridge parties. These involved two or three tables of friends in the drawing room, where we would often be called in to meet them and allowed a jelly from the sweet dishes on the corners of the tables before we were sent upstairs. The bridge tables always had ashtrays and cigarettes balancing the sweets and chocolates, since everyone seemed to smoke in those days, all my adult relatives as well as my parents, and children collected the cigarette cards that came in the packets.

On Saturdays we would go by bus with my father to the synagogue near Marble Arch for the ten o'clock children's service, and in the afternoon to tea with our grandparents, while on Sundays we often went to tea with relatives, especially Uncle Frank Engel and family whose large Victorian house rather overawed me.

We used the car to visit relatives and friends beyond walking distance, but usually only within a few miles, and I don't think we ever crossed the Thames into South London – a failing that still seems to afflict many North Londoners, now we live in the south. We made few visits that needed a bus or tube ride, so apart from the Saturday bus ride to synagogue, I scarcely used public transport.

A rare adventure was Coronation morning, 12th May 1937, when I woke early and set out about 6 a.m. to walk to Marble Arch, on the spur of the moment, to see the procession. I had failed to plan it the night before, or ask for sandwiches. I walked about 3 miles along the way before thinking better of it and returning in time for breakfast, and listened to the ceremony on the wireless in the garden. My parents were quite unperturbed, and said they would not have minded my going to watch if I had asked them. I grew up in law-abiding times when mugging and robbery were rare, but we did allow our 13-year-old David to go off alone to the 1966 World Cup at Wembley.

I was not very nice to my younger brother – it was discovered that I used to pinch his toes in the pram – so I was sent to a local kindergarten called Wycombe House when I was four and a half to keep me out of mischief and improve my behaviour. I have but the haziest recollection of it, and only stayed two terms. I do recall quite clearly Sunbury House boys' school where I went next. It was a large converted early Victorian house in Willesden Lane, run by a tall bald man called Mr Pilliner. As it was well within a mile of us, I walked there and back, and I must have enjoyed it as in later childhood it often featured in my dreams. My clearest memory is of a large school hall, and reciting part of 'The Jackdaw of Rheims' from the *Ingoldsby Legends* there on a Parents' Day. It was one of the first things that I learnt by heart, apart from my prayers, so I can still remember sentences like:

> The Cardinal drew off each plum coloured shoe
> And left his red stockings exposed to the view.

It was jolly Regency anti-Catholic doggerel I suppose, which would not be taught today, but we just saw it as a funny story. Our friend David Howard was a pupil there at the same time, although I can't recall him or any of the other boys or indeed much else, but I certainly learnt my multiplication tables and to read and write fluently before I left, at the end of the summer term after I was eight.

I was to go to boarding school.

# 3

## *Saint Michael's*

Saint Michael's was one of the hundreds of small preparatory schools which sprang up in the late nineteenth and early twentieth century to feed boys at age 13 through the Common Entrance examinations to the public schools. It had been established before the Great War in Tunbridge Wells, and moved during it to a large Victorian house at Uckfield in mid-Sussex. It took boys from age eight upwards, and there must have been about 60 in the school when I was taken down by my parents by car to join in September 1932. I was too alarmed by the thought even to be sick on the way.

I don't remember much discussion beforehand, simply being told that was it, although most of my friends like the Davis boys up the road went to London day schools. My brother Michael joined me three years later when he reached the same age; then I became Tyler I and he the lowly Tyler II. No family ran to more than III. First names and nicknames were only used by brothers or close friends, otherwise surnames.

The founder Headmaster was an Anglican clergyman, the Reverend Harold Hubert Hibbert Hockey. He must have been teased about it at school, but quickly initialled our set cards HHHH. The school was divided into sets, unlike most schools which call them houses – Elizabethans, after his daughter Elizabeth, Lions, Grasshoppers, Druids and Cingalese. How the other names originated was already lost in the mists of time, but we all received a set card booklet each term in a khaki-coloured cover with two weeks to a page and each day laid out for stars and stripes. These were awarded by masters for good or bad work and behaviour, gain five points for a star, lose five for a stripe, so the Headmaster could see and take action if we were running a deficit. On the wall of the dining room was a latticework of five ladders, up which models representing the five sets were moved each week on strings, according to the points gained, so our set progress was always before our eyes. Each boy of the winning set received a silver apostle teaspoon at the end of term, and my five still survive among our cutlery. When we won in Coronation summer, I was annoyed to receive a spoon with the profiles of the King and Queen which didn't match the others.

Mrs Hockey was an early Christian Scientist in this country, so quite a number of the boys were also Christian Scientists as their beliefs would be respected. I think there was no anti-Semitism, even though I was initially the only Jew in the school, because we were divided into those who were obliged to take Syrup of Figs medicine for our bowels' sake and the Christian Scientists, who kept regular by faith alone! Certainly in those days they did not accept doctors, except I think for setting bones, let alone medicine.

Mrs Hockey was very kind to us all, and one of my happier memories is of Sunday evenings when we went to her sitting room by dormitories in our dressing gowns to be read stories. Mr Hockey, who read to the older boys, was known as 'Mr Bean', a name handed down by decades of boys and now given a wider fame by Rowan Atkinson. He was well into his fifties and perhaps easing off a bit, which led to rather lax supervision as there was a certain amount of bullying. Two boys a year or two older picked on me and made my life a misery for some time, but 'sneaking' was such a sin that I dared not complain to masters or my parents for fear of how much worse life would become if I did. Since they attacked me without witnesses in the lavatories or grounds, it would anyway have been hard to prove.

My best friends were Gordon Chambers and Graham Pitt in my form, or class as we now call it, since even in our day we no longer sat on forms, which were school benches, but at battered desks with an inkwell in the corner. Gordon was a small freckled sandy-haired extrovert, Graham a dark-haired quieter type, both good at games. We progressed up the school together for five years, and

19

sometimes exchanged visits in the holidays as they lived on adjacent streets in Wembley Park with touching gardens. Gordon went to the training ship *Worcester* and into the merchant navy, and we kept in touch until tragically he went down with all the crew when his Liberty ship, mass-produced in America during the war, sank without a trace early in 1948 soon after he had been best man at Graham's wedding. I heard the details only recently when I met Graham and some of the others at a Saint Michael's reunion, and 60 years vanished as we remembered. All my form were friends, and amongst others were the Suttons and Frenches, who followed me to Dartmouth and whom I used to meet in the Navy. There were also the Birn and Barling brothers, whose fathers sent them there on my father's recommendation and thereby trebled the Jewish numbers.

We also had our nobility. The tall Earl of Airlie was shown round the school before his son David Ogilvy joined, followed by his younger brother Angus. Angus married Princess Alexandra, and David became Lord Chamberlain. I can remember absolutely no class-consciousness about their living in a castle or us resenting it, nor any concern or even interest in what parents did or how others lived. The only one who suffered was an American boy called Longyear, who insisted that his grandfather had founded Longyear town on the island of Spitzbergen in the Arctic. I think he probably did, which must have made it all the harder that we refused to believe him, especially as his father gave the school its first 'talkies' projector. Previously we had an old projector, which showed a weekly silent film or early cartoon.

We were also fortunate before my time to have had the Astor boys as pupils, and Lord Astor had given the school fives and squash courts which I much enjoyed. Ours were Eton fives courts with a pillbox, based on a game developed round the chapel there, and one hit the ball with a gloved hand. I preferred fives and squash to all the team games, but I haven't seen a fives court since I left the school so it must be almost as rare as the real tennis played at Hampton Court. We played football in the autumn term, rugby in the spring term – 'soccer' and 'rugger' – and cricket in the summer. There was also a .22 rifle range, and an open-air pool in the summer, so all we really lacked was hockey. I was never a very good games player, I think I rose to captaining the football Second XI, but it was compulsory to play or watch. I remember Sussex winters as very cold, with frozen hard pitches where I was tempted to funk a tackle. As it was a small school, more than half were needed to make up two teams for a midweek game, and being small for my age I did not enjoy the damage caused by tackling boys several years older.

We had regular matches against other local prep schools, the traditional rival being the larger Saint Andrew's at Eastbourne, which Mr Hockey had left to found us. It was always a triumph on the rare occasions when we beat them, but we were more evenly matched against Temple Grove and the other Saints – Anthony's, Cyprian's and Bede's. Schools were graded by us according to the standards of the teas provided after the matches. In my last term, with a team featuring most of my friends and with Graham Pitt as Captain, our football First XI won almost every match and even beat Saint Andrew's on their home ground.

When not playing games we went for occasional organised walks in the country on Sunday afternoons, but never got to know any of the local boys or to play any local government schools. Regrettably and snobbishly we referred to the local boys as 'oiks', especially those who played in the 'Rec', the recreation ground beyond the school playing fields. We also had a school Cub and Scout pack, and enjoyed gathering firewood and cooking beans and sausages over a camp fire. I earned a number of Cub badges for simple tests like telling the time or tying knots, but never became a Scout as they had faded out by the time I reached that age. Another activity was gardening; we were all allocated little plots to develop as our gardens. I can't remember any outstanding ones, but I toiled away at mine. The other practical thing we did was basic woodwork in the carpentry shop.

We heard in the spring of 1935 that King George V was coming down for a few days' rest with friends who lived near Uckfield, before his Silver Jubilee celebrations. The whole school assembled by the gate onto the main road, waving the Union Jack and our Scout flag, to cheer him and Queen Mary as their car drove by. The hood was rolled back so that we could see them clearly, the King in his overcoat doffing his hat and the Queen, bolt upright in her turban hat, inclining her head. A roar of cheers followed them along the road, and we went back to our lessons rather disappointed to have seen no uniforms or royal robes. The following January he died, just a few days after Mr Hockey. In December the Abdication crisis burst without warning, and within a week Edward VIII gave way to George VI. Three kings in one year.

Educationally we followed a fairly standard curriculum leading up to the Common Entrance exams. We learnt Latin, French, English, mathematics, history, geography and scripture, with a mid-morning and mid-afternoon break. Typically and regrettably there was no sort of science. Two afternoons a week, Wednesday and Saturday, were devoted to games, and we had chapel every morning before work and church on Sunday morning. Mr Hockey made it clear before entry that everyone in his school must attend the Anglican service, whatever their own beliefs. It did me no harm, as I mentally switched off for 'through Jesus Christ our Lord'. Certainly none of us Jews were converted, and it gave us a useful understanding of Christian beliefs. I might not have sent my children to a school whose motto was '*Per Christum Vinces*', 'Through Christ We Win', but it did not bother my father and I still find myself humming Anglican hymn tunes when gardening. When I became Head Boy in my last year I had the 'honour' of closing the chapel doors, and sometimes reading a lesson.

The masters were mostly young Oxbridge graduates, apart from the Second Master, Mr Gaze, who had helped start the school with Mr Hockey. He taught us maths and drawing, the latter a subject where he correctly found me somewhat untalented. Otherwise, though inclined to be careless, I was quite a good and intelligent pupil and usually near the top of the form. I was best at history and scripture, which was really only Bible history, and I still possess some prize books with the school crest. We had one gay master, who took us on walks to the summerhouse in the dusk, where he fondled and kissed us. We in our innocence thought it rather a treat, as he didn't go any further. Most of us I believe gained his favours, and for all I know it had gone on for years. Suddenly it reached Mr Hockey's ears, and he left overnight. There was no sex education in those days, not even a biology course. Nothing was ever said, but we gathered that such behaviour was unacceptable.

22

The only other sudden change was the death of Mr Hockey himself, after a short illness. We all felt as if we had lost a grandfather; only a few months previously he had broken to me the death of mine – of infection following a prostate operation.

The school carried on as before but with Jim Barber, the senior of the younger masters, as the new Headmaster. I enjoyed working with him as I neared the top of the school, and I am sure he would have been a continued success there, but shortly after I left, Mrs Hockey sold the school. The new owner Cecil Cook devoted his life to Saint Michael's, which flourished in his care but was evacuated to Tawstock in north Devon in 1940 and never returned to Uckfield.

We had long holidays, four weeks at Christmas and Easter and seven weeks in the summer. We worked until the end of July, and returned late in September in good time for Saint Michael's Day. This was celebrated with a special outing and a festival supper, and we had another of those and the staff entertainment before we 'broke up' for Christmas. There was a half-term weekend, and 'days out' about twice a term when parents or relatives could take us out on Sundays. Being not too far away, we would often be driven down to Brighton, or just given lunch at the Maiden's Head in Uckfield if the weather was bad. Its dining room had coloured prints of the coronation procession of King William IV and Queen Adelaide round the walls, which was perhaps why I expected more than a Daimler of King George V.

One half-term when my parents were away I was with my grandfather's half-brother Uncle Sam and we stopped at a village war memorial just before 11 a.m on 11th November, to join those observing the Two Minutes' Silence honouring all those who gave their lives in the Great War. At the eleventh hour of the eleventh day of the eleventh month, the moment the Armistice came into force, the entire country came to a halt. We normally observed it in chapel as the maroons, the memorial shots fired in every town and village, boomed to mark the start and finish of the Silence.

The school uniform was a pink cap and blazer with the school crest, and grey long or short trousers. With the short trousers went grey stockings with two pink bands round the top. We only wore blazers on special occasions, and for every day wore grey V-neck pullovers with a pink band round the neck and cuffs. Everything had to be marked with one's name and school number, with Cash's name tabs sewn into every article of clothing so that it did not go astray on return from the laundry. For years after I left, odd items still appeared in my sock and underwear collection marked 'A. TYLER 46'.

Our clothing, cleanliness and health was looked after by the Matron, Miss Sinclair, whom one rarely saw out of her matron's uniform with its starched headdress. Mrs Hockey worked closely with her, but it was Matron who dispensed the notorious Syrup of Figs. Matron also ruled over the sickroom, which I rarely occupied, except for a mumps epidemic which ran into the summer holidays, when we had a splendid time playing around in the grounds until we were non-infectious enough to be sent home.

The school had a collie dog called George who was everyone's friend, but no other pets, and we were not allowed to keep any. At the rear of the school was a wooden extension called The New Classrooms, with folding dividing walls so as to make a large hall for the annual light opera entertainment and for special occasions. One reached it through the sports changing rooms, above which was the chapel, and to the side was the gym with its parallel bars and vaulting horses for our regular PT sessions. At the side of the school were the other classrooms, and at the front the Head-master's study and the dining room. Food was plain but good, with cereals or porridge, a hot dish and bread and marmalade for breakfast, a filling lunch and supper. A master or Matron sat at each table to maintain discipline, and since they ate with us this may have accounted for the standard of the food. We all had our dislikes, but no real complaints – unlike most schools. I think we also stood well up the visiting teams' tea league table. Upstairs were the dormitories; arranged according to age, and named by their bedspread colours. Each had a different 'lights out' time after evening prep, which was the homework that we were spared at weekends. Privileges came with age, with the first form usually sitting at the Headmaster's table, and having him chat to us infor-mally some nights before 'lights out'.

We traditionally performed a Gilbert and Sullivan light opera each autumn term, so despite the chore of rehearsing as a chorus

24

member and learning to dance in step, not one of my greatest talents, I got to know and enjoy a number of them from *The Mikado* to *The Pirates of Penzance*. After Mr Hockey's death we become more adventurous, producing first *The Rebel Maid* and then in my final term a musical called *Paradise Island* written by the staff.

There was a soothing certainty in the school routine, major events occurring at the same time each year, and after the initial bullying I entered into a familiar routine that went on happily for years with my group of contemporaries and friends. Sadly this had to come to an end.

I had always wanted to go into the Navy, a seed planted so early by Nanny Hawkins that it flourished untended all through prep school. The school had not sent a boy to Dartmouth for years and decided that I needed Greek to try for a scholarship in case I failed the Navy, so I spent more than a year struggling with a new alphabet and the grammar of *thuo*, I sacrifice, before it became unnecessary. I had persuaded another form-mate, Mark Le Gallais, to try for Dartmouth with me, and we went up to London together by train for the interview. Surprisingly I passed and he did not, as I thought he would have made a better impression. We were both down for Charterhouse if we failed, so he went on there. I suppose the interview board, a schoolmaster and group of senior officers in plain clothes chaired by an admiral, knew what they were looking for. The essay we were set to write while waiting was reputedly to calm our nerves and never looked at. All I can remember are some general knowledge questions and making some rather hostile remarks about Mussolini when asked about Italy; I don't remember Hitler even being mentioned in that November of 1937. The invasion of Abyssinia, now Ethiopia, two years earlier had really angered us, and at school we sang a parody of 'Covered Waggon':

Roll along Mussolini, roll along,
For you won't be in Abyssinia long.
You'll be lying on some ants,
With a bullet up your pants.
Roll along Mussolini, roll along!

25

The examinations a few weeks later were a mere formality, based on the Common Entrance exams for which we had been preparing for years, and I left Saint Michael's and my friends for the last time with regret but also with anticipation.

# 4

## *Dartmouth*

The Christmas holidays of 1937 were partly devoted to kitting up with all the uniform required for a naval cadet and set out in a list sent to parents. I found a copy among my father's papers and was surprised to see the vast amount of clothing we had to possess, ranging from 5 trousers, white flannel, at 21s 0d per pair (£1.05) to 12 handkerchiefs at 4d (under 2p) each. 'All articles must be clearly marked with the cadet's name.' '1 rubber name stamp with initials and surname' was to be obtained for marking them. This involved white tape being sewn into even one's football stockings and then stamped in marking ink with the name stamp – an old-fashioned and time-consuming process when Cash's name tapes were obtainable. Naval administration was old-fashioned and labour-intensive, but then so was much of the country; we were even ordered to bring our possessions in '1 Portmanteau (Name to be clearly marked) about 2 ft 8 ins × 1 ft 6 ins × 1 ft 1 in.' Standardisation was reasonable, as they had to be stored in a limited space, but 'Portmanteau' was a dead Regency word for a trunk. Now even trunks are almost obsolete.

A Joining Letter from Captain F. Dalrymple-Hamilton, Commanding Officer of the Royal Naval College, Dartmouth, instructed new entry cadets to join on Wednesday 19th January 1938, and if possible to travel by the train leaving Paddington at 12 noon, arriving at Dartmouth at 4.15 p.m. The journey is not much faster today as the spur line stops at Paignton, but used to run down to Kingswear facing Dartmouth across the river Dart. The letter allowed parents to send us with £1 of pocket money per term, but we might not bring nor receive 'parcels of eatables of any kind'. No Billy Bunters at Dartmouth. Mars and Crunchies had recently come on the market at 2d, as exotic and popular alternatives to bars of chocolate, as had Smarties, and were probably our canteen's best-sellers.

My parents took me to Paddington in good time to find the carriages marked 'Naval Cadets', and to load my portmanteau with its shiny white lettering. I nervously joined several dozen strange boys, all in our new uniforms with a gold button and white twist of braid on our lapels to indicate our cadet rank. We wore the standard naval officer's peaked cap and badge and uniform, but the smaller ones like myself looked more like naval pages at a wedding. I don't remember the journey at all; most of us were too worried and homesick to get into conversation. At Kingswear we were met by College staff in the shape of our Cadet Captains, naval prefects, who shepherded us onto a ferry to cross the river, and then marched us up to the College.

HMS *Britannia*, as the Royal Naval College was known before it gave up its name to the royal yacht, is a handsome group of red brick and white stone buildings on a low ridge above the town of Dartmouth. It was built at the beginning of this century to designs by Aston Webb, to replace the old wooden warships *Britannia* and *Hindostan* moored in the Dart to accommodate and train cadets. King George V had trained in them, and his sons Edward VIII and George VI at the College. The young brothers featured in term photographs on the walls. Training was originally split between Dartmouth and Osborne in the Isle of Wight, but was combined at Dartmouth after the Great War. Eleven terms of about 45 boys, all in four-month age spreads rising from us First Termers at 13 plus to the Eleventh Term of about 17 and preparing for sea, made up the College. It was a combination of public school and naval training college, with the latter very obviously the more important to the extent that schoolwork often seemed like relaxation.

The First Term always joined a day early, so that they could be familiarised with the College, its layout and procedures before the rest returned on the following day. Almost the first thing we had to learn was who to salute and when, from all officers to the

Quarterdeck, which was the main assembly hall presided over by a marble statue of George V in naval uniform. The next thing to learn was the wearing of the lanyard, the length of white twisted braid to which seamen attach their bosun's calls, or naval whistles, which we also had to learn to blow correctly. We had to tuck the knot on the end of the lanyard into our breast pocket, and woe betide anyone who dared attach any unauthorised object to it. The lanyard was pulled horizontally across the lapels by Drakes, and then gradually descended with seniority until it hung almost to the navel. Presumably this was to avoid the enormity of a tall First Termer being mistaken for a senior cadet!

The Drakes were the members of the first two terms, who all lived together in Drake House, before being divided among the five other houses – Blake, Exmouth, Grenville, Hawke and St Vincent – for the rest of their time for inter-house sport and activities. All were named after famous Admirals, but the system had only been introduced very recently to replace the previous arrangements where a term went right through College as a group – hardly spoken to by those above them and looking down on their juniors. The feeling still continued, to the extent that I rarely spoke to Robert French and Robert Sutton, who followed me from Saint Michael's even into the same house, and I recall being spoken to only once by the other Jewish cadet, John Mocatta, who was all of four terms my senior.

The House Officers were all up and coming young officers, Lieutenants and junior Lieutenant Commanders selected for their leadership qualities which were to be developed in those under their care. We in Drake were under Lieutenant Gordon McKendrick, a thin ultra-keen young ball of fire who never tired in urging us on and playing arcane naval games like 'Priest of the Parish' that involved forfeits.

Our days began with a ring on the bell in each dormitory at 0700 – we worked by the services' 24-hour clock – and a dash out of bed through a cold water 'plunge', a sort of shallow swimming bath, which came as a shock in January to sheltered 13-year-olds but soon became routine. The bell was a round brass hemisphere on the wall, rung by pulling down a white plaited bell rope, which when detached became the official disciplinary weapon of Cadet

Captains for beating us on the backside. After breakfast there was Divisions, a full parade of the cadets in blue jackets and white trousers, on the parade ground facing east across the Dart. Inside on the Quarterdeck if wet, but otherwise outside whatever the temperature. As we grew more senior we formed the Guard. Among my sharper memories is sloping arms in the bitter winter of 1940 to grip a brass-edged rifle butt that had refrigerated in the snow while we stood 'At Ease' for Prayers. Rarely in 11 terms did I see a cadet faint. It was a matter of personal pride never to give way, and a useful training for watches on an open bridge at sea. Divisions was where the officers and masters came together. Our Headmaster, E.W.E. Kempson, was an imposing figure and a bit of an actor. Rachel Kempson is his actress daughter. The formal doffing of his mortar board to the Captain was as fine a piece of ceremonial as any we could manage. He and two of the other masters held the Military Cross. One of them, Frederick Whitall, known as 'Weary Wit', was reputed to have an artificial bum after throwing his tin hat over an enemy grenade and then sitting on it to protect his men. It's hard to believe that anyone so quick-thinking would be so stupid, but boys tend to believe what is passed down to them.

Studies commenced at 0910 and continued, with a mid-morning break, until dinner at 1310. We all had a Tutor who kept his eye on our school work, and mine initially was Kenneth Reid, the Head of Science. We were graded for science on arrival according to our Common Entrance Latin results, since science did not feature, so I started in the top group and gracefully moved downwards, which must have been a disappointment to him. Apart from Latin and Greek, we covered all normal school subjects plus some engineering and seamanship. Engineering was carried out in the workshops at Sandquay down by the river, where we learnt to turn metal on a lathe and make various items that one never needed again. I soon proved myself no mechanic.

There was a large seamanship room, with a beautiful model of a battleship's bows on which we practised how to let go and recover anchors and various other activities. We learnt a variety of seaman's knowledge, from tying knots and splicing rope to all the markings on a lead line, which had been used for centuries to measure the depth of water in fathoms, as well as all the signal flags and pendants and the Morse code.

The afternoons were devoted to games, then more studies for two hours after tea from 1640. Evening Quarters, a short parade on the Quarterdeck, was followed by supper, then prep for an hour before bed by 2100. There was virtually no free time except for Make and Mends, free afternoons, on Wednesdays and Saturdays, which usually involved some form of exercise, and a free day on Sunday after an extended Sunday Divisions followed by church. I 'fell out' with the Roman Catholics, and returned to our Gunroom – where we spent our limited leisure – to do my religious correspondence lesson of the week. Jewish cadets were granted leave for the main religious holidays, and that October I travelled up to London to celebrate the Day of Atonement and back again after it. My father felt that with German Jews being thrown into concentration camps for their religion, I must take up the rights granted by the Royal Navy. The following year war had begun, and such travel could no longer be justified. Once a year we had Admirals Divisions during our formal inspection by the Commander-in-Chief, when we marched past him led by the band. We came under C.-in-C. Plymouth, the impressively named Admiral the Honourable Sir Reginald A.R. Plunkett-Ernle-Erle-Drax, KCB, DSO, RN, some of whose surnames grace Wimbledon streets laid out on his former family land, including Ernle Road where our son David now lives.

We were well endowed with sports grounds, offering all the usual games, and we had to do a given number of 'logs' or sporting activities each week. This meant devoting part of Make and Mends to reaching one's target. The name originated with the free time given to sailors to make and mend their clothes, when 'to jew' was to sew or tailor. When there were no organised games one could make up the number with runs, counting as half or one log according to length. We must have been among the world's first joggers, as we trotted and trudged round the lanes behind Dartmouth to such turning points as Nortons Cross in the varied Devon weather. In summer one could sail or row on the Dart to make up one's logs, and we gladly gave up runs. We were taught to sail in naval cutters, gigs and whalers, heavy wooden boats car-

31

ried in ships for lifesaving and pleasure, and also to row in them. Additionally there were little skiffs, in which one could go out with a friend, and ground oneself for a sunbathe. One very soon learnt to study the tide, as pushing even a small boat off smelly mud on a falling tide was no pleasure. We naturally had a swimming pool, where any cadets who could not swim were promptly taught to do so. We had to swim two lengths fully clothed, in case our boats capsized, before we could go on the river.

We slept in dormitories of 30 boys, with a Cadet Captain by the door to keep order. As Drakes, the first two terms slept on opposite sides of the dormitories, each Second Termer responsible for the First Termer opposite to help him follow the correct routine. We were arranged in alphabetical order, so I was between Matthew Todd and Robin Usher and keeping a kindly eye on me from opposite was Victor Smith. Not that we ever used first names to our seniors, or often among ourselves. Nicknames were more common, and I was always 'Wat' after the leader of the Peasants' Revolt. We had heavy wooden sea-chests at the foot of our beds, with top flaps that dropped down like a desk lid to display one's possessions laid out in the approved manner. One's reefer jacket had to be turned inside out each night, folded over to a quarter its size and the bottom tucked under, then placed facing inwards on the left-hand side of the flap. I forget how one's other clothes were displayed, but the whole thing had to be a work of art or one got the bellrope for untidiness. A regular punishment was a kit muster, when one's full kit had to be laid out on the bed in a set order for inspection, similar to the way we later inspected our sailor's kits to check on clothing standards or as a punishment. It bred in some of us an attention to detail that wives find irritating, and my term-mate John Harvey-Jones says he can always tell an ex-Dart by the way he packs his suitcase!

In our Third Term that September we ceased to be Drakes and moved to the five other houses. I became a Blake, with Lieutenant Peter Gretton as our House Officer. He had joined the College at the same time as us, with a DSC for the unusual feat of mounting a naval anti-aircraft gun on a railway wagon in Palestine and shooting up Arab insurgents trying to derail the trains. He seemed to be the fount of all naval knowledge, with a brilliant and enquiring mind, and set a standard that few of us ever attained. He correctly summed me up in my end of term report as 'A cheerful and contented boy', adding 'He is still very young for his age, and he seems to lack concentration. He should do well later.' It is a matter of opinion how well I did later, but I was undoubtedly immature for a 14-year-old, even by the standards of those days, and to be contented was hardly a virtue in the Navy – even if to be cheerful was.

That autumn came the Sudeten crisis, with Britain and France abandoning Czechoslovakia to the dictators at Munich. When Hitler seized the rump of the country the following March we could all sense the approach of war.

My only letter from Dartmouth that survives is an extract printed in the *Saint Michael's Magazine* for summer 1939:

> We have had a good many ships in the river, destroyers and submarines, which we have been allowed to see over and go out in. We have had a busy term with inspections by the First Lord of the Admiralty and by the C.-in-C. at Plymouth. We have had a company here filming for *Sons of the Sea* which is all about the College and brings in First Lords and murdered captains and all sorts of things and everyone in full dress. Leslie Banks is a House Officer and caused great amusement by getting saluted and taking off his cap in reply. The King and Queen are coming down this week-end, which is a great honour for the College as it is the first time a reigning sovereign has come down since Edward VII was thrown by his horse when he laid the foundation stone in 1902.

I don't now remember all those events, but the greatest occasion of our time at Dartmouth was undoubtedly the July visit of the King and Queen and the two Princesses in the royal yacht *Victoria and Albert*. She was as old as *Britannia* became, having been built for the old queen herself, and looked a real classic yacht of the *Belle Epoque* as she anchored below the College in the river flying the Royal Standard. There were Royal Divisions, displays and inspections, and I was overawed to be questioned by the Queen in the library, where I was reading one of the bound volumes of the

*Daily Mirror* of the Great War. I remember her gentle clear voice and soft skin, but not a word of what we said. The Duke of Edinburgh, then Prince Philip of Greece and Denmark, was a Special Entry cadet at the time, one of a group who joined on leaving public school for naval indoctrination and training before going to sea. As a distant cousin he was chosen to escort Princess Elizabeth, and from this first meeting eventually blossomed their marriage. He was also chosen to hoist the White Ensign, which took place every morning at Divisions, when *Sons of the Sea* was being filmed, and it must have been his only commercial appearance. It was a really corny spy thriller, whose naval errors gave us hysterics when it was shown in College. When the *Victoria and Albert* sailed, the entire College and much of the town went afloat in every boat we could lay our hands on to escort the Royal Family out to sea. Reluctantly we turned back, weary, exhausted but full of pride in the occasion which marked the evening – though we did not know it – of the great Empire in which we all believed.

That August the family went on holiday by car to Pornic in southern Brittany, only our second away from Birchington after Sables d'Or near St. Malo two years earlier. The Soviet–German pact burst on us without warning, and it was obvious that war was imminent. We raced back via Versailles, finding it '*Fermé pour la crise*', and crossed safely to England a few days before Germany invaded Poland.

Michael and I were sent to stay at Saint Michael's as part of the mass evacuation of children from London. It was while out on a country walk near Uckfield, about noon on Sunday 3rd September, that a policeman bicycled past wearing a tin hat and blowing a whistle. This represented the first air raid warning, within an hour of Mr Chamberlain's famous broadcast that we were at war. The Great War had become the First World War.

I rejoined Dartmouth later that month, to find that most of our House Officers had been recalled for active service, and replaced by retired officers as part of the war plan. In 1914 the College had closed down and all cadets were sent to sea, an unwise move which completely disrupted officer training, but far worse resulted in the loss of a number of 14-year-olds when three cruisers were torpedoed and sunk by a single submarine.

This time training continued at Dartmouth almost as normal, except that we had to carry our service gasmasks in their khaki satchels with us at all times, the number of Special Entry cadets doubled, and the laid-up shipping surplus to peacetime requirements and clogging the Dart was rapidly manned and put to sea. We had two terms of this 'Phoney War', so called because little moved on land and the RAF was restricted to dropping leaflets. We did have the excitement of the sinking of the German pocket battleship *Graf Spee* in the River Plate, followed by the boarding of the *Altmark* to free her merchant navy prisoners, and the battle against the U-boats had begun.

Chamberlain had brought back Winston Churchill as First Lord of the Admiralty, the post he had held in 1914, and that winter he visited the College and spoke to us on the Quarterdeck. It was not one of his great war speeches, and all I can remember is the gravelly voice. I never saw him as we weren't gathered round, but had to keep our eyes rigidly to the front or our Cadet Captain would have given us hell. Discipline in that way was almost Prussian, and like theirs could repress initiative. It led me to believe for some years that a senior officer could almost never be wrong! As against that, we all thought that nothing could be more inefficient or slow than the Admiralty until we had dealings with civilian firms.

Discipline was strict, but there was none of the 'fagging' common in public schools at the time and virtually no bullying. We were about to serve in the largest and finest navy in the world, and we were taught to look after the welfare of our men, to try and anticipate problems by looking ahead and to act in the best interests of the service. Quite a tall order, but in spite of bouts of individual self-interest nearly all Dartmouth officers lived up to it.

Many of the petty rules were irksome, and we would break them if we could get away with it, but there was complete trust among cadets. There was petty pilfering to make up one's kit for inspection, but although nothing was locked I never recall any money or valuables being stolen. It was not done to refuse a request for help, and all these unwritten codes built up a high standard of behaviour that is still maintained in the services.

Food rationing was introduced only gradually in 1940, but we qualified for armed forces coupons giving much more than the civilian allowances. These were very welcome at home during the holidays. Food at College hardly changed from the plain and plentiful peacetime meals eaten in the splendid wood-panelled mess room. A rationed pat of butter appeared on our side plates, and there was increased appearance of 'Beagle Balls' – the unpopular gristly rissoles whose origin was always under suspicion. The College beagle pack was not popular, except with its devotees.

Germany invaded Denmark and Norway in April, then the following month overran Holland and Belgium. Belgian trawlers full of refugees poured into the Dart, followed by French ones in June as the Germans swept forward after Dunkirk. Most of the masters joined the LDV – the Local Defence Volunteers, who were soon renamed the Home Guard – but this was out of working hours and College routine was little altered except for the disruptions of air raid warnings. We saw few signs of war, as Dartmouth was a minor port used mostly by coastal shipping and not worth bombing. The College, however, was a conspicuous and legal target, so warnings had to be taken seriously.

Cadets were allowed to stay on at College during the summer holidays, while the Battle of Britain was being fought out in the air and the Blitz began with air attacks on London. My parents were working flat out in Civil Defence, and wanted me safe and out from under their feet, so after August in College I was sent to join Michael at Saint Michael's, which had been evacuated to north Devon. From there I returned to Dartmouth in mid-September, as we had long holidays of a full month at Christmas and Easter and seven weeks in the summer. Future holidays were spent at home in Willesden, sleeping in the shored-up drawing room, which had been braced against roof collapse. Apart from an unexploded landmine, which fell in the next door front garden and caused a midnight evacuation, we came through the Blitz unscathed.

We entered our Ninth Term that September, when two major changes took place. The academically brighter boys were 'streamed' into Alpha classes, five in Mathematical and six – of whom I was one – in Literary. The one subject in which I had always excelled was history, where I was usually in the top three of the term, and I was passable at English and languages, so I just scraped in. The principle was rather like A levels, concentrating on one's best subjects.

The other change was that those with the best leadership qualities were selected as Cadet Captains, and more were chosen in the final two terms. Leadership develops early, and nearly all our Admirals and Captains proved to come from those selected at Dartmouth. I was not among them. I was still too immature, as my House Officer recognised, but more surprisingly John Harvey-Jones, a fellow Literary Alpha, was not chosen. Cadet Captains wore a diamond-topped inverted chevron of gold braid on their lower sleeve and the two Chief Cadet Captains from the senior term, equivalent to head prefects, wore one on each sleeve. Ours were David Loram, who reached Flag Rank, and Dan MacKinnon, who became a flying casualty.

We received new tutors on becoming Alphas, and mine was young Count Nicholas Sollohub. He had been smuggled out of Russia as a baby during the Revolution, so was only in his early twenties. He was usually accompanied by his mastiff Sidor Petroivich – an unusual name that stuck in the memory. We were fortunate with our masters, who were mostly characters and made their classes come alive. Among those I remember with affection are Ernest Culme-Seymour with his craze for ancient weapons, demonstrating with his blackboard pointer how a ballista or a lance was used, and Leonard de la Perelle, known as 'Deadly Peril' and still going strong. He was responsible for the long French apology for being late that we had to recite, beginning '*Je regrette infiniment d'être si en retard ...*' Like the dates of the Kings and Queens of England, it is one of the fragments of school learning I can still recite. We were allowed to change languages from French to German in our Seventh Term, and Nicholas Sollohub was our German master as well as my Alpha tutor. One of our history masters was Christopher Lloyd, author of *Sea Kings of Britain*, from which we learnt our naval history, but it was Gerald Brophy who taught us history as Literary Alphas. We were allowed to select the subject for our exam and refreshingly chose Simon Bolivar, the South American Liberator, but discovered that there was not a single suitable book in English. Instead we chose

Napoleon III, and as Hitler's armies drove deep into Russia we studied the scheming nephew of the great Bonaparte who was out-manoeuvred by Bismarck to create modern Germany. Our last term also produced the shock of the *Hood*, the largest warship in the world, being blown up by the *Bismarck* with only three survivors, and the chase and sinking of the *Bismarck* herself. I remember the thrill of seeing 'BISMARCK SUNK' chalked on a blackboard as we went into the mess room for dinner.

We were kept busy that last term preparing for and sitting our 'Passing Out' exams, the equivalent of School Certificate, which we all passed to no one's great surprise. We were hardly likely to be failed when we were needed at sea. The majority of us were in Class I, which gained us a couple of months' seniority towards promotion to Lieutenant, and the rest in Class II. In peacetime we would have had two terms at sea in the training cruiser, but we were to join the fleet as 17-year-olds with no sea experience except the occasional pre-war day at sea in ships visiting the Dart. We were all promoted to Midshipman on 1st September 1941, and had been allowed while still at College to state our first and second choice of postings. I put the Mediterranean first, because much of the action seemed to be going on there, and rather to my surprise I got it.

I enjoyed my leave, visiting various members of the family to say goodbye and be made a fuss of, especially at Merthyr Tydfil, where my grandmother had been evacuated to her nieces and the Welsh cousins gave me a special welcome. I was also invited with my parents to the seventieth birthday dinner of one of their friends, and was seated next to his granddaughter. This was the first time I met my future wife, and she assures me that in my shyness I hardly addressed a word to her the whole evening!

# 5

## *Snotty*

I had already 'put up my patches', the white lapel patches to which the cadet's button and twist were attached to show our new status, when a letter arrived from the Admiralty appointing me Midshipman 'and to HMS *Nile* for disposal'. It was accompanied by a rail warrant to Liverpool for 1st October, to take passage to Alexandria. My father booked me into the Adelphi Hotel for the night, which was rather grand for a 'Snotty', as Midshipmen were invariably known from their reputed habit of wiping their snotty noses on their sleeves. Their full dress uniform, which we never acquired in wartime, carried three brass buttons on each cuff – traditionally to foil this disgusting habit.

I boarded MS *Erria* next morning with three of my term, Brian Wainwright, Nick Walker and David Winterton, and three ex-Special Entry cadets, under the nominal supervision of a Lieutenant Commander, but it proved an absolute rest cruise with no real duties. We were pleasantly surprised to find *Erria* was a comfortable Danish East Asia Line motor ship about six years old. Each pair of us had a large double cabin with bathroom, and meals were almost embarrassingly rich and graced with starched napkins.

We sailed in a convoy of 46 ships but could only proceed at 8 knots, the speed of the slowest ship. However, guarded and escorted by old V and W class destroyers, we eventually reached Freetown in West Africa without incident. There we spent five days anchored in the huge bay with no shore leave, but the natives came out by boat to dive for pennies in the clear water, and to sell baskets of limes, which we hauled up and crushed into delicious real lime juice sweetened with sugar. We sailed on in convoy as far as the equator, where ships were dispersed to their destinations in South America and South Africa at their individual best speed. We reached Capetown in mid-November, Table Mountain towering over the city at its foot, and went ashore for the first time in six weeks before sailing to Durban, where we disembarked. *Erria* continued to India on the route taken by all shipping to the East, as the Mediterranean was closed by Axis submarines and aircraft and the threat of the Italian fleet.

We were given leave by Naval HQ to be at 48 hours' notice to sail, and were taken in by kindly local residents. I spent an enjoyable time with my hosts, and suffered my only war wound when chasing their daughter in the garden and putting my arm through a plate-glass door. It required several stitches and a sling, and I gained enormous respect from passers-by gazing at the poor wounded midshipman.

We then joined HM Transport *Pulaski*, a coal-burning ship of the Gdynia-America Line, along with two companies of Swazis and one of Bechuanas going up as support troops, and other passengers bound for Egypt. We sailed for Aden in convoy with five other transports, escorted by two elderly cruisers as protection against any German raiders. *Pulaski* was quite a comedown after *Erria*, old, grubby and basic, so we were glad to get ashore even in tatty Aden, with its streets of small tourist shops to serve the peacetime liners, and especially to get clear of the coal dust blowing everywhere as she coaled ship. We then dawdled up the Red Sea, as we were not wanted until there was space in Port Tewfik at the southern end of the Suez Canal.

We disembarked with all our baggage and took a train to Cairo, then another to Alexandria, where we arrived on the morning of 21st December after an 80-day journey from Liverpool. We reported to HMS *Nile*, the shore base at Ras el Tin in the harbour, and were sent to stay in hotels as our ship was not in port. Two nights previously Italian human torpedoes had penetrated the harbour and attached limpet mines to *Queen Elizabeth* and *Valiant*, the fleet's only two battleships, which were now out of action sitting on the harbour bottom, so there were more important things to deal with than a group of young snotties. There were no great Christmas celebrations, and it was certainly not a cheerful one; the Japanese had attacked Pearl Harbour earlier that month and were surging through the Far East, the Germans were deep into Russia and Hong Kong fell that Christmas Day. Four days later we received orders to join the cruiser *Ajax*, which had just entered harbour.

*Ajax* was one of the cruisers at the Battle of the River Plate, and had earned further battle honours in the Med. We joined the Gunroom, the Midshipmen's mess, and were offered a choice of jobs. I chose 'Tanky', the Navigating Officer's assistant, and was shown what to do before we sailed next afternoon. At dawn on the 31st we carried out a bombardment of Axis troop concentrations in the Bardia area on the Libyan border, pounding them with our 6-inch guns synchronised with a land assault. We returned safely to Alexandria in time to see the New Year in, and the town surrendered three days later.

All Midshipmen had to keep a journal, issued to us on arrival, which was inspected every month and formed part of our assessment. They were sent home for storage until after the war, when we could ask to receive them, which explains my apparent near total recall of my Midshipman's time, since I have simply consulted it.

The situation in the Mediterranean was grim, as we soon realised. The Royal Navy had lost the aircraft carrier *Ark Royal* and the battleship *Barham* to submarines in November, two cruisers in December and the crippling of the two remaining battleships. The RAF was short of aircraft, Australian ships were being recalled for home defence against Japan, and army reinforcements and supplies diverted to the Far East. The Army had managed to relieve Tobruk and advance to Benghazi, but was so short of supplies that it had to fall back to Tobruk within a month.

Our Commander-in-Chief was Admiral Sir Andrew B. Cunningham, the famous A.B.C. whose bust now faces Trafalgar Square with Jellicoe and Beatty. He kept up a bold front, and was photographed going about his ceremonial duties on the quarterdeck of his incapacitated flagship *Queen Elizabeth* to convey an impression of normality, but he had no heavy ships to oppose the Italian Fleet and preserved his few cruisers for the next emergency.

Consequently we spent January and February on standby in Alexandria, or anchored off Suez as Guard Ship. During the day we snotties were kept busy running the ship's boats, to teach us the art of ship-handling on a small scale, and of handling men in our boats' crews. Normally one had to man the boat by climbing out along the boom swung out from the ship's side and down a rope ladder to which the boat was secured, which also helped develop one's self-confidence. Bringing back drunken libertymen late at night was the biggest hazard, both in maintaining discipline and avoiding accidents. We were also receiving technical instruction, and keeping watch on deck as a break from boats. I happened to be one of the four bridge players in the Gunroom, so occasionally another snotty was persuaded to relieve me for a couple of hours if the others wanted a game.

We were also sometimes granted shore leave when we were not Duty Cruiser, and used it to explore the big city. It was the Alexandria of Durrell's novels, a cosmopolitan city with large European communities, especially British, French, Greek and Jewish, who all ran canteens and social clubs for servicemen. I became friendly with a Greek family, whose daughter Kiki Kampouris was my first girl friend – to such a modest extent that I never even kissed her – and with a Jewish family called Schliosberg who made me very welcome. I also occasionally attended services at the large airy synagogue in the Rue Nebi Daniel, Arabic for the Prophet Daniel. After Arabic the second language was French, but one could always find someone speaking English – if only the shifty character offering 'feelthy pictures' or an 'exhibeesh'. Naturally we took that one up, and were treated to a lesbian act by two leathery-skinned women, which somewhat confused me as I had never heard of such activities.

Middle-class Egyptians dressed in western style and all men, except the poor who wore a white skullcap and a long robe, wore the red fez or tarboosh introduced by a Turkish sultan to replace turbans whose colour revealed the wearer's status. Even King Farouk wore one, and his handsome boyish head before he ran to fat appeared as the trademark in the crown of one that I bought to use as a collar box.

There was a very jaunty Egyptian national anthem which we

soon got to know, as it was played after 'The King' when hoisting Colours each morning. Just as quickly we learnt the ribald version that began 'Tiddly ook King Farouk, Hang your bollocks on a hook ...' The British imperial spirit was arrogantly superior, and all Egyptians were referred to as 'Wogs' – Wily Oriental Gentlemen – which understandably did not make us loved. About this time the British Ambassador sent tanks crashing through the Cairo palace gates to persuade the King to change his pro-Axis prime minister. Necessary in war, but needlessly humiliating.

While we were in Suez bay in February we were given two days' leave to see Cairo, and Brian Wainwright and I rode there in three hours in a Shell lorry – thanks to an introduction from my great-uncle in Shell. We put up at the moderately priced Victoria Hotel for 66 piastres a day all in, roughly 70p, or almost 3 days pay. The hotel fixed us up with a good dragoman – interpreter and guide – and a taxi, and we saw most of the sights. We began at the Citadel, which was also British GHQ, to view the city from the ramparts and visit the Grand Mosque, then drove across the Nile through the outer suburbs to the Pyramids beyond them on the edge of the desert. Nowadays they are almost part of the vast city, but then they were even more impressive as they soared out of the sand. One could climb the Great Pyramid outside or in, but in our heavy blue uniforms on a warm winter's day I was content to go just a short way inside. We admired the Sphinx, excavated in those days to a much greater depth to reveal its rock foundations, and visited the Bazaar, or Muski. We returned with perfume bought there for our mothers, which had mostly evaporated by the time it got home.

At the beginning of March *Ajax* sailed from Port Said to commence her journey home, and received a signal at Ismailia, halfway down the Canal, for us to pack and disembark that afternoon in Suez bay. Back we went by train to Alex, but my new ship, the destroyer *Hasty,* was at sea so I was sent off into town for local leave until she returned a few days later.

*Hasty* was a standard 1930s destroyer with four single 4.7-inch guns, mounted one above the other forward and aft, strengthened for anti-aircraft defence with a 3-inch gun replacing her after torpedo tubes, two oerlikons flanking the searchlights and minor weapons all over the ship. Her captain was Lieutenant Austen, supported by six officers in the wardroom and Midshipman Ollivant and myself. We had four days to get to know the ship and our duties before the fleet put to sea.

We were part of the 22nd Destroyer Flotilla, which with the 14th were to escort the 15th Cruiser Squadron towards Malta to meet the cruiser *Cleopatra* and destroyer *Kingston* and bring them back to Alex. We met them north of Cyrenaica on the morning of the 11th, and raced back at 26 knots, but had been picked up by patrolling aircraft and came under intermittent heavy air attacks all day. My action station was in charge of the oerlikons, 20-millimetre AA guns built to a Swiss design developed at Oerlikon near Zurich. We were on the starboard wing of the destroyer screen, so the planes frequently attacked us out of the sun as they approached the fleet, and we opened up as they came within range. Bombs dropped in our wake and close alongside, but we and the entire fleet escaped without casualties, greatly helped by our being within range of our own shore-based fighters, which disrupted several attacks and shot down three enemy planes. It was my first experience of action, and I was impressed by the speed with which attacks developed and ended, one minute planes all over the sky and guns belching smoke, the next dying smoke puffs and dispersing bomb splashes nearby. We had at least three near misses from sticks of bombs, but you never had time to feel afraid; you heard the whistle of bombs and then the splash before you had time to do more than duck.

Attacks ended at dusk, but an hour later there was a terrific yellow flash to port, lighting up the whole superstructure of the cruiser *Naiad* which had been torpedoed right under the bridge. For a few moments there was confusion, as she was the flagship, but her sister ship *Dido* took charge and ordered three destroyers to stand by the sinking ship and take off her crew. Luckily all but those killed in the explosion were rescued before she sank about half an hour later, but we had lost one cruiser to gain another.

Two days after our return we were off to sea again with our flotilla to escort the cruisers *Dido* and *Euryalus* to bombard the Italian-held island of Rhodes. We went in after midnight, striking in conjunction with an RAF raid so that the first shots were met by

44

an aerial barrage until the defence realised they were under naval attack. The harbour and dockyard were pummelled from a range of 3 or 4 miles by the larger ships, while we patrolled closer inshore to protect them from torpedo-boat attacks. After the bombardment we raced back towards Alex as the RAF came in again to attack the airfields and prevent any daylight attacks on us. A successful operation.

Four days later we sailed with convoy MW10 of four merchantships to bring supplies to the isolated and heavily bombed island of Malta. We were limited to the convoy speed of 12 knots, and joined off Libya by Rear Admiral Vian, torpedoed ten days previously in *Naiad*, and the 15th Cruiser Squadron. Thanks to dull overcast skies we passed safely through 'Bomb Alley' between Cyrenaica and Crete, but not unobserved.

On Sunday morning 22nd March we were joined in the Gulf of Sirte by *Penelope* and *Legion* from Malta and received a report from a British submarine of an enemy force at sea off Taranto. Torpedo bombing attacks commenced at 0930, followed by a lull when we were kept under observation by shadowing planes. At 1425 smoke was seen on the horizon to the north and we assumed battle formation on the enemy side of the convoy. Six and eight-inch shells began falling among us as four Italian cruisers came in sight, and we laid a smoke-screen to protect the convoy. Our cruisers opened fire as they turned towards the enemy, who turned away to the north about 1510 to break off the action. Since our first priority was protection of the convoy, which our forces turned back to cover, this engagement soon ended, without casualties.

At 1648 the enemy reappeared from the north-east, his fleet now consisting of a modern Littorio class battleship and at least six cruisers against our five light cruisers. Admiral Vian ordered us to lay smoke again between the enemy and the convoy, which we did in the rough sea that had come up during the day, as salvos from the battleship came roaring towards us like an express train, landing a few hundred yards away and throwing out huge lumps of shrapnel. Meanwhile, four of our destroyers were sent in through the smokescreen to torpedo the battleship, which suffered at least one torpedo and one shell hit that set her on fire aft. We ourselves made two separate torpedo attacks, but each time found the enemy out of range when we drew clear of the smokescreen, and by 1920 they were out of sight and withdrawing northwards.

Our forces had suffered just three shell hits and no serious damage, so we now left the undamaged convoy and its close escorts only 150 miles from Malta and headed back towards Alexandria into a fresh gale. Fleet speed had to be reduced to 20 knots to limit the wave damage to ships, but at least the stormy weather kept enemy planes away in Bomb Alley and we entered harbour at noon on Tuesday to a rousing reception with all ships lining decks and sirens going full blast. We felt like heroes at this emotional welcome, with signals of congratulation from Churchill and the C.-in-C. We had driven off a superior force and got our convoy through, but the Battle of Sirte was small beer compared to Matapan and the cheers were partly propaganda to raise our spirits at a dark time.

Summing up the battle, I wrote in my Journal:

I had seen little of the Battle from my position, a flurry of smoke covering the horizon, then a rift showing masts and forms pumping out shells, little pinpoints of red light on the horizon which were the enemy, roars as great 15 inch salvos came over, sending up great plumes of white water where they fell, a graceful cruiser moving effortlessly through the water and sending indefinable little thrills through ones body as all ten guns sent a broadside crashing through the smoke, *Zulu* ahead bucking, heeling till the water touched her tubes and righting herself after a 90 degree turn. Occasionally we sprang into action as a plane was seen through the smoke with bursts surrounding but never touching it, and each time we retired under our oilskins again to try and keep out of the waves and spray which regularly broke over us, and wondered what was going on.

I was very conscious that I was living in dramatic times, and recorded the main events of the war in my Journal each month, but my purple prose took charge when trying to catch the feel of battle. Communications were almost non-existent, hand-cranked telephones which no one had time to use, and we received just one message all day from the bridge – to say that the enemy battleship had been hit. To top it all, after the cheering reception at noon, the duty watch was turned out at midnight to load ammunition until 0230 so that we would be ready for action again, but as I sourly noted it was quite needless as next morning we went to 12 hours' notice for steam alongside the depotship *Woolwich* to repair defects!

Our reward came the following week when we escorted the troopship changing over the Cyprus garrison, and had a night alongside at Famagusta. It was then the main port of the island, and we berthed at the wharf below the Venetian walls and Othello's Tower. We walked out of the old walled city that evening into green countryside with primroses blooming in the ditches, and delighted in the contrast with the dust and smells of Egypt. I noted with surprise the lack of defence installations, but the one obvious effect of the war was compulsory currant bread. This was decreed to economise on wheat and to use up some of the surplus currants. Very pleasant for a change, except when you found currants under your fried egg.

I spent my eighteenth birthday at sea, escorting another troopship back to Alexandria, from where we returned to Famagusta with another load of troops. This time we had an afternoon to explore the town, notably the Gothic cathedral converted by the Turks to a mosque by adding a minaret to one corner, then walked across fields full of poppies and buttercups to the new Greek town of Varosha.

This time on our way back to Alexandria we nearly lost our troopship the *Princess Marguerite* to a single enemy torpedo bomber, which coolly made several runs at us and aimed its torpedo at her. Luckily it missed. It was an unexpected attack when the nearest enemy bases were some 300 miles away in Rhodes and Crete.

After one more run to Famagusta and a quick visit to Beirut – a smaller version of Alexandria – we had a week out of action alongside the depotship for a boiler clean and general repairs. During these our RDF was put back in action for the first time since I joined. RDF, Radio Direction Finding, was the original name for the top secret radar, which had only come into the Fleet since the outbreak of war and was still very temperamental. It had a rotating aerial on one of the masts, feeding into an airless cubby hole where an operator peered at a cathode ray tube and made out the blips of ships or aircraft. It proved its value at once by picking up a trawler 4 miles away as we carried out night security patrol in the port approaches.

Our next job was my first Tobruk convoy, as the front line had stabilised to the west of the port and heavy supplies were moved up most economically by sea. We turned round off the port, which we could not see behind its escarpment, and escorted empty ships back. In Alexandria we witnessed an air raid on the harbour for the first time, and saw two of the bombers shot down in the beams of the searchlights.

All April we had been sweating in blue uniforms, but on 1st May in accordance with peacetime practice we changed into white uniforms and shorts instead of long trousers. It struck me as odd that with all the improvisations of war, the date could not have been advanced for everyone's comfort. The next day we set off for another Tobruk convoy, with the Greek destroyer *Queen Olga* as our partner. We two destroyers and four corvettes provided the same strength convoy escort as previously, since with the likely submarine and air attack good protection was needed. At twilight our RDF on top form warned us of aircraft approaching some 25 miles away, though there was little we could do to stop them. It was a pitifully slow convoy crawling along at 6 knots, and although we all put up the maximum anti-aircraft barrage it was a sitting target and fortunate to be hit by only one delayed-action bomb. The *Calderon*'s crew were evacuated in time, but her live-stock was incinerated or drowned when the bomb went off. We were near-missed by a bomb within 100 yards, as were others, and were glad to get through with no worse losses, after a snail's pace 48-hour journey expecting further attacks at any time.

This time we followed the convoy into the natural harbour, a landlocked U-shaped bay facing east and littered with sunken British and Italian ships. We anchored keeping steam at ten minutes' notice ready for an emergency sailing, so could not go ashore, but were invaded by the Army scrounging supplies of all sorts from whisky to flour.

We sailed after a few hours to carry out the night anti-submarine patrol offshore, though there was more risk of us being torpedoed by a submarine on the surface than us picking her up first with our primitive radar. We left next afternoon to escort back to base a now empty convoy. Unusually, the weather was bad, and we saw no signs of the enemy on the even slower return journey.

Two days later the hospital ship *Ramb IV*, fully lit and returning from Tobruk on a publicly announced route, was dive-bombed in the approaches to Alexandria and set on fire. Fortunately it was flat calm and most of the wounded were taken off, but others were horribly burnt to death. We were sent out to relieve the destroyer standing by her, but by then she was too strongly ablaze to be salvageable, and as night fell we were ordered to sink her since she was a blazing beacon pointing aircraft towards the port. Eerily, one huge red cross on her side detached itself in the heat and fell whole into the water. After lobbing depth charges at her to blow in her sides had proved ineffective, we torpedoed her and she broke in half and sank in under two minutes. As we stood by her we were passed by a division of the 14th Destroyer Flotilla off on a secret mission, but on being sighted off the Libyan coast next afternoon their cover was blown and they made for home. Three of the four were sunk in air attacks despite the efforts of our own fighters, and *Jervis* alone escaped to come back after sunset to rescue survivors. We rushed off with two other destroyers to join her off Matruh and escort her home. Relatively few men from the three ships were lost, due to the skilful handling of *Jervis*. We had lost a quarter of our destroyer force in one blow and three of the remaining eight were undergoing repairs. Luckily we had recently been joined by six small Hunt class destroyers, which with five light cruisers were all we could put against the entire Italian fleet.

Next day we sailed to escort a troopship to Haifa, where it loaded troops for Famagusta, and we commenced a shuttle service code-named operation Normal. Apparently there was an invasion threat as we were strengthening the garrison, not changing it, and Greek women and children were brought out if they wished. We were relieved by our sistership *Hero*, which had been refitting in Haifa, and took her place to make good our defects. Just two weeks were allowed, and we benefited from the workforce having

49

just worked on *Hero*. Each watch was given four days' local leave, and refit routine was worked from 0530 to 1230 so that those aboard had a free afternoon.

I knew almost nothing about Zionism or the return of Jews to develop the Holy Land, and the first time I had met Jewish Palestinians was at the Seder service for the eve of Passover which I had attended in Famagusta with the 606th company Palestine Pioneers. It had been a happy evening, and I was impressed by how Jews from all over Europe forming the company were united by their religion and their love for this land.

On a day's leave I toured the Jezreel Valley, stretching from Haifa to the Jordan, to visit a couple of the communal settlements where an idealistic form of socialism held everything in common and everyone shared in developing the land. I was impressed both by their enthusiasm and the standard of their crops and livestock. Another day I visited Acre, the cleanest and most fascinating Arab town I had ever seen, and as a contrast Tel Aviv, the modern Jewish city which was already the largest in Palestine.

When it came to my four days' leave I bussed to Jerusalem, and was thrilled to explore the Holy City which means so much to three great religions but to Jews most of all. I also went down to bathe in the Dead Sea at Kallia, where the Empire Flying Boats used to land on the flight to India, and to cross the Allenby Bridge into Transjordan over the disappointingly small river. Next day among my sightseeing I watched from the balcony of the Services Club as *Hasty*'s guard led a recruiting march through the city — one of the rare occasions that the Royal Navy did so.

I then bussed down to the agricultural college at Mikveh Israel which trained refugees from Europe to be farmers. It was already over 70 years old, and my guide was a young German called Eli Freier who had passed through Nazi concentration camps and internment in Australia before reaching there at 19. We remained friends until his death a few years ago, and he was a witness at my son's wedding in Haifa. From there I bussed back up the coastal plain to rejoin the ship at Haifa, having fallen in love with the country.

We returned to Alexandria at the beginning of June, and I had to leave *Hasty,* having completed my three months' destroyer time. I left with the greatest regret, as I had been proud to be a member of her ship's company. Ten days later her bows were blown off by a torpedo during the next Malta convoy and she had to be sunk, but fortunately only 12 men were lost out of about 150.

I had enjoyed an exhilarating three months, my most exciting of the entire war, but some men had already endured over two years under that sort of pressure with three more to come in different war zones. It is amazing that so many of those who survived were able to resume a normal peacetime life after such sustained calls on their endurance.

I joined up again with my term-mates from *Ajax*, who had also been pulled out of their destroyers, as part of a group of nine midshipmen despatched by train to Suez for passage to Mombasa to join the battleship *Revenge*. We boarded HM Transport *Burma*, an elderly coal-burning merchant ship which took us there at her full 10 knots, calling in at Port Sudan to load cargo, Aden to coal ship, and Berbera in British Somaliland to embark Italian civilian internees to be transferred to camps in Kenya. As we rounded Cape Guardafui into the Indian Ocean the sea changed from deep blue to deep grey-green and the wind came up, reducing the old tub at times to a mere 2 knots. Fortunately, there was no submarine around to pick off this sitting target and after almost a three-week voyage from Suez we entered Kilindini, the naval harbour of Mombasa, to learn that *Revenge* had left for Durban a fortnight earlier for a refit.

We joined instead her sister ship *Royal Sovereign* to await passage, and spent the next few days learning the layout of this class of battleship before embarking in the cruiser *Mauritius* for the four-day journey to Durban. The chief interest to me was seeing her Walrus biplane catapulted off for reconnaissance flights and then land on its floats on her leeward side, to be hoisted in by crane and set back on its cradle ready for its next launch.

We joined *Revenge* on arrival, and were granted a fortnight's leave by Captain Llewellyn Morgan as a reward for our hard work in the Mediterranean. This was indeed an unexpected treat. We were kindly put up by various families in the Durban area, then after five days I went hitchhiking to Johannesburg. In white naval uniform lifts were quite easy. I had an introduction to the Gundle family, who put me up, left me free to sightsee and arranged for me to visit a gold mine. It was rather like a coal mine, nearly 3,000 feet deep, but with no danger of gas explosions open acetylene lamps were used. I cynically noted the enormous expense and work involved in mining and refining the gold so that it could be shipped to America to be buried again in bank vaults! Little has changed. I visited Pretoria, the handsome administrative capital, in their clear cool midwinter, and then returned to Durban.

*Revenge* was by now quite an old lady, having fought at the Battle of Jutland in 1916 soon after completion, and was one of the *Royal Sovereign* class of battleships whose nameship we had already met in Mombasa. As well as her four 15-inch twin turrets, she still had 12 broadside guns, individual 6-inch guns sticking out each side like a throwback to Nelson's navy. Apart from firing at torpedo bombers which had to come in at low altitude, they were of little use as they could elevate barely higher than Nelson's cannon, and in rough weather the sea sprayed in round them onto the adjacent messdecks. The removal of the forward ones and water-tighting the area was a popular part of the refit, which included the fitting of three more modern radars to supplement her single set, and mounting extra anti-aircraft weapons. This took from July to October, as a great deal of other work was carried out, while our time was occupied with gunnery, navigation, torpedo and other courses.

We midshipmen were sent to sea for a few days at a time in South African local patrol vessels for anti-submarine patrol off Durban, and were granted occasional weekend leave to stay with local families. These we really welcomed as our chest flat, the changing space where we stored our clothing in chests, was full of workmen from morning to night, and rivets were heated over coke braziers on the deck below, which made the atmosphere unbearable. Reading our list of complaints, from thefts by workmen to rubbish-littered decks, recalls that even refitting in Durban was not all pleasure. We docked in mid-October to have the ship's sides and bottom scraped of weed and repainted, as marine growth can cut several knots off a ship's speed and we needed all we could raise, reammunitioned and then painted the ship in fresh camouflage colours.

We finally sailed for Mombasa in November, and being Navigator's Assistant again, as in *Ajax*, I was up at all hours helping the Navigating Officer with his star sights and sun sights to work our position along the route. The job holder was known as 'Tanky', because in the old days one of his duties was checking the level of the fresh-water tanks. Almost every job had a nickname, but often its origin was a mystery. We were accompanied by two Hunt class destroyers, *Derwent* and *Blackmore*, as our anti-submarine escort. Two years later I was to join *Blackmore* as her Navigating Officer.

The Commander-in-Chief was Admiral Sir James Somerville, a fighting admiral like Cunningham, with whom he had previously worked from the Gibraltar end of the Mediterranean. Their ribald signal exchanges delighted the Fleet, and one of the best-known was Somerville's on Cunningham's second knighthood: 'Twice a knight at your age. Congratulations'. He had been sent out after the fall of Singapore to form a new Eastern Fleet in Ceylon, but barely had time to assemble it before the Japanese air attacks cost him an aircraft carrier and his two heavy cruisers. It was decided to withdraw to Mombasa so as to preserve a fleet in being, since otherwise it could have been destroyed, and the next few months were spent forming it into a fighting force and getting it working efficiently.

In Mombasa we joined three other modernised First World War battleships as the fleet firepower, but were no match in speed or firepower for the latest Japanese ones, and relied on our large *Illustrious* class aircraft carriers for support. Consequently there were regular fleet exercises offshore to prepare for any sort of action. During target practice I was surprised by the rather pleasant boom of the 15-inch guns, whose vibration was not as great as I had expected when they each threw nearly a ton of steel and explosive at the target. Even in wartime one did not often fire 15-inch shells for practice.

A major event on 1st December, the first pay rise for the services since before the Depression, increased most rates by about a third in recognition of wartime inflation. Our Midshipman's daily pay rose from 5s to 6s 10d, or 34p, though there was little to spend it on at the time.

Occasionally we went ashore in Mombasa, a two-mile walk from the landing place, but it had little to offer after Durban and we usually had better films shown aboard. There was of course no air-conditioning, the electric fans were none too effective in such a large metal box and the cockroaches, which had been building up their strength since Jutland, were a pest everywhere and a frequent unavoidable added ingredient in the food. 'Hands to Bathe' was often piped – orders being 'piped', or preceded by a note on the bosun's call – which made a refreshing opportunity to cool off, and conditions didn't seem too bad after the squalor on board during the recent refit. Between the exercises we continued studying for our Sub Lieutenants' exams, which were due in the New Year, and were given instruction in every type of naval knowledge from rigging and towing to signals and electrics.

New Year 1943 was rung in with the traditional 16 bells struck by the youngest Midshipman. I noted in my journal that the war had already cost the Royal Navy 5 battleships, 5 aircraft carriers, 5 heavy and 20 light cruisers, 100 destroyers and 46 submarines, as well as many smaller vessels and tens of thousands of lives.

We took a succession of exams in mid-January, and my Journal was closed to form part of the Seamanship examination. We had to include in it a nautical illustration at least once a fortnight, also reports on such activities as ammunitioning ship, and, as a would-be navigator, mine was rich in charts and maps as well as diagrams of different classes of ships. I was never a great artist, but at least in those days my diagrams and writing were neat.

Naturally we all passed our exams, for not only had we been given detailed instruction, but – as at Dartmouth – it was almost unthinkable to fail in wartime since we were required as Sub Lieutenants. That ended the best documented year of my life, and from now on I rely chiefly on memory and letters since – although we had to keep full Journals – we were not supposed to keep diaries on active service.

Airgraphs were already in use by 1942, and my parents kept a number of mine. We wrote letters on printed sheets which, after censorship, were photographed onto miniature rolls and flown to England. They were then enlarged to 5 inches by 4, and sent post-free in buff airgraph envelopes to the name and address entered in a box that showed through the slot of the delivery envelope. It was a simple morale booster, that permitted the few available planes to deliver vast quantities of mail to and from the huge forces overseas.

My final airgraph was written on board the armed merchant cruiser *Ranchi* at the start of our journey home and posted at Durban. It was headed 'Sub. Lt. Alan Tyler R.N.', and explained that while we were not officially gazetted Sub Lieutenant until 1st May 1943, we were semi-officially allowed acting rank and had put up our stripes. My commission, signed by three members of the Board of Admiralty, with a reproduction of King George VI's signature, was only dated 10th February 1947 due to the vast backlog of wartime commissions.

I arrived home towards the end of February, much more mature and experienced than the lad who had left only 17 months earlier. Most of us were still virgins, even if we had developed an interest in sex, since VD lectures before we left Dartmouth were intended to discourage it. I remember the curiosity that a dormitory of us displayed in the account by one of our term of visiting a brothel in Algiers, which implied that it was news to most of us. I had, however, come to enjoy beer and wine, though Midshipmen were not allowed spirits, and I had learnt to smoke. I tried every sort of tobacco, South African, Virginian, Turkish and wartime mixtures, as well as smoking a pipe which my father gave me. Smoking was a virility symbol and almost obligatory, but I never enjoyed it and soon gave it up. More importantly, I had absorbed something of the give and take of service loyalty.

# 6

## *Scapa*

My parents had closed up our house in Willesden while I was abroad and moved to Abbey Court in Hampstead. It was a guest house where they had a private room and their meals provided, so that my mother could concentrate on her full-time job of running the Willesden Women's Voluntary Service without the distraction of housekeeping, and my father kept the vestiges of the family business ticking over in addition to his air raid precautions duties as Borough Gas Officer. The government had been keen to encourage exports to pay for the purchases of raw materials in the early part of the war, and even when his City office was destroyed in the great firebomb raid of May 1941 he had set up temporary offices locally. However, as the Japanese occupied most of our main export markets early in 1942, he was able to release his secretary into the RAF and ran the remaining markets with the help of my uncle who had escaped from Singapore shortly before it fell and eventually made his way home.

I was also found a room at Abbey Court, in Netherhall Gardens near Finchley Road station, and returned there for the rest of my wartime leaves. Rationing had become severe by 1943, a few ounces of meat and butter a week for instance, so a serviceman's higher rations were always welcomed. I visited most members of the family during my few weeks' leave, saw one or two West End shows, and discovered music halls. This was their last great boom, as live entertainment was more attractive than the cinema and provided topical jokes that even British films could not keep up with. I used to go to the Metropole in Edgware Road, one of the big old

56

Victorian music halls, all plush and gilt fittings and a wonderful choice of at least a dozen turns an evening including one or two top stars. Gradually the music halls closed in the 1950s and one of the last shows I saw was Laurel and Hardy in Portsmouth on their farewell visit at about Coronation time.

I soon received an appointment to HMS *Mantis*, the coastal forces' shore base at Lowestoft, to fill in time before we began our Sub Lieutenants' courses. I spent about six weeks there as an additional watchkeeping officer on board motor torpedo boats. MTBs and MGBs, motor gun boats, were chiefly based at Yarmouth, Lowestoft and on the south coast to attack German convoys off the French, Belgian and Dutch coasts.

We used to go out towards dusk in these high-speed boats and head across the North Sea towards the Scheldt to try and attack German convoys. We did not have radar, so it was a bit hit and miss, and I was not involved in any of the fierce fast engagements that took place when contact was made. Most of our officers were RNVR, many of them yachtsmen who knew the waters of the area well in peacetime, and life was much less formal, as was dress, than in the fleet units I had known so far. The weather was filthy, cold and rough, for much of the year, and officers and men had great endurance to cope with it month after month. In rough weather I kept watch with a bucket close at hand, but though sometimes seasick I was fortunately never 'sea ill'.

All our term, less those few who had been lost at sea, and our parallel special entry cadets, began Sub Lieutenants' courses at the beginning of May. We were divided into groups of about a dozen and spent several weeks at various establishments in turn, studying its subject in depth and then sitting an exam. We went first to Roedean near Brighton, where the famous girls' school had been evacuated and taken over by HMS *Vernon*, the Torpedo and Anti-Submarine school. The dormitories were reputed to carry the notice 'Ring the bell if you require a Mistress during the night', but if these did exist they had been removed as souvenirs before our time. We then went on to the Navigation and Communications schools, which had expanded into country houses outside Portsmouth during the war, and to HMS *Excellent*, the Gunnery school on Whale Island in Portsmouth harbour. In peacetime this would have taken a year, but in wartime it was condensed to four months with little leisure time. At the end we dispersed on leave, and then off to sea again in September.

I was sent to join HMS *Norfolk*, part of the 1st Cruiser Squadron based at Scapa Flow in the Orkneys. Even getting there was a major rail journey, changing at Edinburgh and Inverness and eventually arriving at Thurso to spend the night and catch the morning ferry to Orkney. *Norfolk* was one of the County class of cruisers, named after English counties, built in the 1920s to the 10,000-ton limit of the Washington naval treaty, with three sloping funnels and high freeboard as their distinguishing features. Her four twin 8-inch gun turrets made her a heavy cruiser, as opposed to the many more light cruisers armed with 6-inch or smaller guns. They were spacious comfortable ships, particularly suited for the tropical stations where most had served before the war. I was to be Sub of the Gunroom, as each cruiser and larger ship had a Gunroom, where the Midshipmen and Sub Lieutenants lived, under the control of a Sub Lieutenant, but quite separate from the officers' Wardroom and the warrant officers' Mess. The Sub was in charge of off duty life and their discipline, as I knew from my own experience. There was a Lieutenant Commander acting as 'Snotties Nurse' to super-vise their training and journals, and the rest was left to the Sub.

We carried six RN midshipmen from Dartmouth, with white patches on their lapels, and six RNR with blue patches. One Paymaster Mid. and one Sub Lieutenant RNVR completed the Gunroom. RNR stood for Royal Naval Reserve, drawn from mer-chant navy volunteers, and their officers wore interwoven wavy stripes, while RNVR stood for Royal Naval Volunteer Reserve, drawn from other volunteers. They wore single wavy stripes, red patches for their Midshipmen, and were known as the 'Wavy Navy'. When provoked they might refer to us regulars as the Maintenance Men who kept the ships running for them to join when war loomed. Rarely until late in the war did the volunteers have command of any but small ships because they lacked the experience, but it was now beginning to happen and certainly I saw no discrimination between the different groups wherever I served. In due course after the war these visible rank distinctions were done away with.

58

In the Gunroom Mess we had our own stewards to serve us, our own separate catering with the Admiralty money granted for victualling plus the shilling or so a day we had to allocate from our pay towards our food, and we ate very well. Midshipmen were permitted a wine bill of about 5s a month, no spirits, and although this was not unduly restrictive at duty-free prices I amplified this by classifying cider as a soft drink until I was bowled out. Gunrooms rarely drank cider, but my father had a friend at Gaymers so we tried it on. Midshipmen tended to play bridge as another virility symbol like smoking, even if they weren't very keen on it, and the one disciplinary act I remember was banning gambling, playing cards for money, and reading them the riot act on the evils of betting. Mostly we were too busy for much Gunroom leisure, but we did have a formal Mess Dinner once a month to dine favoured Wardroom officers, and swapped RPCs – Request the Pleasure of your Company (for drinks) – with other gunrooms. There was a large Home Fleet maintained at Scapa Flow to guard against breakouts into the Atlantic by units of the German surface fleet and to cover convoys to Russia, so one had opportunities to meet friends.

That Autumn we paid several visits to Iceland to pick up convoys for passage to Murmansk and Archangel, where war supplies were unloaded and despatched to the front. I particularly recall Akureyri, right up a fjord in the north and Iceland's second town; it was little more than a village but boasted a chromium-plated milk bar to refresh us when we were able to get ashore. We normally escorted convoys to the North Cape, past enemy warships lying in wait in Norwegian Arctic ports, and handed them over to Russian escorts before turning back, but just before Christmas we went right through to Polyarno, the naval base near Murmansk. The Red Fleet choir came aboard to entertain us, and we went ashore for a walk in the snow, where I used my rusty German to chat with a Russian pilot and exchange a tin of cigarettes for a knife made from a part of a plane he had shot down. There was absolutely nothing to buy except Russian postage stamps, but copies of *Pravda* were given away and accepted as souvenirs even though we could not read a word of them.

On the return journey we three cruisers, *Belfast*, *Sheffield* and *Norfolk*, placed ourselves to the south of the convoy between it and the German base at Altenfjord in north Norway. We spent Christmas Day at Defence Stations, and learnt next morning that the German battleship *Scharnhorst* and her escorting destroyers had put to sea. We immediately went to Action Stations, mine being Turret Officer in charge of our foremost 8-inch turret. We had four twin gun turrets, B on the deck above A forward, and X above Y aft, allowing all eight guns to cover a large arc on each side of the ship. We were well north of the Arctic Circle at the darkest time of the year, so the action was fought in twilight and varying degrees of darkness throughout. Reporting to my parents on the battle I wrote:

It was piped that we would go to Action Stations in fifteen minutes time when we heard she was about, and I got up a weird collection of gear to go into action with. I thought we would have several hours to wait, if we ever saw her, so I prepared myself. The turret temperature is about 40 degrees and falls below freezing at times, so I put on my duffel coat, which is fawn in colour with a hood attached and reaches to my knees, over my oldest reefer jacket with polo-necked sweater and warm clothes below. I also wore socks, woollen stockings and leather sea boots and stayed warm throughout the action. I carried two bars of chocolate and two packets of chewing gum in the food line, and the Bible and the Golden Treasury for literature. I never had a long enough lull to open them, although we spent fourteen hours at Actions Stations that day. I only realised afterwards that I forgot the steel mirror which I usually carry in my breast pocket (to deflect shrapnel), and my brandy flask. We had been standing by for action for three days previously, on watch four hours in every eight, and we were all pretty tired and dirty, but bucked up to full efficiency when we knew there was something doing. We had barely made our preparations when we received the report 'Enemy in Sight' from *Sheffield*, and got off some half a dozen rounds. We claimed at least one hit, announced on the (B.B.C.) News, with another probably. This was very good and she pushed off to give us time for dinner from the galleys, soup and a lamb sandwich.

60

As we were engaging right ahead only A and B turret could fire, so I could claim a 50% chance of helping score the hit. Interestingly the Officer of B Turret, Lieutenant Cheswright RNVR had been present as a reporter at her launch, so was in at her beginning and end. Both he and our Radar Officer, Lieutenant Longley Cook, were old Saint Michael's boys. Contact had of course been made by radar and we had opened fire by radar, but this was still too secret to be made public. By great good fortune our hit put her radar out of action, so she was literally fighting in the dark for the rest of the battle, which probably cost her life.

A couple of hours later in the afternoon, when the blue of day was dying into a brightish night, she came in again and tried to get between us and the convoy. We went straight towards her with our guns blazing as we poured in rapid salvos. This had been decided on previously as our plan of action. Attack is always the best method of defence against a stronger enemy, and she turned and ran. She was only showing us her stern as she ran away, instead of her broadside, which gave us a very small target much harder to hit. Consequently, although we fired a great many salvos we only claimed one hit in this action which headed her off. It is possible that she thought we were a battleship, as we must have seemed very frightening coming towards her at over 30 knots with our guns flaming and our shots falling all round her. It is aston-ishing what a drug and intoxicant action is. One barely noticed the shattering thud of the recoils as the guns kept run-ning back, and we did not feel or notice as their shells hit and fell around us. It was all so exhilarating that everyone almost automatically did their jobs correctly with clear heads. I am very proud of my turret's crew. Some had joined the ship barely a month ago, and many were new to their jobs, but they all acted like veterans and we didn't miss a single salvo due to mistakes. The whole ship worked together excellently, which was why the shell damage was so soon controlled before it was able to spread and affect the ship's efficiency.

*Scharnhorst*, on turning from us, made off South towards

home, but our destroyers headed her off and she didn't dare to dash through them. She turned the only way open to her, with us shepherding her along astern, just out of sight, into the arms of Admiral Fraser the C. in C. coming up in the Home Fleet flagship *Duke of York*. Several hours passed, while we repaired the damage to the turret from heavy seas. They had put out our lights, so that it looked like a Wellsian mine – steel machinery lit up by our emergency lighting like miners safety lamps. About supper time *Duke of York* opened up and she and *Scharnhorst* swapped salvos for some time without much result, as both were heavily armoured, and she looked like escaping as we ate our corned beef stew supper, but destroyers had been detached to torpedo her. They went in most gallantly, four of them, scored three hits which crippled her, slowing her and putting her steering gear and some turrets out of action. Finally the cruiser *Jamaica* finished her off with torpedoes and she sank about 1930 GMT. We went in quite close at the end and could see survivors struggling in the water with boats and rafts as the great ship went quietly down. She fought well, but was defeated by boldness and superior strategy.

We were hit aft in the afternoon action by two of her 11-inch shells, which fortunately caused relatively light damage and only eight deaths and did not reduce our speed. She was using armour-piercing shells, one of which went straight in one side of the ship and out the other, leaving little more than an 11-inch-diameter hole as our light armour was too weak to explode it, and the other went through the casing of X turret, putting it out of action but again not exploding. We were incredibly lucky, as if her shell had exploded in X turret it would almost certainly have set off the magazine and blown up the ship. We had attracted her fire because without her radar she could only fire at our gun flashes, and she could not see those of the other cruisers, which had flashless cordite unlike us. We were also near missed on several occasions, one shell bursting close enough alongside below the bridge to pierce the side, and a couple straddled the forecastle, blowing sheets of water over and into my turret. The shell that passed through the ship produced the usual freak blast effects, cups shattered in the Gunroom pantry with their handles neatly hanging on their hooks, and glasses in the bar intact but the picture above shattered.

Of the *Scharnhorst* crew of around 2,000 only 36 survived this Battle of North Cape, despite the efforts of our destroyers to pull them out of the icy waters of the Arctic. It reminded us how quickly death came from the killing cold, and increased our admiration for the merchant seamen in their vulnerable ships who risked their lives bringing aid to our Russian allies. Fifty years later some of us, including *Scharnhorst* survivors, gathered on board *Belfast* in the Pool of London for a service of remembrance and reconciliation led by the Chaplain of the Fleet and the pastor of the German church in London.

Our dead were solemnly buried at sea on the way to Scapa Flow, where in contrast we celebrated a belated and uproarious Christmas Day before steaming down to the Tyne for repairs. Our Captain D.K. Bain received the DSO with awards for a dozen of the ship's company representing us all, but a more tangible and welcome recognition came in the grant of two weeks' leave. Towards the end of February a group led by the Captain visited Norwich, the city which had adopted us. I was fortunate to be one of the officers selected to represent the ship on that proud occasion when we marched through the city centre past the Lord Mayor, to whom the Captain ceremonially presented our tattered battle ensign at an official reception.

At the beginning of March most of the ship's company transferred to our sister ship *Devonshire*, which was just completing her refit at an adjacent berth. This included myself and the midshipmen and involved many transfers of equipment and stores, so it took time for the new ship's company to settle down. Changing ships en bloc had its disadvantages. Our old hands tended to do things 'the *Norfolk* way' to the annoyance of those already in *Devonshire*, while the watertight doors were often on the opposite side to where they had been in *Norfolk* because the two ships had been built in different yards, so one was halted by a bulkhead in place of an expected door. By the end of the month we were ready to rejoin the fleet, and sailed back to Scapa Flow to work up. This chiefly consisted of gunnery exercises to restore our drill and shooting to fighting standards, and damage control exercises. After our recent action, both were recognised as vital.

The war had turned very much in our favour with the liberation of North Africa and the surrender of Italy, the start of the American advance in the Pacific and the Russians rolling the Germans back towards her borders. The Second Front was expected to be opened in France in the near future, and we all wanted to take part. In the middle of April I was humiliatingly transferred to a hospital ship with a swollen upper lip caused by a developing boil, and ordered to cease shaving. After a very rough passage to Aberdeen I was transferred to the RN Auxiliary Hospital, where it duly burst, to my great relief. Two days later I was declared fit, and rushed back by train and ferry to rejoin as we were expecting to invade at any moment. How wrong we were. D-Day was still six weeks ahead, but I had a new interest – growing my first beard. In the Royal Navy one can grow a 'full set', moustache, beard and side-whiskers, or be clean-shaven. There are no permutations allowed, and one has to obtain the Captain's 'permission to grow'. As I already had a week's growth and a medical instruction not to resume shaving, this was a fait accompli, even though the Captain didn't like beards. It grew well, and I became keen on it as I realised the shaving time it saved and the extra maturity I thought it gave my appearance.

In early May we were visited by General Montgomery, and then by King George VI, who had himself served in the Royal Navy at the Battle of Jutland. We then sailed to escort the aircraft carriers *Victorious* and *Furious* into the Arctic up to 72°N beyond North Cape to launch attacks on the remaining active German battleship, *Tirpitz*. Like her sunken sister ship *Bismarck* she had the potential to wreak havoc if she broke out to attack our Atlantic or Russian convoys, and tied down a large number of our ships that could have been employed elsewhere. The first attack was delayed by bad weather and although 60 strike aircraft were flown off next day they returned frustrated by poor visibility that prevented them attacking. A third attempt the following day was defeated by poor weather and we regretfully returned to Scapa having achieved nothing. There we found a huge fleet assembled, 6 battleships, 3 fleet and 3 auxiliary aircraft carriers, 10 cruisers, 2 French cruisers and many flotillas of destroyers. It was a clear indication that forces were gathering to support the coming invasion. Ten days later we sailed again for Norway with the same ships as before to repeat the previous operation, and once again the first attempt was called off due to the weather, but on 1st June our aircraft drew blood when they attacked the secondary target of a German convoy off south Norway and sank all its three ships. Coming only a few days before D-Day this probably helped to confuse the enemy, as Hitler had a hunch that Norway was a likely target for an invasion. To our everlasting regret we were to take no part in the D-Day support operations, and heard news of it on the radio as we exercised in Scapa Flow.

Scapa Flow, a vast landlocked bay surrounded by various of the Orkney Islands, was developed as a naval base in the First World War, and revived at the start of the Second. There were virtually no amenities, as the attractive little chief town Kirkwall, with its Norman cathedral of Saint Magnus, would have been overwhelmed if the fleet descended on it from its anchorage 5 miles away off the small southern island of Flotta. Here the fleet amenities were established: sports grounds, fleet cinema and canteens; that was about all. I used to go for regular long walks with Hugh Herbert, the RNVR Sub who had joined *Devonshire*'s Gunroom with six RNVR mids, as we were still rank-conscious and it would appear favouritism or worse if I had selected a particular midshipman as my regular companion, and the Wardroom officers hardly looked to the Gunroom for one. Fortunately at weekends we could get ashore on Flotta and stretch our legs if we were not at sea, otherwise we developed a social life with mess dinners every month and exchange visits with other ships. There were occasional opportunities to go sailing in the ship's boats or play a game, but with large numbers of men chasing a limited number of amenities it was not easy to keep up morale in Scapa.

All the action was off Normandy and we were just sitting around in case the *Tirpitz* came out, hence the urge to put her out of action and release ships for the Pacific War. Consequently we tried again in July with a large force of three fleet aircraft carriers escorted by the C.-in-C. in the *Duke of York*, ourselves, three other cruisers and a dozen destroyers. Forty Barracuda bombers with an escort of 50 fighters flew off to attack her in Altenfiord on the 17th, but radar gave the Germans sufficient warning to hide the fiord in a smokescreen, so blind bombing was necessary and only one hit was estimated. Maddeningly a sudden fog prevented the launch of a second strike, so we made our way home to avoid the threat of a U-boat pack attack. I noted that the temperature never fell below 46°F even well into the Arctic above 71° North and I was able to keep watch coatless. Of course there was no night in high summer, and at midnight the sun was still up when the mist let us see it.

Then it was back to Flotta routine, walks, tea at the Officers Club, and the very occasional ENSA show at the Fleet Theatre. ENSA, Entertainment National Service Association, organised entertainment for the forces of every type from variety shows to Yehudi Menhuin on violin, both of which I saw there. Our own Sunday night cinema in the Wardroom in summer used to be followed by a turn on deck about midnight as dusk fell, to look out for the flickering aurora borealis. The country kept its clocks one hour ahead of normal during the war as economy measure, so the summer days seemed incredibly long and winter ones incredibly short, but the cattle and the farmers managed to cope.

We were given a week's break at the end of July in Loch Ewe on the north-west coast of Scotland, within easy reach of Scapa should we be needed. It was splendid rough country for exercises, and I spent a couple of healthy but exhausting days leading a platoon of seamen trying to round up our Royal Marines acting as enemy paratroopers. All large ships carried a contingent of Marines headed by a Captain or Major. They were fully integrated for action, manning X turret in both *Norfolk* and *Devonshire*, but also provided military skills for landing parties and special duties. They had all sorts of nicknames, the most polite one being 'Royals', but we respected their ability to be both sailors and soldiers which their motto '*Per mare per terram*' emphasised. We were able to have a decent meal in the little town of Aultbea, and at the weekend explored the countryside and bathed in the surprisingly warm tarns or hillside pools. Then it was back to Scapa ready to protect escort carriers, merchant ship hulls converted to small aircraft carriers, as they launched shipping strikes off the Norwegian coast.

The battleship *Royal Sovereign* had been given to the Russians earlier in the year, was renamed *Archangel* after their Arctic port, and had become a familiar sight during her two months' work up at Scapa. She was accompanied by four of the four funnelled ex-US destroyers, which we had obtained in 1940 in exchange for leasing West Indies bases, that had also been given to the Russians. In mid-August we cheered them out of harbour as they left for home. In a parody of our Royal Marine bands, a few men in overalls sawed away at their instruments on her quarterdeck as *Archangel* steamed past us. The following day we sailed in a large force, similar to that of the previous month, for one more go at the *Tirpitz*, taking the opportunity to cover a Russian-bound convoy and the vulnerable old *Archangel* and her escorts. Learning from previous experience the danger of an attack on the hour when all ships were changing watches, we changed at ten minutes past the hour and others ten minutes before, since defence is below par when men are just settling at their posts. Once again the weather was foul, and we had to delay 24 hours in Arctic daylight before the attack was launched on the 22nd. Even then bad visibility prevented the Barracudas attacking, but one Hellcat scored a 500-pound bomb hit above the bridge. This time the C.-in-C. was determined to finish the job, risking the U-boat attacks which sank one frigate and damaged one escort carrier, and two days later we went in to within 30 miles of the snow-capped Norwegian mountains. Waves of Barracudas, Fireflys, Corsairs and Hellcats scored three hits and we then withdrew to refuel in the Faeroes, before launching a final air attack and covering a convoy returning from Murmansk. The damaged *Tirpitz* was finally sunk that autumn by British ~~midget submarines~~ Lancaster bombers which penetrated her fiord base.

Our six RN and six RNR midshipmen with whom I had spent a year left us for their destroyer time, to be succeeded by 11 Royal Canadian Navy midshipmen straight out of their college at Vancouver. I began to feel a veteran, but had no time to brood. We were despatched to the Clyde for a welcome few days' break in Glasgow before steaming out into mid-Atlantic to escort the *Queen Mary*, with Winston Churchill and staff aboard, back from their Quebec conference with the Americans and Canadians. That 29° West proved the nearest I ever got to America in my entire service career.

Early in October we were sent down to the Forth to grant leave from Edinburgh, a week to each watch. I had first leave, and took the opportunity to go into the Admiralty and ask for a transfer to a small ship, as I had obtained my Watchkeeping Certificate authorising me to keep watch on my own instead of assisting a more experienced officer, and I wanted to see more of the action. Officers' appointments were handled by the Naval Assistant to the Second Sea Lord and his staff, a group of Commanders, who made it clear that one did not turn up and ask for a change, but proved sympathetic as they had already appointed my successor, who joined just before we left Rosyth for Scapa. Back I came from there by train, a 24-hour journey to London less than a fortnight after leaving. I was not due to join the Hunt class destroyer *Blackmore* at Sheerness until November, so enjoyed another fortnight's leave.

The whole south-east had been under V1 flying bomb 'doodlebug' attack during the summer, but it had ceased by the autumn as their bases in northern France and Belgium were occupied, but the V2s, larger and more powerful, now arrived without warning. Life carried on almost normally, since the only alternative was to spend the time in an air raid shelter, but their threat placed a severe mental strain on those who had to face up to it month after month.

# 7

## *Victory*

Sheerness at the mouth of the Medway was a miniature Chatham, a much smaller naval base known as Sheer Mess, which summed up the general view of it at that time. After five years of war it was drab, damaged and dismal in winter, but that was *Blackmore*'s refitting base after a two-and-a-half year commission in the East, where I had met her escorting us in *Revenge*. I was to relieve an RNR Sub as Navigating and Signals Officer, which I did next day after reporting to the Captain. He was Lieutenant John Kerans, later to be famous as 'Kerans of the *Amethyst*' when he brought her safely down the Yangtze past the Communist gun batteries.

Kerans was a senior Lieutenant who had probably spent most of the last five years at sea under considerable strain, and in his case the escape was drink, which he did not carry well. He sometimes returned aboard the worse for wear and had to be helped to bed, which was embarrassing for the Duty Officer and for morale. He was also not a great ship handler, nor an easy man to work with. All the officers were new, joining during the refit, so we had to get to know the ship and her equipment with workmen all around us. Meanwhile the attraction of Sheerness was its closeness to London, so that I could get home most weekends from dockyard squalor, and away to *Dryad*, the Navigation School outside Portsmouth, for a few days' brush-up. I was even able to invite my parents aboard for lunch as the refit neared its close, which was somewhat unusual in wartime.

The refit ended as 1945 came in, and we were kept busy ammunitioning, storing and completing our ship's company before finally putting to sea. All the Hunt class had been built during the war as smaller slower escort destroyers relative to fleet destroyers. We achieved just under 24 knots during full speed trials after our refit, compared to 34 for a fleet, were about 100 foot shorter than their 360 feet, and 1050 tons to their 1700, but we did have six 4-inch AA guns. Hunts were cheaper and quicker to build, and filled a serious gap for convoy escorts. We sailed up to Scapa for our work-up, and started by getting entangled in the boom. All harbours were protected by booms and nets in wartime to keep out enemy submarines, and they were opened, closed and maintained by boom defence staff. We were soon rescued after slipping our anchors and cables, which had dragged in a gale. After a couple of weeks of exercises we returned to Sheerness and managed to foul a navigation buoy off Southend Pier, where we wrapped its cable round our propeller and spent the night flashing its light at shipping until divers freed us next day. We then escorted our first convoy from Southend through the swept channels between the minefields to Flushing in Holland and brought back a homeward-bound convoy. Most of February was spent escorting convoys to and from Flushing and Ostend to protect them from E-boat attacks, but at this late stage of the war we met no opposition.

At the beginning of March we were sent round to Greenock on the Clyde to help escort a convoy to Gibraltar, breaking off to refuel in Lisbon because of our limited fuel capacity, then carrying on to join the Eastern Fleet. At Aden we were told to sail to Colombo, but had to point out that our fuel would run out on the way, so our destination was shortened to Bombay. This still meant a voyage of some 1,500 miles out of sight of land, which for me as Navigating Officer involved a lot of work with sun sights and star sights, and I was considerably relieved and chuffed when Bombay rose over the horizon five days after leaving Aden. It was also the eve of Passover, so again – as three years earlier in Famagusta – I was able to join a multinational services Seder at the Jewish Community's Forces Club. Next day we sailed with the escort carrier *Khedive* to Colombo, where I celebrated my twenty-first birthday, before proceeding to the naval base of Trincomalee on the east coast of Ceylon to join the fleet.

We were the first of the Hunts to rejoin the fleet, so there was no

70

specific role for us until the others arrived, and we were used for any odd jobs that came up. Meanwhile we explored Trincomalee, a fine large landlocked bay that could comfortably accommodate the fleet but, like Scapa, had only limited amenities and a small town with few attractions. Our first job was to accompany another escort carrier back to Colombo, acting as Crash Boat astern of her when she was flying so as to rescue any aircrew whose aircraft might crash. In Colombo we embarked a specialist Meteorological Officer and his equipment, and sailed for Akyab on the north coast of Burma to act as weather-reporting ship for the reoccupation of Rangoon by the 14th Army at the end of April. We patrolled east of the enemy-occupied Andaman Islands, sending up met balloons and making weather reports, and looking anxiously up at patrolling Liberators which we successfully convinced that we were friendly. We used a communication system called IFF, Identification Friend or Foe, which was supposed to be foolproof but occasionally and expensively failed as recently as in the Gulf War. We fuelled from the cruiser *Phoebe* off Rangoon and embarked a group of brass hats to take back to Akyab, skirting a cyclone whose rough seas did not improve their journey, before returning to Trincomalee. We arrived on the morning after VE Day and 'spliced the main brace', an extra tot of rum for the ship's company and the only occasion when officers receive one, to celebrate the end of the war in Europe. I also received in the mail my official promotion to Lieutenant from 1st April, and put on the Lieutenant's shoulder straps which I had bought in anticipation.

We were out of touch with the world situation, relying chiefly on the radio and the local newspapers when we saw them, and expected at least a further year or two of bloody battles against Japan before she was forced to surrender. Reinforcements of all three services – of which we were a minor symbol – had begun flooding out East as the war in Europe approached its end, and it was generally assumed that we would be invading Malaya in the near future to link up with the Australians and Americans in Borneo and the Philippines, although our main naval strength was in the British Pacific Fleet to support the coming invasion of Japan.

First we had a minor overhaul in Trincomalee, which allowed

two of the three watches a week's leave up in the hills at Diyatalawa Rest Camp. As the 200-mile bus journey took all day we were quite ready for the rest when we arrived, and enjoyed the coolness and lower humidity after tropical Trinco. Fortunately we were normally at anchor there, pointing into what wind there was so that the metal windscoops fitted into the scuttles, as naval portholes were called, scooped in any breeze. Not that a puff of warm, damp air made much difference, nor indeed did the limited number of electric fans, and those who could slung their hammocks on deck at night. Athlete's foot and dhobi itch were rife, naturally, but no more serious sickness, despite the climate. We went back to our Crash Boat job for the escort carriers and other exercises, varied by a day's break in Madras while crash boating in June, and early in July joined other ships' companies for a pep talk by the charismatic Admiral Lord Louis Mountbatten. He was a handsome fellow, and knew it, and had the knack of making his audience feel that he was taking them into his confidence as part of one big team.

The following week our engines packed up after limping home from an exercise, not very surprising after more than three years active service, and we spent nearly three weeks alongside the depot ship *Woolwich* repairing the bearings and undergoing a general overhaul while leave parties were sent up again to Diyatalawa for a rest in the hills. On the way back this time the bus stopped in the old Ceylonese capital of Kandy, where we caught a glimpse of its historic buildings and the famous Temple of the Tooth guarding one of the Buddha's teeth.

On 6th August the first atom bomb was dropped on Hiroshima, and three days later the second one on Nagasaki. Russia declared war on Japan and invaded Manchuria. Next day Japan offered to surrender if she could retain her Emperor. The Japanese Empire suddenly collapsed, surrendering on 15th August, but that morning we sailed for Colombo so we were at sea on both VE and VJ Day and missed the celebrations. We made up for it next day in Colombo, splicing the main brace and celebrating in town. To add to my pleasure *Devonshire* arrived in harbour a few days later to join the fleet, so I was able to meet up with old friends aboard and hear how they brought the King of Norway back to Oslo at the Liberation.

We had been sent round to Colombo to be docked and have our bottom scraped of weed to increase our speed, so once this was done we returned to Trincomalee for our Crash Boat work while the escort carriers continued deck landing training. Meanwhile our full Hunt flotilla had assembled, to join in the naval preparations for the liberation of Malaya. Landings at Port Swettenham, now Port Kelang, the gateway to Kuala Lumpur the capital, had already been planned for September to launch the invasion, and these were to be carried out by landing craft to test the plans already made.

The fleet sailed on 4th September for the Malacca Straits, we in a group led by the cruiser *Royalist* with six escort carriers and eight destroyers. With our limited range we had to fuel at sea from one of the carriers, as did the other three Hunts, and we anchored at dusk on the 8th about 30 miles off Port Swettenham, ready to cover the next day's landings against any opposition. There was none, but unexpected mud banks would have left some of the landing craft sitting targets, and we were detached to join Force 64 proceeding south to free Singapore. We anchored at the western end of the Singapore Strait the following day and fuelled again while waiting for the fleet to assemble. Next morning, the 11th, we weighed anchor to bring up the rear of the line. As we passed Raffles lighthouse the order was given to Invert the Line from the Rear, so we swung out, increased to 19 knots and steamed past the rest of the destroyers, the cruisers, the escort carriers and the great French battleship *Richelieu* – on her way to reoccupy Saigon – to lead the liberating fleet into Singapore. I as Navigator was crouched over the binnacle checking our bearings, and we anchored off the city about an hour later with the fleet all round us. Only later did we learn that we had sensibly been given the leading position so that if the Japanese minefields were not accurate the smallest ship would be the first casualty! What still irks me is that no effort was made to instruct us to muster the maximum number of hands on deck in case we did strike a mine, and indeed it was quite some time later before we even heard the mine story.

Next day, Wednesday 12th September, Admiral Mountbatten as Supreme Allied Commander in South-East Asia accepted at the City Hall the formal surrender of the Japanese Southern Armies in the presence of the official representatives of all the Allies. We were allowed to go ashore once the surrender had been signed, and found the green-grassed Padang in front of City Hall turned brown with a covering of thousands of surrendered Japanese troops. The streets were decorated with valueless Japanese occupation currency notes strung across them, and the pavements littered with Japanese office and company signs torn down with delight by the Chinese who had been so cruelly oppressed. One of those signs reading 'TOKYO MARINE AND FIRE INSURANCE CO LTD.' with the appropriate Japanese characters above, which I picked up as a souvenir, still decorates our garden shed.

My father and uncle had many friends in Singapore and Malaya, so I did my best to find and assist those they had listed. They had all been interned, civilians as well as military, in local camps, where they were fed a starvation diet and were often close to death by the time liberation came. My father passed on to the editor of the *Mercantile Guardian* a letter which I wrote him, and this extract gives a contemporary account of the situation:

On Thursday I went ashore with a case full of clothing to present to some of your friends. The Japanese had seized their office, and had sold all their papers as waste. All the European offices were treated the same, and records of all goods in godowns (warehouses) were disposed of, so that it is most difficult to pick up the threads of business. A friend in an internment camp received some cheroots from outside wrapped in his own banking account records. I saw an Attorney's agreement trodden in the dirt outside Union Buildings. Your friends have got their office back undamaged, with most of the furniture, used by the Japanese, intact, but they must start from scratch and were busy tracing their pre-capitulation Chinese staff and giving them a month's pay and registering them for employment. Everyone had a bad time under the Japanese. They were fed on a little rice, a few vegetables and some occasional fish – always bad. The Red Cross parcels the Japanese sold to the public for their own profit. There were medical supplies, but the Japanese held them back. All who I met say they owe their lives to the

74

Chinese who smuggled food and tobacco and medicines to them at risk of their lives. In another three months nearly half of them would have died of weakness or despair. We only just arrived in time.

Singapore could not have been a pleasant place. The leaders of the Chinese community announced that the Japanese had murdered 20,000 Chinese and some estimates put the figure higher. Chinese heads were exhibited all over the city while Japanese officers were signing the visitors book at the untouched Anglican Cathedral. Of the synagogues one was converted into a Japanese temple and the other into an ammunition store. The mosques were spared. All Jews were arrested and interned in Kranji Gaol, and later at Sime Road Camp with the other British civilians. Yesterday I met one recently released. He had lost all his family, and his godowns and stores were officially robbed by the Japanese. They commandeered all his goods as enemy property, which is what they did with all the European stores. Whiteaways is bare and empty, as is every big store and building. Raffles Square is dead. Every building, empty but undamaged, is defaced with Japanese boards and nameplates and the ramification of Japanese firms are everywhere, branches of the Yokohama Specie Bank, and agencies for Nipponese businesses established in our places.

They seem to have had little pride in their great new city, and it is shattered and unpainted. They have not even troubled to remove British inscriptions, not even the enamelled wall signs of well-known British products. Union Buildings still has the name over the door and so has Albany Buildings, with the names of the firms and representatives still unaltered in the hall. The Japanese have done little but put subheadings under our road signs. They seem to have realised that Japanese was not understood, as all their own firms showed their names in English and Japanese. I think few places in Asia have been more grateful for liberation. The Nips killed Chinese on any pretext and hung them or sabred them. Every prisoner and internee had to bow to every Japanese or Korean, and they were beaten up if they didn't. The Koreans were very varied types. Some were war criminals worse than the Japanese, while others risked their lives to feed our men. I saw the signed testimony of a colonel to the loyalty of one of them, yet others were devils. The Nips seem to have turned some to their own creed and raised others to a patriotism and loyalty to the Allies never dreamed of before. The bad will certainly be punished, but I hope we will not forget to reward the Chinese, many Koreans and a few Japanese who saved our men's lives and helped in every way they could. The best currency is still cigarettes. I was offered four dollars for a tin of fifty, but I kept them for a family I was calling on. The Japanese never issued any coins but ran off notes from one cent up. You can understand that if ten dollar notes were used for street decorations the one cent notes are lying in the gutters. They are too small for kindling and too coarse for cigarette paper.

On the surface Singapore, with its buildings undamaged, looks to have trade in full swing. There is plenty of food visible if you can afford it. Japanese occupation money nearly broke the local people. It started at par but by August an egg cost fifty dollars and by the time we arrived the price was three hundred dollars. Now they are ten cents Straits currency and other foodstuffs seem to be coming back to normal. The black market of course is thriving. The native shops have managed to hide or save a portion of their stocks, but the Japanese imported little except cheap mass-produced necessities and the whole country is desperately short of decent manufactured goods. There will be unlimited demand for any kind of goods, although Military Government is in force and is expected to control trade for at least six months. I am sorry this is such a morbid letter, but I thought you had better know something of how the Japanese behaved before your friends return home.

I was able to find one of my father's good friends from the First World War, a Dr Bruce Wallace, ex-RAMC, who had run a rubber plantation in Kedah between the wars and joined up again for local defence. I met him several times after his release from

Changi Camp, and was amazed how tough these elderly men were, probably due to acclimatisation and in his case to his medical knowledge. The released were known as RAPWIs – Released Allied Prisoners of War and Internees – and put up in Raffles and other hotels to ease them back to sufficient health for the sea journey home to recuperate. Bruce insisted on buying me the set of Japanese surrender photos which I still have. Another souvenir I hold is several copies of *The Syonan Shimbun*, the English-language newspaper that the Japanese printed on the seized *Straits Times* presses. By the end it was down to about the size of two sheets of A4 paper, on whose back and front was packed a surprising amount of slanted news. The one I prize is that of 21st August, announcing that 'Tenno Heika has graciously granted an Imperial Rescript for suspension of the war'. Tenno Heika, Son of Heaven, was one of the imperial titles, and Syonan, or Southern Capital, was the new Japanese name for Singapore.

Another victory had taken place a couple of months earlier. Labour had decided to leave the wartime coalition government after the defeat of Germany, so Churchill formed a temporary Conservative government to carry on the war and a General Election was held in July. All servicemen overseas and over 21, which was then the age limit, voted for their home constituencies and their votes were flown home to be counted along with the rest three weeks later on 26th July. Naturally election addresses couldn't be sent all over the world, so servicemen in particular voted on the party records. The large majority of servicemen and the majority of the country blamed the Conservatives for the pre-war unemployment and appeasement of the dictators, and Labour won by a landslide. I remember the cheers from the lower deck and the gloom in the Wardroom as the results were announced over the radio, though our gloom was more for the loss of Churchill as war leader than worry over a Labour government led by men who had been part of the war cabinet for the past five years. I voted Conservative in tribute to Mr Churchill, but also because I believed that the Conservatives could be relied upon to lead the country best.

With the surrender of Japan, the government was anxious to reduce the huge number of men and women in the armed forces and demobilise then to fill our factories. Britain had built up an enormous war debt, owing hundreds of millions of pounds for wartime purchases and suddenly now had to pay for all supplies from America due to the abrupt end of Lend-Lease loan arrangements. Austerity soon exceeded even wartime levels as we lacked the foreign currency to buy the food we wanted from abroad, and the government was blamed for circumstances beyond its control.

We remained anchored in Singapore Roads for several weeks, sending parties ashore to help restore services as required, and made one journey as far east as Bali to escort a ship bound for eastern Borneo, before being informed early in October that we were to be sent home as part of the reduction of the fleet. Our flotilla was an obvious choice, as our limited range made us a bit of a liability on a station where long voyages were required. This was proved again on our return to Trincomalee, as we had to call in at Sabang island off the northern tip of Sumatra to refuel so that we could complete the journey. By now I was navigating with confidence and enjoyment, and was reasonably certain that Trincomalee would indeed appear over the horizon a couple of days later. It did.

By wartime standards I was now a rich young man. As a newly promoted Lieutenant I was earning 17s a day, plus 2s 6d Japanese Campaign Pay introduced to reward those still fighting after VE Day. £350 a year was a good sum for a young man with no liabilities, free accommodation and a token charge for food, a free health service – which the services had for ages before the National Health Service came in – duty-free cigarettes and gin and whisky at an old penny or two a tot. The government, anxious to damp down inflation, introduced a new pay code which would effectively have left us out of pocket, so my pay was artificially subsidised right up to 1949 to ensure that I was maintained at my lordly wartime level of 19s 6d a day while newly promoted Lieutenants had to get by on 17s. It was the only time I won on a pay change, and on my return I blew a month's pay on a silver tankard for my father on his sixtieth birthday.

From Trinco we sailed again round to Colombo, where we took on a large draft of 34 ratings for early release, to replace men in higher age groups who were landed for further eastern service.

Most of our ship's company were HOs, Hostilities Only ratings. I doubt if even 10% of the lower deck were still RN by the war's end, and release was based on age and service so that the older men who had served longest were first to be demobilised. It was a very fair system, but meant a bulk change of about a quarter of the ship's company – men whose understandable interest was to get home and out of the service – so considering that they did very well. Fortunately we had two weeks in Colombo to settle down, as it was decided to remove and replace a damaged propeller before the voyage home. I enjoyed Colombo, being able to afford good hotels in my affluent state, and meeting up with old friends. I was delighted to make contact with my old *Devonshire* friend Hugh Herbert in the corvette *Tulip*, and John Birn, son of my mother's close friend Gertie, who as a Lieutenant in the US Army had been involved in cloak-and-dagger operations behind the Japanese lines.

We sailed from Colombo as a half flotilla of Hunts, four of us led by *Bicester*, at the beginning of November. After a final shopping and fuelling call at Gibraltar we left the others off Ushant to berth at Devonport in early December, to discharge our men for release and prepare to put the ship into Reserve. The huge wartime fleet was being rapidly scaled down as men were demobilised, and only the best and most modern ships were to be kept manned.

We now had a chance to cease living for the day and to think about the future. We had seen the first sign of peacetime cost-saving when we were ordered to proceed from Bombay to Aden at our economical speed of 12 knots, the speed at which we covered most miles to a ton of oil. We also had a brief chance to think of the greater cost when we observed the pre-war Two Minutes Silence at 11 a.m. on Armistice Day, to remember for the first time the dead of two dreadful world wars. I was fortunate to have lost none of my family – unlike most British Jews who had relatives murdered in Europe – no close friends from school or Dartmouth, and to have come through the war without a scratch, but we all knew how lucky we were when we paused to think about it; a bomb or a shell striking just a little to one side and we or those we loved would not have survived. Although I might thank God, it struck me as inappropriate to do so when God had more important

79

things to do than ensure that I was not killed. It was too great a burden to believe that God had preserved one for some mighty service to humanity; I preferred to attribute my good luck to chance.

Christmas was now approaching, with most of the ship's company on leave. The American aircraft carrier *Wasp* was berthed just across the basin, so the few of us remaining in the Wardroom, with the inborn confidence of a British destroyer in its home port, invited two of their officers over for dinner. Ensigns Collier and Swanson were their representatives to spend an evening with us, that ended with coffee and talk aboard *Wasp* until 3.30 a.m. We really hit it off, and they joined us again for Christmas Eve dinner in town and nightcaps aboard us into Christmas morning. Swanson was unfortunately killed in a flying accident a few years later, but Felton Morland Collier – who claimed descent from the Felton who killed Charles I's favourite the Duke of Buckingham – remained a friend of the family until his recent death. On Christmas Day we entertained the petty officers before lunch, and the forward messdeck was at home to visiting Wrens, Women's Royal Naval Service, in the evening. A good time was had by all without any disciplinary consequences. Leave parties changed over, and I arrived home just in time for New Year's Eve 1946. Like the others I received three weeks' leave, then returned to *Blackmore* to complete putting my areas of responsibility 'into mothballs' as it was called, before leaving her for good. She had not been a very happy ship, and I was glad to be gone.

All regular servicemen were awarded a month's 'End of War Leave', and it was just my luck to be given it during a cold, miserable and underheated February. Fuel was in short supply, gas pressure low, and my abiding memory is of crouching over a low gas fire much of the time as my reward for Victory.

I was a keen stamp collector, encouraged by all stamps from overseas letters being torn off and kept in a drawer in the office for Michael and me to dip into, so several cold days were spent bringing my collection up to date, including those sets I had bought at post offices during my overseas journeys. Interesting and attractive many were and still are, but as an investment few things pay worse than such uninformed impulse buying. The prize example is the Military Administration set issued for the re-occupation of Burma, which is barely worth the 30 shillings I gave for it over 50 years ago and would buy now less than one shilling did then.

My parents had recently moved back home to 63 Exeter Road. I had my old room back, and was able to unpack my limited possessions and resume the life interrupted when I went to sea. A house-warming party in January, to mark their return home from their wartime lodgings in Hampstead and my father's sixtieth birthday, provided an opportunity to meet up again with many of their circle. My mother's sister Lizzie and her children Anne and Brian were back from their wartime evacuation to Australia, so I saw quite a bit of my cousin Anne before she started her National Service in the Wrens. There were visits to my grandmother in Hove, to my mother's brother Lawrence near Diss, and to various relatives whom I had not seen properly for years, theatre outings, dinners in the West End, and visits to my favourite music hall, the Metropolitan in Edgware Road, to enjoy Max Miller and other leading comedians. Keen as ever on historic events, I queued for two hours one afternoon in January outside Central Hall Westminster to witness an early meeting of the new hope of the world – the United Nations Organisation. I noted it in my diary as 'Rather humdrum but interesting', and went on to the Metropolitan to see the pantomime *Cinderella*. It must have been panto of the year, as I had seen it the previous week at a lesser music hall, the Kilburn Empire, to which we had taken my younger cousins Rosemary and Bill. I finally saw my brother Michael again, when he got weekend leave from his Royal Signals base at Catterick, where he was being initiated into his National Service – as conscription for 18-year-olds was imaginatively called. I went up by train later in the month to spend a weekend in a hotel at Catterick Bridge to meet him there, and be given a conducted tour of that vast base. It made me appreciate having chosen the Senior Service.

Cinemas were far more of an attraction than today, not merely because there was no television but because they always provided a two-film programme as well as a newsreel. We possessed at the nearby State in Kilburn the largest cinema in Europe, whose opening week's show I had attended before the war, with Harry Lauder appearing on stage. On this leave I saw *Brief Encounter* and *The Count of Monte Cristo* in a not unusual four-hour performance, which always included a break for a performance on the Wurlitzer organ rising up from below the stage. We certainly got our money's worth.

I had already been informed by the Admiralty of my future, courses and then a destroyer in the Mediterranean, so I went straight from my End of War Leave to RN Barracks Portsmouth for a week's radar course. The wardroom was a fine late Victorian building and the cabins cosy, each with its steward-tended coal fire, which I appreciated after civilian austerity. Radar had made enormous progress since the experimental RDF of the early war years, and its role in gunnery was now well established. As a Gunnery Control Officer elect – the job for which I had unwillingly been selected – one needed to know all about it. The next week was spent at the Royal Naval College Greenwich, my first experience of dining in the magnificent Painted Hall, which is probably the finest services mess in the world, for a Current Affairs course. It was a five-day compressed general education course to broaden our outlook, ranging from British trade figures to Imperial, not yet Commonwealth, relations. A week living at home was next, for a Damage Control course in London, followed by a week at the navigation school outside Portsmouth on handling all the information coming into a ship's control room and plotting tables. That filled March, as a prelude to our course in HMS *Excellent*, the Gunnery School on Whale Island at Portsmouth, which puts the snap into the Royal Navy as its drill as well as its gunnery school. We had an intense six weeks there, smartening us up and giving us the knowledge of the latest destroyer control systems and guns. Four of us were going through the course before joining the same flotilla, and in mid-May we all passed our exams and were sent off on our embarkation leave. This climaxed with my acting as best man to my Uncle Douglas, who in his early fifties finally got round to marrying Josie, whom he had been courting for years. On 5th June we went down for the ceremony at Hove Registry Office, followed by an excellent lunch, and two days later I joined the troopship *Orontes* at Tilbury with my three

82

fellow Gunnery Officers for a comfortable journey to Malta. As we steamed down the Channel on the 8th, the ship's radio broadcast the Victory Parade marching past the King in London.

# 8

## *Chevron*

My destroyer *Chevron* had been the first of her newly built class of eight to commission, just after VE Day. All their names began with the letters 'CH' and they formed the 14th Destroyer Flotilla based at Malta. As *Orontes* entered Grand Harbour, *Chevron* steamed past into the dockyard to commence her first annual refit.

Malta dockyard consisted of two long narrow bays, facing the capital Valletta across Grand Harbour. Practically the whole island, especially the harbour area, had been fortified by the Knights of Saint John when it became their base against the Turks in the sixteenth century. Fort Saint Angelo, on the headland guarding the northern bay called Dockyard Creek, had become HMS *Saint Angelo* and the headquarters of Flag Officer Malta. Behind the fort lay the town of Vittoriosa, facing its twin sister Senglea on the next tongue of land which divided Dockyard Creek from French Creek on its southern side, and the town of Cospicua linked the two other towns round the head of Dockyard Creek. They were known as the Three Cities, and had been practically destroyed during the war by Axis bombers trying to wipe out the dockyard on which the Royal Navy depended. Dockyard Creek had supported the galleys of the knights, and the slightly wider French Creek had become the main RN Dockyard, shielded to the south by the barren heights of Corradino, so we were effectively boxed into a long stone coffin in high summer and never seemed to catch a breath of air.

Perhaps it was as well to start what was to prove the happiest of commissions under the worst possible conditions, since after that dockyard refit anything was bound to seem an improvement. I soon got to know my way around Malta, finding the innumerable little offices and sections ashore which serviced the fleet and which I would need in future, from the Confidential Book Office, which supplied our CBs, to the RN Film Corporation, which provided our shipboard films. As much local leave as possible was given to get us out of our sweat hole, and while most of the ship's company were sent to a services rest camp at Taormina in Sicily, we new arrivals had to make do with Saint Paul's Bay rest camp. Saint Paul had traditionally been wrecked there on the north coast of Malta on his way to Rome. It certainly made a pleasant change from the dockyard. Another break was a week's Musketry course at the Royal Marines Training Centre at Ghain Tufficha nearby, which also provided a sandy beach for afternoon relaxation after a long and gruelling exercise session from 7 until 1. The Maltese language is Semitic, close enough to Arabic to be mutually understood, and Ghain, pronounced Ain, is their common word for a spring of water. The 'gh' is silent in Maltese, whose *dghaisa*, pronounced daisa, is their version of a gondola.

We gratefully undocked after the worst ten days of the refit, when our upper deck was at dock level while our bottom was scraped of weed and our propellers cleaned. On 1st August the refit ended, and the same day we changed our number from the wartime 14th, which I had known at Alexandria, to the peacetime 1st Destroyer Flotilla, and removed the 4 from the 14 previously painted on our funnel.

It was a new experience for me to serve in ships painted a uniform grey instead of wartime camouflage, and to accustom myself to peacetime standards of spit and polish when in wartime polished brass could give off a dangerous reflection. The Mediterranean had been the premier fleet before the war, or certainly fancied itself so, and this spirit continued. We were the victors of a long and bitter war, and without rival in the area. France was recovering from occupation and heavy naval losses, Italy from defeat with a much reduced navy, there was no other fleet of any size and Russia was as yet no naval threat, but we were financially crippled by the war, and visits were restricted to soft-currency countries to conserve foreign exchange. We rarely went west of

Malta, as Spain was a pariah fascist state and our Treasury was short of French francs. The fleet was concentrating on getting back to pre-war standards of appearance and operations, complicated by the constant change over of crews as officers and men were replaced and demobilised.

We had a splendid ship's company and officers led by our captain Lieutenant Commander John Bush, DSC**, which meant he had been awarded the Distinguished Service Cross three times during the war. Under him were three RN Lieutenants who had all commissioned the ship with him, plus myself, Lieutenant Commander (E) Michael Hodgson, DSC, our engineer officer, a Sub Lieutenant and Warrant Officer Gunner and a ship's company of about 180. For those days accommodation was quite good, most – except the officers who had bunks in their cabins – still slung their hammocks, or slept on deck in hot weather in harbour on camp beds. Food was good and morale was high as we rejoined the fleet. We moved round to the small ships harbour in Sliema Creek, on the other side of the Valletta peninsula from Grand Harbour, accompanied by our own *dghaisa*. He proudly displayed 'HMS CHEVRON, GEORGE' behind the seat to show his loyalty, and George always received priority over his rivals when anyone wanted to go ashore. Our main armament of four single 4.7-inch guns were my chief concern, and our brief work up included shoots against targets to check that all was in working order, before we left for Greece to join the rest of the flotilla at Port Drepano on the west coast for the traditional peacetime Flotilla Regatta. We had been preparing for these rowing races in ship's whalers, and came a close third of the eight in a good-humoured Derby Day spirit of fun.

While in Malta, the Captain had said to me quite casually in the wardroom that he assumed I had no objection to serving on the Palestine Patrol, and equally casually I said that I had not. He knew that I was Jewish, as did the officers and most of the ship's company, yet during the next nearly two years I never heard a single hostile or anti-Semitic remark, even from a drunken liberty-man, despite the many patrols we carried out. It was all remarkably clear-cut at the time. Our government had restricted the number of Jews who could enter Palestine; Jewish extremist groups in Palestine – the Stern Gang and Irgun Zvai Leumi, or IZL – were attacking British servicemen and taking their lives. The King David Hotel had just been blown up with heavy casualties – I didn't know until years later that the evacuation warning was ignored – and to me there was no question of not intercepting the 'illegal' ships whose passengers probably included potential terrorist recruits. It was as straight forward as a British Catholic serving against the IRA in Ulster, whatever his views on government policy.

Six of the flotilla went on from Port Drepano to Haifa to relieve our opposite numbers of the 3rd Destroyer Flotilla and mount the patrol. This ran for about 75 miles from the Lebanese border to south of Tel Aviv some 10 miles out at sea, and took around five hours, while another patrol roughly on the 3-mile limit waited to intercept, and the other ships in Haifa Bay were on call to back up. The country was thus effectively sealed off to seaward, backed by radar surveillance, and we saw the first result when the *Fede* was intercepted on 2nd September and towed into Haifa. Her 1,200 passengers were transferred to a transport ship that we escorted to Famagusta, where they were disembarked for internment until they qualified under the legal immigration quota. No violence, but considerable frustration and bitterness for these concentration camp survivors to be towed into Haifa and then deported to another camp – even though it bore no resemblance to those in which they had suffered. We saw their camp at Karaolos a couple of miles outside Famagusta, Star of David flags flying from many of the huts, as we bicycled past to visit the nearby ruins of Salamis. Back at Haifa towards the end of the month came an anonymous warning that a charge had been laid 500 yards from the harbour entrance. To the annoyance of the oil companies, as it delayed shipment from the Iraqi pipeline ending in Haifa, our Captain (D) in *Chequers* closed the port and searched the harbour entrance area without success, but finally found a powerful charge attached to the oiling jetty which could have destroyed a warship fuelling there and caused a disastrous fire. We also stood by the minesweeper *Rowena* as she boarded a caique, a local sailing schooner, which slipped down the Lebanese coast using an auxiliary motor, hoping to beach herself at the Jewish township of

Nahariya near the border. All 'illegal' ships adopted a Hebrew name, and this one was called *Palmach* after the elite Jewish defence force.

Jewish limpeteers had attacked and damaged the transport *Empire Rival* as a reprisal against the new policy of deporting immigrants to Cyprus, so explosive charges were dropped at intervals by ships in the bay to discourage any further attacks. They often provided the bonus of fresh fish for breakfast. Men could only take leave in pairs and armed, in restricted areas of the city, so everyone was glad to get away when our five weeks' duty ended.

We paid a short visit to Port Said to be present for the Commander-in-Chief's visit in his flagship the cruiser *Liverpool*, and witnessed the glorious disruption of ceremonial as she came in with her Royal Marine band playing on the quarterdeck to be met by a launch packed with Egyptian bandsmen, engaged by the chief contractor Jim Irish, blasting out such less ceremonial tunes as 'She'll be coming round the mountain when she comes'. The C.-in-C., Algy Willis, was Clem Attlee's brother-in-law and a similar rather dry type who was unlikely to have seen the joke.

We went on to Larnaca to join the Fleet Autumn Cruise, and from there escorted the cruiser *Phoebe* to Heraklion in Crete. The breakwater where we berthed was soon lined with men, women and children anxious to barter poultry, eggs or Greek money for clothing, cigarettes or chocolate, which were almost unobtainable locally. The Nazis had bled Greece dry and starved the people, there were almost no industries still functioning and reconstruction had barely started. There was little to do in the damaged town, but we made the excursion to Knossos a few miles away to see the part-excavated, part-reconstructed, Minoan capital city and sit on the king's marble throne, which I am sure is not accessible nowadays to tourists' backsides. We sailed back to Argostoli bay in Cephalonia for the Fleet Regatta, a much expanded version of our earlier Flotilla Regatta This included the Small Ships Regatta, which we won, and to our great delight the Cock of the Fleet title. One of the races we won was the officers', where I coxed a wardroom crew; we had all aroused some astonishment in Heraklion as we got in practice there. Each race crew was accompanied by a 'chuck-up' party in the motorboat in fancy dress, cheering them on with musical support, and at the end a wooden cock was mounted in front of the bridge to represent the silver one safely stowed below. On a less happy note, ashore we visited a Greek church near which the Nazis had built their war cemetery. So hated were they for their cruelty that the graves had been uprooted and the bones thrown into a charnel house beneath the church. The island was famous for its grapes and raisins, the latter for sale round the landing pier, and an austerity British Christmas was brightened for many naval families by Cephalonian raisins.

We escorted the flagship back to Malta after the regatta, and had a few weeks there boiler-cleaning, making small repairs and doing some sightseeing. I took the opportunity of the cooler weather to explore the historic capital Valletta, and especially the splendid Palace of the Grand Masters. This had mostly survived the bombing and was full of portraits of them wearing their black robes emblazoned with the white eight-pointed Maltese cross. It had become the residence of the Governor, now Mr Douglas, the first non-service representative since Britain captured the island from Napoleon's troops after they drove out the last Grand Master. A civilian had been appointed to symbolise the planned change to self-government under the new constitution that he was drawing up, but meanwhile the Council of Government met there. It was open to the public, so I went along one afternoon and found it rather like a town council meeting in a very grand tapestry-hung chamber.

We also had plenty of opportunity for sport, and after playing cricket for my Quarterdeck Division, for the first time since Dartmouth, I now took up hockey again. These games and the drinks which followed were a good opportunity to get to know one's men off duty. I had acquired extra duties, chiefly Victualling Officer, where I relied heavily on a splendid Stores PO and had taken on a self-created job of producing a one-page ship's newspaper, *The Chevron Chronicle*, about once a week to report on places we were about to visit or offer humorous articles or interesting news. It had begun with articles on Heraklion and Argostoli, then on Malta featuring R. Sole, my naval equivalent of Tommy Atkins, attuned to sailors' humour level. Television language after the 9 p.m. watershed was normal on the lower deck, but they would never dream of using it in front of their families in the way it is needlessly done today. The next issue was on Palestine to mark our return to Haifa, to try and explain Britain's half-promise of it to both Jews and Arabs, and the deadlock caused that now involved us all.

On 8th December we witnessed a total eclipse of the moon, the first I had ever seen and very impressive at sea with no shore lights to dilute it; then we were diverted to the tiny island of Sirina in the Dodecanese, where an illegal immigrant ship had grounded and sunk on the way to Palestine. They had managed to send an SOS, on their portable transmitter, and we were to investigate. We arrived off the small rocky island, about 2½ miles long by 1½ wide, next morning, and sent in our motor boat with supplies. The *Athina*, an ancient steamship with a Greek crew, had embarked nearly 850 Jewish refugees at a Yugoslav port, and had been driven ashore or run aground in Sirina bay in rough weather. The ship heeled over, and almost all the passengers were able to scramble ashore before she slid off and sank in deep water within an hour.

The eight inhabitants were completely overwhelmed and unable to provide food or shelter, so the food and blankets dropped by RAF planes from Palestine were received with tears of relief some hours before our arrival, as the passengers had been surviving on a soup made of local snails. Next morning we were instructed to embark all survivors, which we did in groups of 40 in the motorboat towing the whaler. I was in charge of this operation, greatly helped by an embarkation party on the rocky shore guiding them aboard. The children were delighted to be hoisted into *Chevron* in sacks, but their mothers were somewhat less enthusiastic. After a break caused by rough weather, all survivors were embarked by early morning by us and the minesweeper *Providence* which had arrived to help. Despite the weather not a single refugee was hurt beyond the odd scratch or cut, which was a fine achievement. They were quickly disinfected, given a hot meal and allowed to rest while we sailed for Crete. There they were transferred to a tank landing ship for internment in Cyprus, but before they left a delegation visited the bridge to thank the Captain for their rescue and good treatment aboard.

As our reward, along with a congratulatory signal from the C.-in-C., we were sent to Piraeus for a break in Athens, where we were joined by my first ship the cruiser *Ajax* on a flag-showing visit. We travelled the 10 miles to Athens by train, or by British Naval Mission trucks. These streaked up the long straight road towards the city nicknamed the 'Mad Mile', and rightly so in view of the driving. The city was having its coldest December in years, with icy winds sweeping down from the snow-dusted mountains, and one soon learnt that *Krio* was the Greek word for 'cold'. The Parthenon was floodlit, possibly for the first time since the war, in honour of a visit by the South African premier General Smuts, and we took the opportunity to visit it and the other temples on the Acropolis. We were also shown the pocket-sized stadium built for the first modern Olympic Games just 50 years previously, and the Fix Brewery on the Mad Mile turning out beer for our servicemen under NAAFI control. The only things in good and cheap supply were beautiful natural sponges, whose sellers stood on street corners with their wares on strings, and dolls in Greek national costume.

We sailed on to Kavalla in Greek Macedonia at the request of the British 10th Brigade, who wanted a warship for Christmas, and who gave us the most alcoholic one I ever experienced. The brigade was there to train the new Greek army and help them keep order in the province, which was menaced by Communist guerrillas supported from over the Bulgarian border. On Christmas morning we were visited by a choir of shy Greek girls to sing us Greek carols, a touching gesture as their Orthodox Christmas fell some 12 days later. The ship was dressed with evergreens at the mastheads and yardarms, and all the messes with flags and streamers and other decorations. The official cavalcade led by the Captain wound its way slowly round the ship, lengthened by a tail of young ratings in borrowed officers' uniforms, and paused for a drink or snack in each mess. As we had done the same routine the previous evening round the army officers' and sergeants' messes until the early hours, it is surprising that we survived to eat the traditional heavy Christmas dinner and then be host to the Army for the rest of the day. Later in the week officers and men were invited out to stay in isolated Army posts, bumping over torn-up roads at a maximum of 20 m.p.h. I went with a group to join the Durham Light Infantry at Xanti, where even the officers were living in an abandoned tobacco factory since the War Office refused to supply tents as men might not sleep under canvas after the end of October. The obtuseness of the War Office almost reconciled us to the peculiarities of the Admiralty. New Year's Eve brought the news of the captain's promotion to Commander at the early age of 32, which led on to full Admiral in due course. This made the party all the happier, ending up with a joint service gathering in the RASC Sergeants' Mess to see in 1947.

Unfortunately we had to sail next morning, seen off by a sizeable Army group in heavy rain at the end of our best ever liaison visit to the Army. Even more unfortunately, that forenoon had been selected for a full-power trial, and tearing into a rough sea brought back the previous evening for most of us in a very unwelcome way. We returned to Sliema Creek in Malta, and spent most of January enjoying its mild winter climate while Britain was suffering one of the coldest of the century, when Churchill rose in the Commons in his overcoat to belabour the government for the fuel shortages which almost brought industry to a halt. We took the opportunity to explore the Maltese countryside at weekends by bus. The buses had suffered from six years' hard running during the war without replacements, and the way the Maltese crossed themselves at the start of a journey seemed not just piety but also effective travel insurance since I never heard of an accident to those rickety old vehicles. Almost no-one had a private car just after the war, and I can't ever remember using a taxi, so it was bus or walk, except for the old coal-burning ferries built in the 1880s which still ran from Sliema to Valletta after surviving the wartime bombings.

It was back to Haifa again in February, broken by a visit to Beirut, from where we made excursions by bus to Damascus and Baalbek. Lebanon had only been independent of France for a few years and its flag was not yet well known. Several of their coasters came under suspicion of immigrant running for flying 'the Austrian flag with a Christmas tree central', as it was described by one captain who did not recognise the cedar of Lebanon.

A Commodore Palestine had recently been appointed, with his

headquarters at Stella Maris on the slopes of Mount Carmel, to be in charge of the immigration patrols in place of a constantly changing senior officer afloat. He was Commodore de Salis, who came aboard to give us a very balanced talk on our responsibilities without any bias against the unfortunate would-be immigrants. We saw the avoidance of another near disaster when the caique *Merica* was towed in soon afterwards with nearly 650 'illegals' aboard, after she broke down and drifted on the high seas well away from the coast. It says a great deal for the seamanship of the Palyam, the Haganah branch organising the ships, that she and the *Athina*, wrecked on Sirina, were the only two of the dozens of mostly decrepit old ships they were able to purchase that did not reach Palestine in the course of three years.

At the end of the month we were involved in our first interception, the steamship *Ulua*. She was flying the flag of Honduras, a Central American republic with lax registration laws but possibly also favoured because its flag resembled the future Israeli flag. She claimed to be bound for Tel Aviv with Jewish survivors of a shipwreck, but then announced her change of name to *Chaim Arlosoroff*, a Zionist leader, to which our senior ship *Chieftain* replied, 'Happy Birthday'. When we reached the 3-mile limit of territorial waters two minesweepers were ordered to board, but by skilful manoeuvring she broke away and ran aground at the foot of Mount Carmel. Unfortunately for her she grounded opposite an army barracks and all her thousand immigrants were arrested. Despite strong resistance to the minesweepers' boarding parties, which left two sailors seriously injured, no firearms were used by the Navy and not one immigrant killed – an example of the restraint used on all occasions in the face of a barrage of missiles. Fifty years later I returned to Haifa as part of a Royal Navy team to take part in symposia there and in Tel Aviv on these conflicts. It was almost like one of our naval reunions the way we were greeted by our former opponents, including the master of the *Ulua* Captain Gad Hilb and his commander Lova Eliav, later a distinguished Labour politician. Tributes were paid to the behaviour of the Royal Navy, and relief expressed that it was us and not the French or the Americans they were up against in their struggle, or it might have been a much more bloody affair.

It was at this time, anchored in the bay between patrols, that I composed the following bitter poem, which appeared in my synagogue magazine and sadly in part still remains relevant:

## THOUGHTS IN HAIFA BAY 1947

Mount of Elijah
City of Carmel,
Haifa the squarebuilt
Formal and modern.

Harbour of stone blocks
Built for world shipping,
Frowned on by buildings
Ranged up the hillside.

Long range of Carmel
Nature made backbone,
Marks out the skyline
Bare but not jagged.

Aloft on the Point
Stands Carmel Convent,
Perched like a watchbird
Brooding o'er Babel.

Warships of Britain
Rest in the Bay,
Ready for duty
Firm but not harsh.

Large cooling towers
Rise grey by Kishon,
River of Galilee
Tomb of Baal's prophets.

Curved on its hillock
Sleeps ancient Acre,
Dreaming of chivalry
Death and Napoleon.

Cloud flecked blue sky
Forms gentle cover,
To it from Lebanon
Reaches white Hermon.

Brown hills of Galilee
Sacred in history,
Bathed in old glory
Rise from the plain.

Christian nonentities
Mocking their teachings,
Squabble for precedence
With rival priesthoods.

Semites of Palestine
Mad Jews and Arabs,
Plot greater violence
Hateful and evil.

Is nothing holy
In this most holy land,
Nothing but Nature
Naturally clean?

Promised forsaken land
Dear love of many souls,
Wake now reborn again
Jerusalem rise.

Build up the true faith
Out of this hatred,
Trust between all men
Peace on this earth.

94

The week after the *Ulua* we intercepted another 'illegal', also flying the Honduras flag. She was a smart modern diesel yacht called the *Abril* with an American crew, who proved co-operative. I addressed them in English and German over our loud hailer, which I was to use in future for a standard warning that they would not be allowed to land and should not resist as force would be met with force. It may have been tactless to use the language of the hated Nazis, but it meant that most of the immigrants knew the position and could not be misled so easily by troublemakers. This time it certainly worked, as our boarding parties met with no resistance and were actually offered fudge and tomato soup from her modern galley. I only learnt at the recent symposia that she was the one IZL 'illegal', funded by the American writer Ben Hecht after whom she was renamed, but her prospective captain had run off with most of the funds and a girl in Marseilles, so the crew saw no point in starting a fight.

She was berthed in Haifa harbour in the middle of the night, and by dawn her 600 passengers were on their way to the internment camp in Cyprus. *Abril* was later to become one of the first ships of the Israeli Navy after the end of the Mandate, as all the arrested ships piled up in one corner of Haifa harbour, while lawyers tried to determine to whom they belonged.

After these interceptions shore leave was given in Haifa, which was quite exceptional, and the officers went for a shopping trip along Herzl Street. We found the Jewish population surprisingly friendly and life going on so normally that we ended up with a cream cake tea in a cafe. We were also able to complete the flotilla football competition with a win over *Charity* to gain the cup with a record of 7 wins against all our 7 flotilla mates. It was a fine welcome to our new captain, Lieutenant Commander Robin Mayo, who had taken over command between our two interceptions. We also gained a new First Lieutenant and reliefs for others of the original officers who had been with the ship since she was commissioned.

Our duty ended, we enjoyed a short cruise, first to Beirut, then to Poros island in the Gulf of Athens. Poros was renowned for its lemons, which were in season and so plentiful that we could pick and suck them like oranges. They quenched the thirst without being too bitter. We were due to go on to Piraeus for Easter in Athens, so when King George II of Greece died suddenly on 1st April we made hurried preparations to parade a guard at the funeral. Fortunately the C.-in-C. arrived in his flagship to spare us that chore, and we witnessed the funeral procession on our western Easter Sunday. I was impressed by the Greek soldiers along the route standing at the Present Arms for more than an hour as the whole procession passed, and the former Regent, Archbishop Damaskinos, on a small throne carried by priests, turning from side to side to bless the crowds.

On Good Friday the wardroom had made an excursion by truck to Corinth, with a good view on the way of the canal – still blocked by the bridge which the retreating Germans had blown down into it along with part of the 200-foot cliffs. We passed through the little town of Isthmia, which gave its name not only to the isthmus through which the canal was cut, but to every other narrow land bridge in the world, and explored the excavated old city of Corinth. The visit was cut short by my messmates so that I could be back in Athens for the eve of Passover service – just one example of the consideration they so often showed. It was a sad and moving occasion to join in the synagogue the remnant of the Athens community who had returned from the concentration murder camps.

We left for Malta with over a hundred Greek sailors to take over former British ships awaiting them, and did a short work up on arrival to settle in our new members, since demobilisation of wartime servicemen drained off a batch of them every month or two. Weekend leave was granted when in Malta, and I took the opportunity to travel by bus and elderly ferry across to the smaller sister island of Gozo, more laid back, fertile and quiet. It seemed to be a standing joke in Malta that 'my brother in Gozo' could usually get hold of whatever was wanted, but a visit proved that it was a euphemism for the black market, laying the blame unfairly on the Gozitans. The full flotilla assembled in Saint Paul's Bay for exercises, and then sailed together to Port Drepano for the Flotilla Regatta. This time we just pipped the flotilla leader *Chequers* – in which the Duke of Edinburgh was to serve as First Lieutenant a couple of years later – to become Cock of the Flotilla, combining this with Cock of the Fleet Small Ships gained the previous October. A tremendously cheerful party followed, with the cock paraded round the flotilla and our wardroom at home to all the other seven. Our return journey provided the rare sight of a full flotilla of eight handsome sister ships racing through a blue summer sea in a combined full speed trial. We secured in Sliema Creek, the only time we were ever all together in Malta and so unique that the C.-in-C. came round in his barge to admire the sight.

We were now due for a month's turn of duty in the Adriatic, one of the most popular areas, and set off gladly for Trieste. It is the most northerly harbour in the Mediterranean, well north of Sebastopol in the Crimea, a beautiful city and a lovely place to be in summer. It was the chief port of Austria for centuries until they lost it to Italy in 1918, and two years before our visit the New Zealanders and Yugoslavs met in the city at the end of the Second World War. The Yugoslavs wanted it, although the population was Italian, but were persuaded to withdraw to just outside, and we and the US were holding the fort until a peace treaty was signed. We were regarded very much as liberators from the backward and Communist Yugoslavs and made most welcome, helped by a weak Italian lira which enabled us to holiday like well-bankrolled tourists. Trieste was supposed to become a Free City, as the Russians wouldn't agree to it returning to Italy, and we were its protectors. As the Victualling Officer, I took the opportunity to truck up to the attractive old Venetian inland town of Udine to supervise the drawing of our vegetables, which for some inter-service reason had to be drawn from the Army there instead of purchased locally, and we gave a free ride to anyone who was pre-pared to sit on potato sacks on the way back.

Too soon we had to move on to Pola, 50 miles to the south, which was an important Austrian and then Italian naval base. Under the peace treaty it was to pass to Yugoslavia and become Pula, and already the vast majority of the population, who were Italian, had upped and left, stripping their former homes down to the doors and plumbing, and the remainder were hostile and wait-ing for us to leave. The town boasted one of the finest surviving Roman amphitheatres, able to seat thousands of people until the

Venetians carried off its marble seats to build some of their palaces. There was little else to see, and the Army kindly let us share their lido as the harbour was too polluted for swimming. The officers held a Midsummer's Night picnic on the beach of a little island in the bay, to learn later from the Army that it was full of unswept landmines.

Our next call was Venice, where we embarked a pilot offshore and entered through winding channels to berth near the heart of the city and Saint Mark's Square. I was thrilled to explore this famous and tourist-free city where we were still almost an occupying power. The great Danieli Hotel was an officers' club, and the Lido beaches ours for the asking. The city had escaped war damage but life was not easy for the local people without tourism, and some resorted to theft. We were a popular and soft target, and gondolas slipped past in the early hours to steal bedding, clothing or anything else within reach through the open portholes. I lost my sheets the first night, and we had to post extra security guards, but that did not restrict our enjoyment. We went over to the Lido to bathe, though in that tideless sea the sand was already distinctly grubby without a natural daily wash, and to Murano to see the glass blowers, as well as the city sights, shops and bars.

My parents were holidaying in Switzerland, and the Captain granted me a week's local leave to visit them in Zurich We had a happy few days together before my 30-hour return journey, as rail services were still painfully returning to normal. Many changes were necessary, including an overnight sleep in the waiting room of Milan station before the morning train to Venice, and the evening train via another change in Udine back to Trieste to rejoin just in time before midnight. Overstaying one's leave is a major offence, and a missed train connection is no excuse, especially as we sailed next morning for Malta, so it was quite a nerve-racking journey.

We were soon off again on the Fleet Summer Cruise, calling in for a short two-day visit to Athens, then on to Istanbul for the first official fleet visit since before the war. We anchored in the Bosphorus just north of the city, where we were welcomed with boxes of 50 Turkish cigarettes for everyone, dinners for the ratings, and for the officers an official reception and lunch by the

Commander Active Fleet at a seashore hotel. His flagship was the former Imperial German battlecruiser *Goeben*, renamed *Yavuz* and still impressive in her old age. She anchored downstream of us with the bulk of their fleet to greet our two cruisers, two light aircraft carriers and four destroyers. We had a splendid view of the walls, domes and minarets of old Constantinople from our anchorage, and conducted tours of the city were laid on by the Turkish Navy. For all the official functions we wore our neck-high starched white uniforms, under which the sweat gently soaked our trouser tops in the hot and humid July weather, especially during the fleet's official return cocktail party on *Ocean*'s flightdeck when the Royal Marine band rose up on her lift to Beat Retreat in its usual incomparable way.

We sailed up the Bosphorus to turn just short of the Black Sea, a journey we had already done in the British Embassy yacht as part of our entertainment, but now to show the flag to the residents, then down past the city through the Sea of Marmara and out through the narrow straits of the Dardanelles. We saw the tall Anzac memorial on Cape Helles, honouring those who died there in the failed 1915 attempt to take Gallipoli, then separated from the fleet to visit Greece's second city, Salonika. We had to anchor offshore as the port was so small, and found our Christmas friends from Kavalla had been moved down there. Friendships were renewed and they gave us a good time, since the poor city, crowded with refugees from Communist guerrilla attacks, had little to offer. Alexander the Great had founded it in honour of his sister Thessaloniki, the Greek name it still retains, and its Saint George's Church is one of the world's oldest, a converted Roman temple surviving since Saint Paul's visit. Most of the old city was destroyed by fire during the First World War, and it was still recovering.

We joined up with the fleet again at Nauplia for the Fleet Regatta. It had been the temporary capital of Greece while the Turks still held Athens; their first President Kapodistrias was assassinated there, and the bullet marks were preserved under glass on the church door-lintel. The new King Paul and Queen Frederika of Greece came round from Athens in a destroyer to watch the regatta, and although we were unable to hold on to the

Small Ships Cock this time it was another very cheerful occasion. For the third time I coxed the Officers' Whaler, which was beaten into second place after two previous wins. Army alcohol in Salonika took the blame, but we were not up to the previous standard.

No sooner were we back in Malta than we were fuelled and stored and despatched to Marseilles, to watch over three ferry ships anchored nearby off Port de Bouc. The story began a month earlier when some 4,500 Jewish Displaced Persons – the official name for concentration camp survivors with no homes to return to – had sailed from Sete near Marseilles in an old Mississippi steamboat called the *President Warfield*. As she approached Palestine they renamed her *Exodus 1947*. She offered violent resistance to the boarding parties, leading exceptionally to three Jews being killed and many injured before she was brought into Haifa. There they were loaded into three ferry ships normally taking 'illegals' to Cyprus, and sent back to France. With very few exceptions the Jews made it a point of honour not to disembark, and there the ships lay, since the French refused to accept back any who did not land voluntarily. Finally Foreign Secretary Bevin redoubled his error by delivering an ultimatum to land within 24 hours or be carried to the British zone of Germany and forcibly landed there. Not a single Jew agreed to disembark.

We patrolled up and down for eight days in case of need, transferred stores to the ferry ships, and had a close up of conditions abroad. They really looked prison ships, with the decks boxed in with wire netting to prevent the Jews jumping overboard or breaking out to take over the ship. It was Saturday, and we could see a group of Orthodox Jews wrapped in their praying shawls conducting their Sabbath service. It was the one time I felt ashamed, to be taking part in such a heartless and insensitive operation, but unknowingly Bevin was building up international support for the United Nations resolution three months later that led to the establishment of the State of Israel. We now formed part of the escort of the ferry ships to Gibraltar on their way to Hamburg – a sad police duty for proud warships. There we gladly turned them over to ships of the Home Fleet, and had a couple of days' relaxation before returning to Malta at the end of August.

100

We were to stay there as it turned out until mid-December, and Mrs Mayo arrived to join the Captain. They set up home in a little villa at Saint Paul ta Tarja and regularly entertained the officers there, which made the island more enjoyable. On 8th September it was Malta's National Day, the anniversary of both the lifting of the Great Siege by the Turks in 1565, and the capitulation of Italy in 1943 which ended the second siege. The towns were decorated, public buildings floodlit and fireworks went off all over the island. Every town has its own saint's day with fireworks and brass band performances, but this was the lot rolled into one. In Valletta even The Gut was *en fête* with flags. The Gut was the nickname for Straight Street, a peculiar name since the whole town was laid out as a grid of straight streets. It was almost entirely full of bars to serve the fleet and other servicemen, and was definitely Ratings Only. It was clearly understood that officers did not go there to be an embarrassment to their off-duty enjoyment, and each ship had its favourite bars with often the ship's crest and photo. The next three months were a boom time for *Chevron*'s favourites.

The worst of the economic crisis had just hit Britain, leading up to the November devaluation, and expensive items like cruises were cut, along with the fleet. Demobilisation was moved into top gear, reducing the size of the fleet, and we did little but exercises and a few Crash Boat days escorting *Ocean* until our refit. This was a repeat of the one I had met on arrival, but fortunately in cooler weather, and this time the local leave was in Cyprus. I formed one of a party taking passage to Famagusta in the frigate *Cardigan Bay*, an unusual experience to be a passenger in another ship, then spent a fortnight based on Army rest camps. From these I explored much of the island by bicycle in each main area which I reached by taxi, except between Famagusta and Nicosia, where I rode the long since departed little train on the island's only railway. Usually there was only one train operating, so the driver could mentally switch on autopilot and read his paper until the train reached its destination. I covered most of the island from Kyrenia to Limassol and the Troodos mountains to Nicosia, and enjoyed its scenery and its ruins, then back to Malta by ferry ship.

Malta had received its new constitution, for which Governor Douglas had been sent out, and the King delegated his brother the

Duke of Gloucester to open the new parliament, following the election of a Labour government under Doctor Boffa. As Gunnery Officer I was naturally in charge of our section of the street-lining party, resplendent in my shiny black gaiters and sword. The Destroyer Platoon led the march down the main street Kingsway to the Governor's Palace, where parliament met, and platoons from the various services and regiments lined the whole route. Each platoon commander ordered 'Royal Salute, Present Arms', but the street was so narrow that we were forbidden the full sweeping sword salute for fear of slashing the crowds pressing close about us. All went well, with trumpet fanfares and a 21-gun salute, and democracy was restored to a people who had fully earned it.

We had an unpleasant surprise to discover that we were to spend several more weeks in the dockyard to change all the superheated steam tubes in our boilers as some had been found defective, but it did mean that we were able to listen to the wedding of our future Queen to the Duke of Edinburgh on the BBC's overseas broad-cast. Due to the rapidity of demobilisation, three-quarters of the ship's company had left in three months and, though we were now almost all regulars with very few of the new National Servicemen, we needed a proper work-up to reach fleet standards. This we had in early December, with exercises ashore and at sea, so as to com-plete the only full flotilla of eight seagoing destroyers in the entire Royal Navy for the next year, as the rundown and removal of the Hostilities Only men almost halved the seagoing fleet at a stroke, and the other flotillas were at only half strength.

Back we then went to Haifa as, though the United Nations had voted for Partition, Britain remained in charge until the Mandate expired on 15th May, and immigration controls were maintained to placate the Arabs. We embarked from our predecessor the boarding platform introduced since *Exodus 1947* – a cross between a high diving board and a meccano set, designed to ease the boarding party's assault on high-sided ships. Christmas Day was spent on patrol, with only token celebrations, and Christmas dinner postponed until we could eat it next day at anchor in the bay. The year ended with our escorting another 'illegal' into port, the sailing ship *Maria Giovanni*, which looked beautiful as she approached the coast in winter sunshine with all her sails set, flying the Star of David flag and with her passengers lining the deck. She had been renamed *Haganah Ship 29th November 1947*, the date of the UN resolution approving a Jewish state, and following our usual loud hailer address about not resisting, she lowered her sails before sunset and continued under auxiliary engine. No resistance was offered as she crossed the 3-mile limit and we boarded, disembarking her 700 passengers for transfer to Cyprus.

The delayed Christmas Concert held on the forward messdeck on New Year's Eve ended 1947, then we weighed anchor just before midnight. A ship's concert is an occasion for everyone to let their hair down with acts of various degrees of humour and imagination emphasising our shared experiences, and this one helped weld together the new and older members of the ship's company with its ditties and jokes about patrols and naval routines. That night we saw one more major immigration problem solved, as two large groups of immigrants totalling some 15,000 passed us in the *Pan York* and *Pan Crescent* under escort direct to Cyprus for internment. They had sailed from Rumania and been shadowed since entering the Aegean. The Jewish authorities had decided not to risk their lives by resisting boarding, and agreed for them to proceed direct to Famagusta. There may well have been some strategic planning to divert our attention while key personnel slipped in, as we were sent out again late on New Year's afternoon to investigate a ship aground off Naharia near the Lebanese border. She proved to be a schooner called *United Nations* which had successfully crept down the coast and beached herself when all eyes were on the two '*Pan*' ships. She was one of the few successful blockade runners.

It was about this time that I gave up eating bacon and pork, not because I was suddenly smitten with remorse at breaking a biblical injunction, but as an outward sign of my Jewishness and a form of self-discipline which I have continued ever since. Since it was one of the few things that most people knew about Jews, I felt it wrong to be eating forbidden food even though I regarded it as far less important than obeying the moral code of loving one's neighbour as oneself which Jesus repeated from the Laws of Moses.

We had a few days in harbour mid-month, when leave was granted provided men remained in groups of four or more, of whom at least half were armed, and did not leave the main streets. This was in Haifa, a mixed Arab and Jewish town, traditionally the most tolerant in Palestine, with Army Bren gun carriers at the junction of Jewish and Arab districts to prevent clashes. In Jerusalem and the Tel Aviv–Jaffa areas there had already been riots, deaths and destruction, but Haifa tried to maintain an uneasy peace. It was the citrus season, with oranges and grapefruit piled up at the port in crates waiting to be shipped. Ripe fruit that could not survive the journey was weeded out, and the loaders were pleased to trade a dozen for a cigarette. Deck ukkers, ludo played with huge wooden dice on a board 6 foot square, was a popular relaxation when we were in port, with different parts of ship competing for a cup, also regular tombola, since with no sport and limited leave it was otherwise easy to get bored.

Before we left for Malta at the end of the month we had all earned the Naval General Service Medal with clasp PALESTINE for completing 28 days' operational duty. The award had been introduced the previous autumn, and was contemptuously known as the 'Bevin Star' after the Foreign Secretary by those who had earned real combat medals only a few years earlier. We were in Malta for the first post-war Carnival in February, a miniature version of the Riviera Mardi Gras processions with decorated floats and tableaux constructed and peopled by representatives of almost every town on the island. These promenaded slowly round Valletta, up and down the various streets for hours to the delight of the onlookers as it represented another part of the return to happy pre-war days – though there were still great gaps among the houses from the wartime bombing. Town bands led their floats, one preceded by a man on 10-foot stilts who never once slipped on the steep streets, and children in costume escorted their town floats in a real people's festival. A few days later came the island's own festival, the day of Saint Paul's shipwreck on Malta, with religious processions and a great service in Valletta's Church of Saint Paul for the devoutly Catholic people.

Soon afterwards we sailed to escort the Commander-in-Chief in the cruiser *Newcastle* on his farewell visit to Alexandria, where there was much ceremonial but little leave as anti-British feeling was so strong that it was not advised. A strange sort of official visit, not very diplomatically timed when treaty negotiations were bogged down. We escorted him from there to Haifa and on to Beirut, where we were invited to a reception at the Officers' Club. The marble staircase was lined by the Garde Republicaine in ceremonial dress, who snapped to the salute with drawn sabres as we drew up and had to remain thus while we sorted out enough Lebanese money to pay off our anxious taxi driver.

From there we escorted the C.-in-C. down to Port Said and through the Canal for a farewell visit to King lbn Saud in Jeddah. We crossed into the Tropics in the Red Sea for the first time in the commission, and changed gladly into white uniform as the mercury rose. A local pilot led us through the reefs into the inner anchorage off the city, gleaming dazzling white in the sun and freed only the previous year of the old city wall which had deflected any breeze up and over it. The town was almost unaltered from the days of Lawrence of Arabia, as the oil revenues were yet to flow. We were offered the famous Maria Theresa silver dollars, still being minted in Vienna dated 1780, and large silver riyal coins for our Egyptian pounds, but few took them up except as souvenirs since there was little to buy. The King's son Emir Feisal received the Admiral, and we mustered a naval team to play cricket against a local British team on a smooth sandy portion of the so-called golf course outside the town. The local team did well to force a draw, their star bowler being an Indian doctor in a tarboosh, and our Sub Lieutenant Mike Garnett scored a century not out.

The alcohol restrictions must have been less fierce in those days, as the team and spectators were treated to beer and sandwiches in a tent after the match. In return we put on a firework display in honour of Saudi Arabia, with special emphasis on the green and white of their national colours, which involved a huge stock of rockets and flares embarked for the occasion. The full ship's company, in tin hats as a protection against falling rocket sticks, took part in the finale holding flares, while salvos of rockets burst overhead. As Gunnery Officer in charge of it I felt like a firework impresario, but the sheep enjoyed it less. With limited warning a boat had arrived alongside that morning with 20 live sheep, rice, fruit and vegetables as a royal gift, and *Newcastle* received a larger supply. Our sheep were penned on the quarterdeck, where one had its leg broken by a rocket stick, before they were despatched in a bathroom converted into a temporary abattoir where they were shot, skinned, disembowelled and prepared for the cold room over the next two days by men with slaughterhouse experience. They considerably reduced our mess bills, and proved surprisingly tender and flavoursome.

We returned to Malta in mid-March, where we made some minor repairs, and the officers took several of their 'Runs Ashore', which began with dinner at the Union Club in Valletta, the former Auberge de Provence of the French Knights, and often ended at 'Aunties'. Auntie had been a star of the British music halls in the Naughty Nineties and later settled in Malta, where her bar was decorated with photos of stars she had worked with or known long before we were born. Her hostesses were not much younger, and it was an unusual contrast to our other raucous haunts to stop off at Aunties in Kingsway.

Easter brought out women in the faldetta, the old national dress of black robes and curved plywood headdress covered in black cloth, which one rarely saw otherwise in the towns though it still lingered on in the villages, and the churches rivalled one another in the beauty of their decorations and flowers. On April Fool's Day I shaved off the beard I had worn since before D-Day, and enjoyed the surprise of those who did not recognise me. The following day I entertained my messmates to dinner at the Marsa Club, a more relaxed version of the staid Union Club, to celebrate my twenty-fourth birthday.

We returned to Haifa later in the month, and as we approached the city on the 22nd were surprised to see boats full of Arabs leaving the harbour and heading north for Acre and beyond. The end of the Mandate was little over three weeks away and Haifa was to be the site of the final British withdrawal, so the Commander British Forces had apparently decided that he would not intervene in local battles since Haifa had been allocated to the Jewish state by the United Nations partition plan. He withdrew British troops into the port area, and by the time we arrived two days later the

Jewish defence force Haganah had captured the whole lower Arab town. Many Arabs fled north by road, or by sea after taking refuge in the British guarded port. Meanwhile we were keeping up patrols to the last while the country behind us disintegrated into civil war, and on the 24th we joined our sistership *Chieftain* to intercept the modern Italian motorship *Vivara*. She had been renamed *Haganah Ship Mishmar Haemek* after a settlement that had recently beaten off heavy Arab attacks, and after my usual loud-hailer address asking them to cooperate we were able to escort her 800 immigrants into Haifa. As always, on principle, she stopped her engines when boarded at the 3-mile limit, and had to be towed into port, where even at this late stage her passengers were deported to Cyprus. Two days later we joined *Chieftain* again to intercept the French trawler *Tadorne* and her young and spirited group of passengers. They renamed her *Haganah Ship Operation Kastel* to mark the capture of that key village on the road to Jerusalem, painting the new name round her bridge as we watched, and after a show of defiance they gave way in face of a barrage of firecrackers and were boarded without resistance. We rescued two of *Chieftain*'s boarding party who had fallen overboard and took them and a sick immigrant into port. We were then shifted to the inner patrol to look out for arms runners, and could see the skirmishing near Tel Aviv marked by curving tracer in the night sky.

At the end of the month we were sent for a rest break to Beirut, but communications had been interrupted and we were not expected, so had to wait offshore until the Chief Pilot returned from his mother's funeral accompanied by his relatives the other pilots. We took the opportunity as usual to book excursions led by our friend Tony Karam, the proprietor of Liban Tours, who was so pro-British he had been interned by the Vichy French and had named his son Churchill. This time he included a visit to his uncle Elia, the Orthodox Patriarch of Lebanon, who greeted us with sugared almonds and sweet wine. After a long speech in Arabic he gave us all a reproduction of a local ikon of the Virgin and Child reputedly painted by Saint Luke, and blessed us. It was encouraging how warmly the Lebanese always welcomed us, and how high was Britain's standing; we had even been asked during the

C.-in-C's visit who Britain wanted to win their elections. As we had no idea of the situation, it was easy to give a diplomatic answer. In the harbour we were shown round Hitler's former yacht *Grille,* which flew the Red Ensign as her post-war purchaser was a Lebanese with a British passport, Mr Arida. We were interested to see the ship's bell engraved with an eagle and swastika, Enigma cypher machines which meant nothing to us, 'Eva Braun's Cabin' for Hitler's mistress, and the ship's bridge. Steering was by pressing a red button to turn her to port, green to starboard and an emergency button for sharp turns.

We were back off Acre within a few days to support a British-negotiated truce with a show of force, but all appeared to be quiet ashore and we returned to our usual outer patrol the following day. *Tadorne* seemed to have been the last of the 'illegals' – there was no point trying to run a blockade which would cease within a few days – and we saw no likely arms runners which again would be biding their time. We were relieved the next week, and spent the last three days of the Mandate at anchor in Haifa Bay. Italian, French and other foreign warships had been coming to Haifa and Jaffa to evacuate their civilians as the certainty of war increased, and now a large force of British warships arrived from Malta to be present for the end of the Mandate and be on hand to protect the withdrawing British troops.

On Friday 14th May, the last day of British rule, I went ashore to supervise the collection of victualling stores from the Army base near Athlit, then dropped off in Kingsway to discover what was going on. Suddenly a convoy approached led by armoured cars, and I recognised and saluted General Sir Alan Cunningham, the departing High Commissioner, in army uniform in the central car, which was flying his standard. Despite all that must have filled his mind, he still found time to return the salutes of us servicemen in the street. I then called in at the Post Office to see what was on sale, and found it full of servicemen and civilians buying up as souvenirs the Jewish National Fund stamps overprinted *Postage* in Hebrew that had replaced the withdrawn Palestine stamps. Everything was ending in improvisation as Britain withdrew without any attempt at continuity.

The High Commissioner boarded the cruiser *Euryalus*, and

about 1130 that evening the British fleet sailed from Haifa, six destroyers escorting the aircraft carrier *Ocean*. As midnight approached we all directed our searchlights to form a cone over *Ocean*, then *Euryalus* drew up from astern between the lines of escorts, the High Commissioner's flag illuminated at her masthead and General Cunningham standing on the front of her bridge. The Royal Marine Guard of Honour on *Ocean*'s flightdeck presented arms, and her Royal Marine band played the National Anthem, followed by 'Auld Lang Syne' as the cruiser passed between us and *Ocean*. Three cheers were followed by a final fourth as *Euryalus* drew ahead on her voyage to Malta. The Mandate might have ended disastrously, but at least the Royal Navy had marked its end with dignity.

We then all dispersed along the coast to cover the withdrawal of the British forces from Sarafand near Jaffa to the British bases in the Canal Zone. The first column moved off at dawn and we shadowed it down to the border at Rafah by about 9. We went to Action Stations when they came under small arms fire in Gaza from Arabs who may have thought they were the Haganah, but they suffered no casualties and we did not have to intervene. We then turned back to join *Volage* covering the second and final column, which completed the journey by evening without incident.

Our first column passed the Egyptian army vanguard as they crossed the border, and we watched the smoke rising from their bombardment of the isolated Jewish settlements in the Gaza area as they moved north towards Tel Aviv. There the Jewish National Council, meeting on the Sabbath eve, had proclaimed that the State of Israel would come into being at midnight. Next morning the armies of five Arab states, Egypt, Transjordan, Iraq, Syria and Lebanon, crossed the borders on all sides in a co-ordinated attempt to crush the new state at birth. We were seeing the Egyptian thrust, which like the others was eventually halted short of the main Jewish areas. We withdrew to seaward overnight and returned to the coast in the morning, to support if need be the small British rearguard waiting near Rafah for any stragglers who might come in. As all was quiet we stopped for 'hands to bathe' and a waterpolo match, but in the afternoon an Egyptian Spitfire circled us doubtfully so we decided to identify ourselves – as during the

Spanish Civil War patrols – by spreading a large Union Jack on our forecastle. That night we were recalled to Haifa, as it was rightly thought unwise to keep us in the war zone without good reason.

Our naval contractor Aaron Tweg, a tall thin Iraqi Jew whom I had got to know well over the last 20 months, came aboard with supplies and news. The Israelis were falling back to defend the Jewish areas which they seemed sure they could do despite their shortage of weapons. The Star of David flag of the new state was flying all over town and over the captured 'illegal' ships berthed in the harbour, of which the best were being prepared for the new Israeli Navy. Several American ships were flying the flag at their mastheads, the normal mark of respect to the country one was visiting, since the United States had already recognised the new state, and ships were bringing in supplies to help the beleaguered Israelis. The British fleet dispersed rapidly, and soon we and *Volage* were left alone to take it in turns as Duty Destroyer. This began to mean something on Saturday the 22nd when Egyptian Spitfires attacked the airfield at Ramat David in the British enclave, destroying several planes on the ground and killing four of our men. The RAF were ready when the second attack came in, and shot down five of the six Egyptians. It was probably a genuine misidentification of an Israeli airfield, but after that we kept our close range weapons manned. Volunteers and arms had been flowing into Haifa to assist the Israelis, so Bevin's next move was to close the port to all but military traffic. It could be argued that this was an even handed policy, but to me and the Israelis it was blatantly hostile when the British-officered Transjordan Army was attacking them. Britain did not evacuate Haifa until 30th June, effectively sealing the only major port at a vital time for the new state, when evacuation could have been completed more quickly.

The British enclave extended about 10 miles south past Athlit, where we went several times by truck to bathe from the sandy beach below the ruined crusader castle, but we were heartily glad to leave when our relief arrived early in June. We took the opportunity to send home our final food parcels, which we had been doing regularly during our patrols to help out the family rations. Israel can not have been short of food in those early days as I despatched a 6-pound tin of tongue. Israel had advanced its clocks two hours to double summer time to reduce electricity consumption during the war, but Malta was not using summer time at all, so we put back the clocks one hour each evening of our three-day return journey to Malta.

We went straight into the dockyard for our half-yearly docking, and I had the opportunity to show much of the island – which I now knew well after two years – to my Uncle Douglas and Aunt Josie. They were holidaying at what was then the only large hotel, the new Phoenicia in Floriana just outside the walls of Valletta. I made a point of taking them to the old capital, which shared the Maltese name Mdina and the Italian name Notabile. It stands on a hill in the centre of the island, and is a delightful group of old stone buildings surrounding the handsome domed cathedral. Around it spreads the modern town of Rabat, with the catacombs in which the Maltese buried their dead in Roman times and from which you could take away the macabre souvenir of old bones. During the month I became the ship's 'oldest inhabitant', the only one to have served aboard over two years, and *Chevron* established her record as the ship longest with the fleet after three years. We persuaded *The Times of Malta* to carry an illustrated write-up, which was good for morale, and gave everyone a cutting to send home. This was followed by our captain being promoted to Commander Robin Mayo – our second commanding officer to get his 'brass hat' in 18 months.

Early in July we set off for the Summer Cruise, joining the aircraft carrier *Triumph* at Port Trebuki, a landlocked bay at the southern end of the island of Skyros between Athens and the Dardanelles. It was a thinly inhabited island seldom visited by the Navy, and we had been sent there partly because no check had been made since the war on the grave of the poet Rupert Brooke who had died there during the Dardanelles campaign. We found a tiny 'foreign field' containing about a dozen olive trees, and in their centre a marble tomb surrounded by green painted railings. The flat stone was engraved with a large cross inscribed 'Rupert Brooke' at the head and '23 Aprilio 1915' at the foot. A working party cleaned the stone and repainted the railings for the poet who died so young upon Saint George's Day.

We joined up with the fleet at Argostoli for the Regatta, where *Chevron* maintained her standard by coming third in the Small Ships Regatta in the usual carnival spirit of the event. Being summer the raisin grapes were available in profusion for eating before the main crop was dried. Smaller than a pea, pipless and very sweet, they looked like small black currants and we ate them in handfuls off the stalk. From there we went with *Chieftain* to visit Messina, which proved to be a southern Trieste with all the attractions of a fine Italian city. It claimed to make the best ice cream in Italy, which was quite a boast, and we soon learnt to order *gelati*. As it was an official visit by Flag Officer Destroyers in *Chieftain*, the Italian Navy made us very welcome, to the extent of making the wardroom honorary members of the officers' brothel! We also discovered the attractions of vermouth, three of us consuming a bottle each one evening without any hangover next day. On our way back from this spree we bought a huge watermelon for breakfast which we accidentally dropped in the main square, where it burst like a bomb, to the amusement of those out of range. Our final visit was to Corfu, seat of the British Governor of the Ionian Islands in the nineteenth century before we returned them to Greece. We did first teach them cricket, which survived to be played each summer. On our first day we played the Byron Cricket Club, and the Greeks staged more games during our stay. The attractive town was dominated by fortresses built by the Venetians to resist the Turks, but had the misfortune to be bombed by almost everyone during the war so it was remarkable how much survived. As always the local people made us very welcome, and organised bus tours to show us this most beautiful of Greek islands.

On our return to Malta in mid-August we had to endure water rationing. The island never has sufficient rain, but after only 9 inches the previous winter the water supply had been cut to only four hours a day. The Maltese beer always grew noticeably more salty in summer as the water sank in the underground reservoirs, but now it was so brackish that even tea was almost undrinkable and the island was plastered with 'Save Water' notices.

The Captain and I were soon joined by our reliefs from England, but it took several days to turn over my duties, as not only did all the victuals have to be checked to the last can of baked beans but also the costly radar valves and gunnery spares that were my responsibility or 'on my slop chit'. It had been a most happy commission during which I had typed with one finger of each hand nearly 100 issues of *The Chevron Chronicle* among my sidelines, and in my farewell edition I wrote: 'There are many happy memories I shall retain of my first post war commission... comradeship and enthusiasm ... and just the pleasure of having a good ship and messmates to return to from shore.' I meant every word of it.

# 9

## *Hebrew Student*

As there was no troopship due to call for some time, I arranged to join the cruiser *Phoebe* for passage as she was returning to England. It was a pleasant cruise home, calling on the way at Tangier. It was still an International City separated from Morocco and reputedly the sin, sex and drug centre of the West. We saw little sign of it, being very hospitably entertained by British residents, and when we reached Chatham I was discharged.

Luckily I went up to the Admiralty almost immediately to enquire about my future, as I discovered that I was due to join London University less than three weeks later. Every year an Admiralty Fleet Order was published asking for officer volunteers to learn a long list of languages from Arabic to Swahili, and that spring I had noticed Modern Hebrew included for the first time and put in a formal application. No one had acknowledged it or informed me of my selection, but I was to join the University's School of Oriental and African Studies at the beginning of October. Luckily my parents lived in London, or much of my leave would have been involved in finding and moving into suitable accommodation. I also lost several weeks' leave entitlement, but one doesn't complain when given a soft billet.

I shared the house with my brother Michael, who was home on release from National Service in India and Singapore with the Royal Signals. He had originally applied for a permanent commission and then changed his mind but, as he was not allowed to withdraw, deliberately failed his interview board by giving the most unsuitable replies to their questions. He enjoyed himself saying that he had applied 'for the social prestige', and otherwise pulling their legs. He had decided to join the family company, Tyler Brothers, which was working flat out exporting severely rationed textiles to a waiting world. Quotas were allocated by government control, and it was more a case of obtaining some pieces of cloth for a particular market or customer and granting them as a favour than competing to make a sale. Quotas were so limited that no great profits could be made, but at least there was full employment, though it was an unnatural business climate which was soon to change as competition developed from our war-ravaged rivals. The company was still operating from a small shop in Cricklewood Broadway five minutes' walk from home, after being firebombed out of the City in 1941, so there were no travel problems for my father or for Michael when he was not away at manufacturers learning the textile business. We both joined the Berkeley Reunion Group, the synagogue youth group for young adults back from the forces, and he also joined its amateur dramatic group the Berkeley Players, where the film star Leo Genn had first taken the stage before the war.

I took the Tube, as the Underground is still often called, to Goodge Street daily to check in for my tutorials at SOAS, as the School of Oriental and African Studies was invariably known. It was a pleasant change to be out of uniform, and quite astonishing to be free of all responsibilities at the end of the working day, not on call as Duty Officer, no watchkeeping, no one to report to or deal with and no extra-curricular activities. I was able to get to know post-war London, its theatres and entertainments, its parks and museums, and to involve myself in the social life of my contemporaries.

It was not pure holiday, however, as even my Hebrew alphabet was rusty from lack of use, and I could barely follow a Hebrew prayer book let alone pick out the headlines in a Hebrew newspaper. I was given just one day to go away and memorise all 22 consonants, some of which take a different form at the end of words and others a different pronunciation with or without a dot in them, as well as the various vowels formed by different dot and dash groups over and under the consonants. Vowels at first look like a sort of mad Morse code, but later I advanced to reading unpointed Hebrew newspapers made up of consonants only, where one's knowledge of the language and the context supplied the correct vowels and pronunciation. It is rather like recognising M J R for Major in English from its context, a bit of an acquired art. For an assimilated Jew like myself with little basic knowledge of the language it was not easy. In a Semitic language where only a few religious words like *amen* and *halleluyah*, that don't come up often in daily conversation, and a very few borrowed western words like *bank* or *telephone*, are recognisable, almost every word had to be learnt from scratch. It became easier after one learnt the roots, the mainly three consonant verb bases from which all tenses and nouns and adjectives were formed, as one could often guess or later remember them from a root one knew. Linguistically it was fascinating, as a military vocabulary was being adapted, often from biblical words, but it was a hard slog for an ungifted sailor like me.

My senior tutor was Isidore Wartski, a roly-poly little man who had come over from Eastern Europe as a lad before the First World War, and loved Judaism, Hebrew and England almost equally. His pain during the last years of the Mandate can be imagined, as his beloved England was virtually at war with the Jews of Palestine. He probably taught me more about my religion, almost by the way, over the next 18 months than I had learnt before, and was one of the finest Jews I ever met. His assistant Ben Segal is still active, at that time a youngish man recently out of the forces, and later a leading light of our Reform Judaism.

We had a common room and a few student sporting, social and political activities, but there could be little university life as such for a university in the centre of London. I made a number of acquaintances, notably an ex-colonel who was learning Arabic to work for an oil company in Kuwait, which was so newly producing oil that I had never heard of it, and one friend we have kept until today. He was then a young student from Israel, now a retired professor of the Hebrew University in Jerusalem – Jacob Landau. He was just commencing the studies which have made him an international expert on the last decades of the Ottoman Empire.

I had a very full social life as all my childhood friends, as well as the new ones I was making at university and through the synagogue, seemed to be holding birthday and other parties, often given by their mothers in the case of girls as the best way of finding likely boyfriends or husbands for them. In the case of Jews this was most important, as it was then almost unthinkable not to marry another Jew, so every effort was made to involve Jewish boys. Initially I just enjoyed the parties and the sophistication, but after a few months it began to dawn on me that this was the best opportunity I might have in years to find a wife, and particularly a Jewish wife. My parents were very broad-minded and would have accepted anyone I chose, but it never occurred to me to look outside my own faith. The different faiths did not mix as easily as they do today; it was unusual even for Catholics and Protestants to intermarry. Church- and synagogue-going was then more common, and formed the basis for many friendships and marriages. In my case Michael was being produced in the Berkeley Players by Jill Woolf, whom I failed to remember from her grandfather's seventieth birthday party many years before, and whom I would not have met if Michael had not sometimes asked her home, since she lived in West Byfleet. I began to take notice of her as 1949 wore on, asked her out several times and decided that she was just the girl for me, good-looking, intelligent and kind. Eventually on 13th August I took her out in a boat on the Wey with her spaniel Shandy, and proposed to her on my element. She accepted and I noted in my diary 'Both very happy'. Give or take the occasional argument, we still are.

Various other things had occurred earlier in the year. Britain finally decided to recognise the Jewish state officially, and missions were exchanged. In those days only the more important states exchanged ambassadors; a small state like Israel sent a minister. I was one of the large crowd that cheered the hoisting of the flag at the newly established Israeli Legation in Manchester Square on 31st January, and used the opportunity to visit the Wallace Collection almost next door.

In the Easter vacation I joined a National Union of Students tour to Italy. Trains were slow, with several changes, and it took us from 10 on Monday morning at Victoria until 9.45 on Tuesday evening to reach Verona. After sightseeing there and in Venice we went on to Merano in the Italian Tyrol for a week's walking holiday. The Austrian-style cream cakes and beercellars appealed to me almost as much as the dramatic Alpine scenery. We returned via Milan, where I saw *Lucia di Lammamoor* at La Scala, then had my first visit to Paris on the way home. This was followed in July by a holiday in the Lake District, where I explored the countryside by bus, taking steamer journeys on the lakes, and climbing Skiddaw and Saddleback on the same day. I had a wonderful time there, and Jill felt that I must be getting serious when I sent her a postcard. I then went on to Lancashire to stay with old gunroom friends, before returning to London to resume work.

In addition to my Hebrew studies I had been writing a book during the year about my experiences in *Chevron*. Although eventually completed, and the first half passed by the Admiralty, it never got into print due to the wedding and other more important things to attend to, but it provided a good basis for the previous chapter, and some idea of naval life for Jill as she helped to type it.

Jill's parents were on holiday in Cornwall when we got engaged, so we had to tell them by telephone and wait some time before seeing them. I left a note for mine before I went to bed as they were out, and was woken at 1.30 in the morning to receive their delighted congratulations. Jill had already fixed her summer holiday in Majorca, and went off by rail early in September via Barcelona to meet her brother Maurice, who was studying in Spain. This gave me time to sort out some wedding plans, including arranging an arch of swords from among my former *Chevron* brother officers then available in England, before I met her at Victoria on her return.

The wedding was fixed for Tuesday 13th December, as my parents were going on a Far Eastern business journey before Christmas and I might be off to sea again by the time they returned. The 13th held no threat for us, having already become engaged on it, and we saw no reason for a long engagement. The four months passed very quickly in a round of engagement parties and invitations, as I had to take Jill to meet my various relatives and she take me to meet hers. We chose an engagement ring, went to theatres and out to dinner – including *Aida* at Covent Garden followed by the Savoy Grill, where we stood next to the legendary

Winston Churchill as his son Randolph helped him into his coat and we heard him say a gruff 'Thank you, my boy.'

I had been down to Jill's home several times in the summer, and by now knew her family quite well. She had two elder brothers, Maurice and Brian, who had been in the Navy and Army respectively during the war. Maurice had been up at Cambridge reading modern languages, and Brian at Birmingham taking an engineering degree, and both were still living at home. The Woolfs had taken in two little sisters from Berlin in 1939, when Jews unable to emigrate were sending their children for fostering in Britain in the hope that they could follow. Ines and Anne were almost four and two when they arrived that July, their mother having already died, and never saw the rest of their close family again. They soon spoke perfect English, German forgotten, and had recently been legally adopted when no trace of their family could be found, as they had vanished in the extermination camps. They were now enjoying preparations to act as bridesmaids, while Michael was to be my best man.

The two families vaguely knew each other, being members of the same synagogue, and the Woolfs made me very welcome into their family. They were a confusing couple, being step-brother and sister. David Woolf's mother had married Gladys Harris's father after the early death of her first husband, Maurice, left her with just one teenage son. Gladys, who loathed that name, was known as Bill all her life as her father Alfred Harris had wanted a boy. He created quite a scandal in 1916 by divorcing her mother, formerly Constance Druiff, for being unfaithful to him. It must have been a traumatic event for 16-year-old Bill, her younger twin sisters Eileen and Olga and her young brother Alan, whom she had to mother. A few years later Alfred married Lizzie Woolf, née Davis, who understandably had no wish to be the second Mrs Harris after what happened to the first, and persuaded him to change his name. He fancied Hamilton to keep his initial, she King, so they compromised to become King-Hamilton. Hence their son, Judge Alan King-Hamilton, QC, and Jill's only blood uncle. He had lived with her parents until his marriage, and she took this to be a normal family, so when playing with her doll's house, she had to have a father, a mother and an uncle. Alfred was a solicitor and the law ran on in the family down to Alan's grand-daughter, now a young barrister.

The Saturday before the wedding I read the Torah, the 'First Lesson', from Genesis in Hebrew and Jill the Haftarah, the 'Second Lesson' from the Prophets in English. We had both known Rabbi Harold Reinhart since we were children, when he came over from America to act as Senior Minister at the West London Synagogue. He and his wife Flora were childless but loved children, and he regarded those of the congregation as his own. They were family friends, but his greatest claim to the community's gratitude was the number of German Progressive rabbis he had been able to rescue and bring to England before the war by finding them employment. One of these, Rabbi Bruno Italianer, was to conduct our marriage with him.

I had arranged with my cousin Edward Cohn and his cousin Henry Solomon that they would act as my ushers. On the eve of the wedding they took me first to Henry's RNVR Club for dinner, he having been a Paymaster Lieutenant during the war, and then on to Edward's Pathfinder Club for drinks, as he had been a Lancaster navigator, but they handled me carefully to avoid the traditional wedding hangover. My friend Lieutenant Peter Davis, RM, Jill's distant cousin, was fortunately available to brief the rest of my ex-*Chevron* guard of honour on synagogue routine. Covering their heads was easy enough as they came in uniform, and the rest was simple. The wedding canopy was wreathed in flowers, the bride looked lovely in white as she entered on her father's arm and we recited our vows in front of a mass of relatives and friends. Jill showed her strength of character and practicality by declining to recite her words in Hebrew, which she did not understand, and insisted on saying them in English. I am a great believer in tradition, and chose to use the old Hebrew words that have been recited for thousands of years, so between us in two languages we said 'With this ring I thee wed, according to the law of Moses and Israel'. Short and sweet. Then we left under an arch of swords in the winter dusk for our reception at Claridge's. This was too short for us to speak to all our friends; Uncle Alan gave one of his elegant and witty speeches, and it was time for us to change and dash for our train.

We caught the 6.30 from Paddington to Bristol, and spent the night at the Grand before travelling on in the morning to Saint Ives to honeymoon at the Tregenna Castle, one of the top GWR hotels recently nationalised into British Railways. It was several days before the marriage was consummated, both of us being shy and inexperienced, unlike most marriages today. The Tregenna Castle was almost empty ahead of the Christmas rush, but every table was laid and decorated with flowers, and everything maintained and presented to pre-war standards. We walked for miles during the week, as Jill showed me some of her family's favourite holiday places and we visited some of their Cornish friends. We also bussed out to Land's End and other local sights, since I did not drive and saw little point in learning while petrol was still rationed and I could hardly afford to buy a car. We moved on to the Headland Hotel at Newquay for Christmas, where we again explored the area by foot and bus, and enjoyed a succession of parties and dances in that rather gaunt hotel before returning by train to London.

My parents had left for a business journey to the Far East, so we returned to live at the family home with my brother Michael, but went down to West Byfleet to see in the new year with Jill's family. It was Jill's first and only experience of running a house with servants, and she did not enjoy it – especially as the servants were some 30 years older – but she coped womanfully. Meanwhile I got down to preparations for my Interpreters' Exams, having not completely neglected revision even during our honeymoon, as they were due in mid-February. There was still time for plenty of enjoyment, including a visit to the local State cinema in Kilburn to see the International Ballet dance *Swan Lake*, my first full-length ballet, and as a contrast *Charley's Aunt* revived in the West End. Several evenings were devoted to revision before a full day of written and oral exams in London. The following week came the General Election, in which Attlee's Labour government just held on to power, but lost a great number of seats, including that of my tutor Ben Segal's brother. We had tea with him and his wife as the results came through, before going on to *The Mikado* at the Golders Green Hippodrome. Jill had always been keen on the theatre and was rehearsing *Thunder Rock* with the Berkeley

Players at the time, and I had my first chance to immerse myself in drama of all sorts during that period. I also saw King George VI and the Royal Family proceed in state for the opening of the new Parliament on a warm Monday in early March; my first glimpse of peacetime full-dress ceremonial. We went to the Ideal Home Exhibition at Olympia, to gather ideas for when we had our own home, and to Kew Gardens, where the admission fee was one old penny right up to decimalisation, when it rose sharply to one new penny!

I was fortunate that there did not seem to be an immediate job for me, or I was being allowed the overseas leave missed on my return from the Mediterranean, as I was left on leave until the beginning of May. Towards the end of March my parents arrived home from the Far East and we met them off the P&O *Corfu* at Tilbury, after which we based ourselves mainly with Jill's parents at Byfleet. During my visits there I had shared two differing interests with her brother Brian, playing squash and swapping cigarette cards. Up to the war these had been issued in sets, usually 25 or 50 on subjects from insects to warships, one in each cigarette packet, and collecting sets was a great hobby.

I had been directed to take passage in the *Empress of Australia* from Liverpool on 4th May to join HM LCT 4001 in the Mediterranean, and found that I was one of ten Lieutenants sharing a cabin. We had few duties except to keep our eyes on the naval draft taking passage, so we kept out of the cabin as much as possible, sunbathed, read, and took part in any deck sports that we could. Most of the naval party disembarked at Malta, and I was left in charge of the remainder until we landed at Port Said.

The following day I took passage up to Famagusta, where I found LCT 4001. Developed during the war, an LCT was a Landing Craft Tank, a smaller version of an LST, or Landing Ship Tank, and she was the only one serving overseas. She had been sent out some 18 months earlier to conduct secret beach gradient surveys of the southern coast of Turkey, in case we needed to come to her aid if she was attacked by Russia. There were three officers, all Lieutenants, of whom I was the junior, and a crew of about 30 plus a naval hydrographer and a Royal Engineers contingent led by a Major and a Lieutenant who conducted the surveys.

She was having a rest break in Cyprus, and sailed for Turkey immediately I had taken over my duties. As soon as we were out of sight of land we all changed into civilian clothes and lowered the white ensign. We had no number painted on the side, and masqueraded as a former naval vessel sold to a civil company – as many had been at that time. We carried a Turkish naval liaison officer to sort out problems with the local Turks, which was essential as none of us spoke Turkish, and picked him up at Mersin, where we based ourselves. It was quite extraordinary to carry on naval routine without flag or uniform, offenders being brought before the Captain and made to doff their trilby hats before their offence was read out, but discipline continued normally despite this.

We worked eastwards along the coast, anchoring and sending the survey party ashore in their craft, and soon arrived at Iskenderun near the Syrian border. We spent an interesting evening there entertaining an intrepid John Godley and his companions, who were driving out from England across Asia to Christchurch in New Zealand to celebrate the centenary of its foundation by his great-grandfather. Driving across Asia in 1950 was still quite an adventure, and we were suitably impressed; I assume they made it. Iskenderun was founded by Alexander the Great, after whom it is named, and is the port of the ancient city of Antioch, which we visited by bus. Its church of Saint Peter, carved out of a hillside, is reputedly the oldest in the world, and we lunched by the attractive Harbiye waterfalls nearby. Then the area was quite unspoilt, but no doubt today it is overrun with tourists. We spent some time surveying the area, as the sheltered bay provided the best anchorage for hundreds of miles, and this completed many months of Turkish surveys. Regretfully changing back into uniform, we returned under the white ensign to Cyprus and conducted similar surveys around the coast of the island where the details needed updating, before proceeding to Piraeus for a short break. We then commenced our Greek surveys in Navarino Bay, famous for the battle which settled the Greek War of Independence when an allied British, French and Russian fleet 'accidentally' got involved in a fight with the joint Turkish and Egyptian fleet and sank all 99 of them – a truly decisive result.

We spent several weeks carrying out hydrographic surveys along the western coast of southern Greece, sending out our teams to update the pre-war information, before returning to Malta late in July. Our surveying duties were completed, so we discharged our Royal Engineers and hydrographer and prepared to pay off into reserve. First Lieutenant 'Tug' Wilson and I had already applied for our wives to join us, and now began searching for suitable accommodation as there were no married quarters for sea-goers. Elsie Wilson and Jill were flown out on the same plane, so were able to share their nervousness at never having flown before, and we met them at Luqa airport. I had unwisely booked us into the Westminster Hotel in Kingsway, Valletta's main street, and the heat, humidity and clanging church bells gave her a dreadful welcome after a long noisy flight. Fortunately we only had to endure it for a week before our lease was signed and we moved into our first home.

It was at 2 Gunlayer Street in Floriana where we rented a large first-floor flat in a typical nineteenth-century Maltese house, stone-built with enclosed wooden balconies and stone floors. The furnishings were sparse and old-fashioned, the cooking and plumbing facilities almost primitive, but it was our first home and it was fun to be on our own. We explored the island by bus, finding little bathing beaches where we could be almost alone, Mosta village church with its third largest dome in the world, and goats being milked at the housewife's door. Jill got to know local shops, did her housekeeping and flat-cleaning and had my supper ready for my return from work. I used to walk down to Grand Harbour in the morning and take a *dghaisa* across to the ship, a most romantic form of commuting, and return the same way to avoid a long bus ride.

We were slowly preparing to pay off into reserve when we were suddenly ordered to go into reverse, as we were to land the C.-in-C.'s car for his official visit to Rome. We sailed in mid-September to Ischia in the Bay of Naples for what amounted to a few days' holiday. We enjoyed our short stay, including a circum-navigation of the island by motorboat with swimming breaks, then sailed to Anzio, just north of Rome. We went alongside the cruiser *Gambia* for her to lower the cars into our hold by crane, then anchored aft and lowered our ramp onto the jetty with our bow doors open so that they could be driven ashore safely. To further justify our visit we carried out a port survey for future visiting ships, but most of the week was spent granting leave to Rome. It was Holy Year, with pilgrims from all over Europe visiting the Vatican and main churches, but nothing like the crowds one meets today. We saw all the sights quite easily, thanks to the tours laid on for us by the Italian Navy. The Pantheon impressed me most with its simplicity, and I brushed the film world by meeting Leo Genn, whose bridesmaid Jill had been, filming *Quo Vadis*; then we re-embarked the cars and returned with them to Malta.

Jill and Elsie had been exploring Malta in our absence, so we had further places to visit while we commenced reducing to reserve again. We were getting settled in our flat now, washing in a ewer-filled basin though we did have a shower and flushing loo. Our big double bed had a splendid Victorian frame, whose brass balls on the four bedposts rattled like mad at any movement. We discovered that they could be unscrewed, did so and put them away in a spare ewer. Months later in Jerusalem, we realised that we had forgotten to replace them. I was expecting to be drafted to another ship, having only been abroad a few months, when I was suddenly informed that I was to be sent to Israel for further Hebrew study as I had not reached the required standard in my Interpreters' Exams. I had my tutors to thank for this, as they had pointed out the difficulty of achieving fluency without living in the country. The Admiralty expected me to leave Jill in Malta or send her home, but she decided to follow me to Jerusalem. However, I had to go ahead, having written for advice to the Vice Consul, who found me accommodation in the YMCA, and Jill was able to follow me only a fortnight later after packing up our possessions for eventual shipment by stores ship to Haifa. Handing back the flat and doing this was quite a worry for a young wife abroad on her own for the first time.

Late in October I flew by BEA from Malta to Rome, as the future British Airways was then divided into short-haul British European Airways and long-haul British Overseas Aircraft Corporation. I renewed my passport at the British Embassy and obtained an Israeli visa, then flew on to Lydda by BOAC. A taxi carried me up to Jerusalem in the dark, and deposited me at the YMCA. The YMCA was a city landmark, stone-built in the 1930s with a tall domed central tower and two long wings on either side, facing the more famous King David Hotel. I had only been in Jerusalem for a couple of days in 1942, when my sightseeing was concentrated on the Old City, so I was not even aware of this splendid building with its concert halls and squash courts, library and restaurant. During the 1948 fighting the city had been divided, with Transjordan occupying the Arab eastern suburbs and the old walled city including its Jewish quarter. These and most of eastern Palestine had been united into the recently proclaimed Hashemite Kingdom of Jordan. The rear of the King David therefore looked out beyond its gardens across ruined buildings and barbed wire to the walls of the Old City in Jordan, and as the YWCA was cut off in Jordan the YMCA had become unisex, putting up ladies and families as well as men. There was no religious restriction on its residents, who ranged from United Nations employees and bank managers to missionaries and students of all creeds and nationalities, and the staff were equally multi-ethnic.

The arrangements for my course had been left to me as little was known of the local facilities, and on the Vice Consul's advice I registered for a Hebrew course at the Hebrew University and for some of the lectures to improve my understanding of spoken and written Hebrew. The Hebrew University had been one of the first institutions set up by the Jewish community under the British Mandate. It had been opened by Lord Balfour, who as Foreign Secretary had issued the historic Balfour Declaration of 1917 declaring the British Government's support for the establishment of a Jewish National Home in Palestine. The university expanded rapidly on Mount Scopus, greatly helped by the influx of German Jewish academics in the 1930s as refugees from Nazism, but was cut off from Jewish Jerusalem during the fighting. The buildings were preserved as a United Nations guarded enclave in Jordan-occupied territory and could not be used, so temporary arrangements had been made to continue in the west of the city. Terra Sancta College behind the YMCA, on what was still called King George Street, had become its temporary main premises, and there I attended their limited Hebrew language classes and my other lectures.

As term had not started, I arranged to spend a week on a kibbutz, or communal settlement, and was sent to Tzuba in the Judean hills, which had been founded by Palmach veterans a couple of years earlier. The Palmach was the elite of the Haganah, or Jewish Defence Forces, under the mandate, a sort of cross between the Commandos and the Guards without the ceremonial. Tzuba was a group of about 80 young enthusiasts creating a communal farm in the hill country, and sharing everything in common in an idealised form of socialism. I was surprised how readily they accepted a member of the former 'occupying forces'. I turned my hands to various jobs, from hoeing in the tree nursery, dull tiring work, to cutting up and putting screw threads on lighting rods for the chicken run, during my time with them before returning to the YMCA to greet Jill on her arrival. She also had to fly via Rome, as there was no direct route. The Admiralty still regarded Israel as Palestine for allowances, and ten shillings a day didn't get us very far. We had to take bed and breakfast terms at the Y, but could not afford the other meals so ate at various cafés or bought unrationed food for snacks in our room. Rationing was severe in Israel at that time of *Tzena*, or austerity. The meat ration was almost non-existent, a small allowance in some weeks only, but most dairy products and fruits were among the limited number of unrationed items.

Jill was fortunate, due to her former job with a publisher, to obtain a post in the YMCA library, cataloguing and issuing books, and with her wages plus my pay and allowances we were able to make ends meet. We ate all over the city for the experience, as we could walk to the main shopping streets, Ben Yehuda and the Jaffa Road, but our 'local' was Levi's café at the bottom of King David Street, where we could always be sure of excellent vegetable soup, *dag memullah* – the Israeli version of gefilte fisch, or fish balls – cream cheese and bread. Jill rapidly learnt '*Shtay kosot mayim*' for ordering two glasses of water, and '*Tapuchay adamah*', a direct translation of *pommes de terre*, for potatoes.

Jerusalem was still the city of the Mandate, with no new buildings yet. It was divided almost north to south by the ceasefire line, which skirted the western walls of the Old City but left Mount Zion overlooking the southern wall in Israeli hands. One was able to climb it and visit the Tomb of David in a former mosque, and listen to oriental Israeli soldiers chatting with the Arab Legion guards above the Zion Gate. There were no incidents along the line and the sole crossing point, open only to diplomats and the United Nations, was the Mandelbaum Gate in the north of the city, named after the house of a Mr Mandelbaum who had lived nearby. There had been violent rioting after Partition was announced, when much of the Jewish commercial centre near the Jaffa Gate was gutted, followed by fierce fighting to prevent the Arabs breaking into the Jewish areas. Now a belt of ruins formed a no man's land between the two front lines almost everywhere. Many buildings had been wrecked during Jewish and Arab terrorist attacks before the Mandate ended, and gutted buildings marked the approach to Levi's café, but much of the city had escaped damage. There were many fine stone buildings, thanks to the decree of Sir Ronald Storrs, the first British Military Governor of Jerusalem, that all buildings were to be at least faced with local stone.

We had been given a number of introductions and received much hospitality despite the rationing, so we soon found our way around. We met a number of fellow students and friends whom I had known at London University, notably Jacob and Zipora Landau, who had returned to settle in an old thick-walled house in the Street of the Abyssinians near the Abyssinian Church. It was cool in summer and warm in winter, being designed for the climate. The university year opened belatedly on 13th November, delayed by all the necessary improvisation in new quarters, and the following day there took place the first municipal elections for 15 years, which explained the assorted alphabetical posters plastered everywhere, as the many parties were each allocated a letter of the alphabet as their symbol.

I had chosen courses on Jewish history and archaeology as my chief interest, and attended lectures by some of the outstanding scholars of the time who were professors at the university. Lecturers included Professors Sukenik on the Dead Sea scrolls, in whose recovery he was so deeply involved, Tor Sinai on old Hebrew inscriptions and Pravar on mediaeval Jerusalem. All fascinating, even though I missed a lot due to my restricted vocab-

128

ulary, and naturally I was also attending the Hebrew courses for those not yet fluent. There were no lectures on Friday afternoon or Saturday, the Sabbath, which were our main exploration opportunities. We covered all the city on foot as it was still relatively small, and walked out sometimes beyond it through Bet Hakerem to Ein Karem in the countryside – the village of John the Baptist. One day we found a baby tortoise there and brought it back to keep in our room. It seemed to thrive on milk and grass but was not house-trained, so we soon released it back into the wild. Another time we walked down to Ramat Rahel, a kibbutz guarding the southern approaches to Jerusalem which had been heavily shelled but held out against the Jordanians. From there one could look down towards Bethlehem and back to the city, from the shell-scarred dining hall.

At the beginning of December we went down by train to Tel Aviv to report to the Military Attaché at the Legation. The cease-fire line left the railway line just inside Israel, west of Jerusalem, and it then wound down the mountains to Lydda in the plains, under 40 miles in an hour and a half, where we changed to catch another train for the 10 miles on to Tel Aviv. This was the only railway under the Turks, and didn't seem to have improved much since then. One of the novelties on a later journey was seeing Orthodox Jews praying as they travelled, and spinning round like tops to keep facing Jerusalem as the train corkscrewed through the hills. The Attaché was my mentor, passing any official letters to and from London, though it was clearly understood that I was to do no spying in Israel but I was to report on my language progress and any unclassified information of interest. We were invited to one of the Minister's diplomatic cocktail parties, and then dropped back at our hotel on the seafront. Tel Aviv was already the country's largest city, with over a quarter of a million people, less than 40 years after its foundation as a Jewish suburb of Jaffa. We took the opportunity of our visit to make a week's tour of the country, as it was the Chanucah holiday, the Jewish Festival of Lights, marking the freeing of the Temple and the country from idolatrous Syrian-Greek rule about 150 BC. From Tel Aviv we walked into Jaffa through the no man's land of shattered housing between the two cities, destroyed in the battles for independence, and up to the

Yarkon river. This formed the city's northern limit and its banks were a tree-lined, park-like oasis of calm.

I was so engrossed in our holiday tours that I completely forgot Jill's twenty-fifth birthday, which fell on the 5th – a sin of omission that I have never repeated. That day we took a bus to the Northern Station, as the railways did not then link up, to catch the train to Haifa. In two and a half hours we chugged some 60 miles up the coastal plain, stopping at every town. We were met by our former naval contractor Aaron Tweg, who put us up for the night and showed us round the city next day. We then took the bus down to Beth Shan in the Jordan Valley, a run-down little town with a Roman amphitheatre, and another bus to the nearby religious kibbutz of Sdeh Eliahu to see Eli Freier. He had shown me round Mikveh Israel, where he was training in 1942, and we had stayed in touch ever since. He was a rabbi's son from Breslau who had escaped just before the war, and he and his wife Ruth had settled down there for life. They showed us round their fields and farm, and the basic huts for housing in which they bore the intense summer heat below sea level – and the occasional winter cold. We saw photos of the previous winter's snow – the first in living memory – and the trees planted with the money I had sent them to mark the end of the Second World War.

We bussed on to Tiberias on the Sea of Galilee, then an unattractive town of old black basalt buildings but with a lovely lake outlook. Back in Halfa we had tea with Dr Joseph Bentwich, a leading academic at the Technion, the Institute of Technology, on the introduction of his elder brother, Professor Norman Bentwich of the Hebrew University. Jill had been told to look up the Professor, and actually met him on her flight to Israel when she found herself sitting next to his secretary. Their father was an early British Zionist, as were his two sons and nine daughters. They were all musicians who had each been required to play an instrument in the family orchestra. A slightly eccentric but delightful family, of whom we met several sisters in Jerusalem, where we returned next day at the end of our holiday.

Hotels and restaurants were graded in what was to us reverse order, from first class like our little Levi's café to fifth class top hotels like the King David. We sampled one a few days later when we dined and danced at the Eden Hotel to celebrate our first wedding anniversary, and recognised Golda Meir and other ministers at a nearby table. We also became actors, even I for the only time in my life, by rehearsing and recording radio plays for Kol Zion Lagolah, Israel's Overseas Radio Service, which in those early days was almost as amateur as us. Being Israel, there were lectures at the university on Christmas morning and afternoon, and we then attended a tea dance at the Y. On Boxing Day we went to the Y's Christmas Dinner, but there was little Christmas spirit, nor for that matter spirits as the Y was dry.

I was busy with my studies as we entered the new year 1951, translating articles from the Hebrew newspapers and attending lectures, but progress seemed to be slow, so I took to lunching at the Students' Cafeteria for more conversation. There were few sports or club activities, everything having been uprooted from Mount Scopus, where even the library was trapped, and still so disorganised that in January the university was closed for a week by a students' strike in protest at no exam dates having been fixed. Unfortunately most Israeli students wanted to practise their English and the *Anglo-Saxonim* – the incongruous Israeli word for Jews from English-speaking countries – tended to lapse into their mother tongue. Socially we also tended to meet the Anglo-Jewish community who stayed on, and were often invited to Friday night supper at the Moss Levy's. She was the principal of the Evelina de Rothschild School for Girls, the Roedean of Israel, and a generous hostess. They were very Orthodox and we were not aware of all their customs, so Jill caused consternation one Friday night by switching off the light when the ladies left the kitchen after clearing up. We hadn't met previously the ban on using light switches as a form of Sabbath work. Since there were no Reform Jewish communities in Israel, I rarely went to synagogue, as the long repetitive Orthodox services did not appeal. I did go in Tel Aviv at Chanucah, and to the main Yeshurun Synagogue in Jerusalem occasionally for their pleasant and decorous Sabbath evening and morning services, but then they did regard themselves as the most western of Jews.

The State of Israel was under three years old, and many arrangements were still provisional. There were few links with

Malta, so we were still living out of the suitcases with which we flew in, awaiting the arrival of our trunks with the rest of our clothes. I went down to Tel Aviv for the day to follow up these matters at the Legation and to meet my mentor, the new Military Attaché. He was a Japanese interpreter, selected because he was unlikely to be biased against Jews or Arabs! I went down by bus in two hours, quicker than the train, and returned by Sherut taxi in an hour and a half. The Sherut shared taxi system was one of the better Israeli ideas. One queued at a starting point in one city where taxis filled up for another city for a modest charge and dropped off each passenger at his desired destination. It would be impractical in really large cities, but worked well – and still does – in the small Israeli ones. Visas had to be renewed quarterly, so we registered as temporary residents and received ration cards after our first three months. Jill had just become pregnant, so qualified for extra rations including an allocation of bananas, which were very scarce and could not be had in restaurants.

Our baggage finally reached Haifa in mid-February, and I went down in a consular truck to collect it at the Legation, got it uncrated at the Y and up to our room. It was good to have more winter clothes, as Jerusalem can be quite chilly though we didn't have snow that year, and some English chocolate and other luxuries that Jill had packed. I continued my various courses and visited the Knesset, the Israeli parliament, one day when I was able to follow the gist of a foreign affairs debate. Progress though was still slow, and when I heard that an *ulpan* was starting up in Jerusalem I immediately registered for it. This was at the end of February, but it was mid-May before I was able to join the four-month course, living a Hebrew-speaking life all day with new immigrants from all over the world. Meanwhile I set off on a kibbutz tour in mid-March, to live in Hebrew-speaking surroundings in case the *ulpan* did not materialise.

I left Jill behind working in the Y library, and went first to Sdeh Eliahu, where I had already visited Eli and Ruth, and helped gather and box their carrots, then to Ein Gev on the eastern side of the Sea of Galilee, where I hoped to work on the lake and pick up some nautical vocabulary. Not a hope. They did not fish in the lake and were busy replanting their banana groves destroyed by the

Syrians during the war, so I spent a healthy but exhausting week marking out new groves and carrying and planting sticky banana saplings. By the end of the week I was a temporary expert on the subject so I moved on, after maintaining the Navy's reputation by diving off their pier into the clear water of the lake and recovering, by good fortune first go, a toy some child had dropped in. I diverted for a sightseeing tour of Nazareth on my way to my third kibbutz, Hulata on the shore of the since drained Lake Huleh. Their main occupation was fishing in the lake, so I spent a useful few days in their boats laying and recovering nets, and gathering in and salting the fish. The small lake, about 3 miles long by 2 wide, was fed by the Jordan running in from the north and out south toward the Sea of Galilee. It was shallow, full of bullrushes, reeds and beds of water lilies. Navigating was not easy, but I did pick up some vocabulary and more interesting experiences. On the Sabbath I decided to walk south along the Jordan to the next kibbutz, not realising it was a demilitarised zone, but luckily the Syrians were not trigger-happy, or saw no threat in one unarmed civilian, and I only learnt of my error on my return. I moved on via Safed, the picturesque Galilee hill town, to my final kibbutz, Rosh Hanikra, just south of the headland forming the Lebanese border. The kibbutz was little more than a year old, some 60 young Sabras, native-born Jews, establishing a strategically defensive farm near the coast. They had a jolly almost gunroom-like mentality, with a serious resolve behind it. I learnt to plough with a mule, loaded orange and grapefruit peel to feed to the cows, planted beans, and had the good fortune to be there for an open-air wedding of two kibbutzniks.

Jill joined me for a couple of days' holiday in Tel Aviv before we returned to Jerusalem to receive her mother, who flew out from England with cold fried fish, greaseproof-wrapped, to nourish her pregnant daughter. Like Jill she had never flown before, and it was quite an adventure then for a middle-aged woman to fly off to another continent. We were able to book her a room in advance at the Y, and enjoyed showing her all our favourite corners of Jerusalem. She was there for the Passover Seder service, which we spent at the Moss Levy's, and her visit fitted in with the Passover holidays at the university, so after she left I made a quick two-day

133

visit to the south. I went first to Beersheba, the country's small shabby southernmost town, where I caught a bus as far south as I could go. This was the remote kibbutz of Revivim in the central Negev. As the bus ran only twice weekly, I left on it early next morning after briefly experiencing living out in the desert miles from anywhere in this small settlement, maintained by reservoirs storing the water from the wadis which flowed briefly during the winter rains. The Israelis were already trying to recreate the farming achieved by the Nabateans there nearly two millennia ago, and one had to admire their stamina and resolve. Back in Jerusalem there was a big military parade, including 24 Sherman tanks, to mark the third anniversary of independence in May, with the city decorated with flags, and young people dancing the national dance, the *hora*.

After that I finally joined my course at Ulpan Etzion in Bakaa in south Jerusalem. Each class consisted of about 20 immigrants from Iraq, Rumania, Hungary and most parts of the globe, whose only common language had to be Hebrew. Everything was taught in Hebrew, all conversation had to be in Hebrew, and we were at work from 8 or 9 in the morning until evening most days, reading the Bible and newspapers, having discussions and lectures. There were various grades, advancing from the basic to the fluent, and I came somewhere near the middle. There were concentration camp survivors, resistance fighters, refugees from Arab countries, idealists from Western Europe, a fascinating cross section. One very attractive girl had been interpreter to a Russian general in Romania, and I gathered various details for passing on to Naval Intelligence, but that was just a by-product.

Early in June we were invited down to Tel Aviv for the King's Birthday Party at the Legation. We went down in a car with Sir Leon and Lady Simon. He had been the head of the Post Office Savings Bank and had come out to advise the Israelis on how to run theirs. Before we drew up at the Legation, Lady Simon opened her handbag and produced an enormously long pearl necklace which she proceeded to wind row after row round her neck in a way that nearly reduced Jill and me to hysterics. We were then recruited by the Military Attaché to join him in leading the singing of the National Anthem at the appropriate moment.

The ill feeling over the bitter end of the Mandate had mostly evaporated after three years, but the spirit of the country was reminiscent of Britain during the war, with everyone devoted to a common cause. There was an almost spiritual feeling even among the non-religious of being involved in rebuilding the Jewish state after 2,000 years, cemented by hostility and threats from the surrounding Arab states. One of our scores of acquaintances was Major Shaul Ramati, ex-Captain Rosenberg of the Gordon Highlanders and now head of the Israeli side of the Joint Armistice Commission sorting out incidents on the various borders, from whom we learnt how close was the threat of renewed fighting. The main fear at that time was of a Syria-Iraq union and attack, and the papers were full of rumours of wars.

Jill's mother had flown out with the Lipkin family, settling their daughter Mavis in at the Y to study Hebrew. We became close friends, particularly as she joined the same *ulpan*, and we met her again decades later in Wimbledon. Our *ulpan* teacher was a short jolly girl called Malkah Jaffe, jolliness being a rather unusual Israeli characteristic, who encouraged our individual progress, and got us discussing matters of interest to improve our conversation. *Ulpan* priority in those early days was given to professional people needed to develop the country, whose two-thirds of a million Jews at the end of the Mandate had more than doubled in three years. They had filled all the homes abandoned by the Arabs, and the newcomers were now put in transit camps called *maabarot*, unattractive hut-type temporary homes. Those with skills and professions were put through these intensive courses, so that they could get to work as soon as possible to help the others. Newspapers were published in all the main languages of Europe for the benefit of the immigrants, while the old *Palestine Post*, renamed the *Jerusalem Post*, served the *Anglo-Saxonim*.

Winter in Jerusalem had been delightful, rather like spring at home, but early summer brought the *hamseen* – the hot humid desert wind which could raise the temperature well into the 90s, and then drop it sharply to the 60s as a cool spell followed. We found the flat roof of the Y made an ideal sunbathing area, and I enjoyed the squash and tennis facilities. Jill's pregnancy followed its healthy course, making her very exhausted if the humidity was

135

bad, but otherwise our pleasant work and social life continued uneventfully. Often at weekends we walked out through the attractive suburb of Rehavia to the olive groves around the Greek Orthodox Monastery of the Holy Cross, where we picnicked and read in the shade. No public transport ran on the Sabbath, and there were few other such pleasant places nearby.

While at the university I had amplified my Hebrew studies by taking private lessons with a Mr Rosen, who had contacts with the radio service and recruited me to act as his pupil 'David' in a series of Hebrew lessons recorded and broadcast twice a week during the spring and summer. I welcomed it as extra practice and a generous £1 a session, which compared favourably to my £1.50 a day naval pay. The Israeli pound was officially at par with sterling, but worth only about half as much on the free market, so to encourage tourists there were Tourist Shops – as in Soviet Russia – where one could buy luxuries more cheaply in foreign currency. There was one opposite us in the King David, where we spent our few hoarded pound notes on export chocolate and other items not available in the shops.

Jill finished her work in the Y library at the end of June and had a month of leisure before flying home. As women more than seven months pregnant were not accepted by BOAC, there was a deadline. During July we gave several thank-you and farewell dinner parties at the Eden Hotel, and a number of tea parties when we used one of the Y's lounges. On the 20th Jill had invited Mrs Wright, the Vice Consul's wife, over from the Jordan side for lunch, and her husband to join us for tea and to take her home. Suddenly she received a phone call from him that King Abdullah had been assassinated when leaving the Al Aksa Mosque after Friday prayers, the Mandelbaum Gate had been closed and a curfew imposed. We were able to obtain a room for her at the Y, Jill lent her toiletries and clothes, and at lunchtime next day an anxious Mr Wright shot over when the gate was opened for diplomats to offer their condolences and rescued her. We had no idea how close Israel and Abdullah were to a formal peace. Secret negotiations had been under way for some time, but extremist Arabs knew and acted accordingly. Israel was on the alert for a *coup d'état* and more trouble, but fortunately the situation remained stable. Israel itself was in the midst of a General Election campaign, with 15 parties competing, and the election at the end of the month returned a Labour and Religious parties coalition to power again. The city walls were plastered with election posters in various colours, which were not cleaned off afterwards and left the city looking scruffy as they frayed away.

When Jill left I moved into a single room while completing my course and waiting instructions on when to leave, as I had been entered by the Admiralty for the Interpreters' Exams in London in mid-September. The *ulpan* course conveniently ended on 31st August, with exams which were a useful practice for the ones in London, and a half-hour talk in Hebrew on a chosen subject. I spoke on Mediterranean ports, since when I ran out of things to say or the word I wanted, I could move on to the next port. The following week I checked out of the Y and caught the weekly BOAC plane home via Athens and Rome – a full day's journey of 12 hours – back to England and the Royal Navy.

# 10

## *The Bomb*

I joined Jill at her parents' home in West Byfleet, where our first child Mary was born, ten days earlier than expected, on 28th September. She was a healthy baby and a relatively easy delivery, so Jill was soon up and about again. Previously we had visited the Festival of Britain, of which only the Royal Festival Hall remains, where they had to open a turnstile to let through a very pregnant visitor. The Festival celebrated Britain's post-war recovery and the centenary of the Great Exhibition, but I recall it only as a succession of small pavilions full of exhibits and a miniature Royal Mint stamping out souvenir Festival Crown coins. I spent a day in London sitting my Hebrew interpretership exams, which I naturally found much easier after the extra study in Israel, and qualified this time as a First Class Interpreter in Modern Hebrew and the welcome award of £90 for doing so. One was also paid five shillings a day when called on to use it, but the requirement only arose once, so the course was hardly one of the Navy's best investments.

I was now appointed First Lieutenant of the River class frigate *Plym* and joined her in Chatham dockyard, where she was refitting out of the Reserve Fleet. I knew that she was to be involved in some special operation, and blueprints for her conversion had been provided, but it was some months before I discovered that the large space forward that was marked 'W.R.' on the plans was to be the Weapon Room into which I was to hoist Britain's first nuclear weapon. Lieutenant Commander Peter Draisey was her commanding officer, and we spent the rest of the year supervising the refit and planning her commissioning. I found lodgings in Chatham for Jill and the baby, a sitting room downstairs and bed-room upstairs, with shared kitchen and bathroom, in a semi-detached house with the widow owner. I forget her real name since we always referred to her as 'Mrs Demon' after her favourite phrase 'I'm a demon for this or that'. Jill coped gamely with this form of housekeeping, and taking Mary to the medical centre for routine weighings and health checks. At weekends we would usu-ally return to her parents or visit mine, and the months passed pleasantly. It was then that I gave up cooked breakfasts to save Jill, as a nursing mother, the trouble of preparing them before I went off to work – a kind thought that has helped me keep a trim figure ever since, though a dislike of most fried food has certainly helped.

I was fortunate when drawing up my ship's orders to find my Dartmouth term-mate Brian Wainwright as First Lieutenant in a nearby frigate. He kindly lent me his ship's orders on which I was able to draw when preparing my own. All ships require a fairly similar basic framework for their routine, and this has to be set out in print. Of course the key man during a refit or conversion, far more than the Captain or any other officer, was the Engineer Officer. Jill and I became very friendly with him, Lieutenant Commander Denny Marsh and his wife Chris, and saw them again in the 1980s when one of his former stoker mechanics, Stan Murray, organised several reunions of ex-*Plyms*.

One evening early in December, a rumour reached us in the barracks of a terrible road accident. A bus had ploughed into a column of RM sea cadets marching in the shadow of Chatham dockyard wall and killed 24 of them. It is one shocking accident that I have never forgotten. That month we also had a visit to inspect progress by Rear Admiral A.D. Torlesse, who was to be in command of our scientific squadron as it was known, and I told him that it was to his former Nanny Hawkins, who later came to us, that I owed my naval career. Junior officers rarely discuss nannies with their Admirals, but he took it very well.

We were shocked by the sudden death of King George VI in his sleep early on 6th February 1952, and saw the barracks gun car-riage crew rehearse their drill for his funeral when they drew his coffin through the streets of London. We wore a crêpe mourning band round our sleeves for a month, and all social activities were suspended. Previous to this I had taken the opportunity as a member of the barracks officers' mess – since we could not eat aboard during the refit – to invite my father and father-in-law and some male friends and relatives to the regular Tuesday night mess dinners. These formal dinners with the officers in mess undress uniform and miniature medals, guests in dinner jackets, were a popular means of entertaining. For the Christmas Ball, when ladies were welcomed, we brought Mary in her carrycot and put her to sleep in one of the bathrooms, since I lived ashore so had no cabin. She behaved perfectly, taking her midnight feed in these unusual surroundings.

*Plym*, formally commissioned on 19th February, was one of the first ships to join *Her* Majesty's Navy since the death of Queen Victoria 51 years earlier. 'Her' had been handwritten over 'His' throughout the commissioning warrant that was read out by the Captain in front of the assembled ship's company.

We moved aboard the ship two weeks later, just before the refit ended, and I described the occasion in our ship's newspaper *The Plym Pudding*:

Eventually on Friday 7th March came our great day. We moved in. It was indeed a great day, and a wet filthy one too. At 1030 loads of stores arrived, and at 1100 the Commander in Chief paid his official visit. Seldom can a stranger ship have received him. The spuds and the Dockies were just swept off the gangway in time, as he walked the plank over floods from burst hose pipes and blocked jetty drains. A salute of bosun's calls and windy hammers greeted him, and was repeated at 1430 in honour of the Admiral Superintendent. Meanwhile the ship's company had come aboard to live, and an outnumbered party of Stokers and Signal ratings had just forced an entry onto the forward mess deck against the well organised defence of air conditioning maties. The Refit ended officially that evening, but work was still in progress on the following Tuesday, when derricks were tested and pipes bolted up all over the ship in probably

140

the biggest refitting day of all. Even the following forenoon when we sailed, Dockies were hustled over the side complaining bitterly at having their breakfast disturbed, while teacans, caps, half-eaten sandwiches and other souvenirs of their stay still come to light daily in the oddest places.

A certain poetic licence may have embroidered that report, but getting order out of chaos demanded a quick escape from dockyard to 'shake down'. We steamed down the Medway the few miles to Sheerness to fuel and spend the night, before carrying out engine trials off the east coast. After work-up exercises we returned to Sheerness and endeavoured to paint ship and appear more like one of HM ships despite our complete lack of armaments and the strange added superstructure and derrick acquired during the refit. Easter leave then intervened with ten days for each watch while the other kept things ticking over and met all the needs and requests of visiting scientists – or 'boffins' as they were invariably known. We moved between Chatham and Sheerness as various additional modifications in the dockyard were required by the scientists, and finally on 14th May Rear Admiral Torlesse hoisted his flag in the escort carrier *Campania* as Flag Officer Special Squadron. The Prime Minister, by now Winston Churchill again since the previous October, announced in Parliament that the test of the United Kingdom atomic weapon would be carried out off the Australian coast and gave details of the ships involved and Australian cooperation.

Jill and I had given up our Chatham lodgings, and moved in May into our first house at 62 Manor Drive in Hinchley Wood – an inter-war township that had grown up between Surbiton and Esher in Surrey, just outside London. It was a pleasant three-bedroom detached house, which Jill's father had bought for her as a sort of dowry. She was to spend most of the next four and a half years there and I about one of them in broken periods. In those days of shortages we furnished it with tough plain 'utility' furniture, and spent much of our wedding present money on the then luxury of a small refrigerator.

Meanwhile back at Sheerness a lighter came alongside one May day. We opened the forward hatch leading down into the large space now revealed as the Weapon Room, and swung out the derrick. With one red and one green flag for Stop and Go I then carefully hoisted Britain's first nuclear weapon out of the lighter, and lowered it gently down into its housing in the Weapon Room, where it was firmly secured. Various scientists were in attendance, but the actual transfer was no more dramatic or complicated than loading a crate of food. In our ignorance we assumed that it was primed, so grasped the steadying lines firmly, but in fact the worst we could have done was to dent the outer casing. All we ever saw was the casing of the bomb, which looked like a huge steel egg, and was solemnly inspected at regular intervals to check that all was in order. We assumed that the scientists aboard knew what to do if it was not, and hoped that by then it would not be a bit late to take action!

We finally sailed on 11th June in company with *Campania* for Gibraltar, as the idea was to suggest that we were escorting her and she carried the weapon in case there was any attempt at sabotage. We continued via Freetown to Simonstown, the Royal Naval dockyard and base outside Capetown, for our 'runs ashore', accompanied by warnings that apartheid had been introduced and the wartime friendly atmosphere had changed. Conditions were still quite amicable, and we enjoyed the break. We sailed on to Port Louis in Mauritius to fuel and sightsee, then across the Indian Ocean to Fremantle in Western Australia. It was the port of Perth, the capital, and proved the most popular visit of our journey, but after a few days we moved on to our destination. This was the Monte Bello islands, a group of islands off the coast about 800 miles north of Fremantle that form a central lagoon in which we secured with strong cables to buoys laid by the advance party of Landing Ships Tank. The islands were discovered by the French and named after one of Napoleon's marshals, who was Duke of Monte Bello, but did not live up to their name. They were neither mountains nor beautiful, but low rocky islands covered in scrub and creeper and uninhabited except for lizards, turtles and the descendants of cat and rat survivors of shipwrecks. They lay about 80 miles from the township of Onslow on the mainland, from whose airstrip our mail was flown. *Campania* carried one of the first naval helicopter squadrons, whose aircraft were ideal not only for mail collection but for moving the scientists and work parties quickly about the islands to erect their observation and other equipment. I had my first helicopter flight in one of them, and was much impressed by their versatility.

We had reached Monte Bello early in August, and were busy for several weeks offloading scientific stores, destoring the ship and carrying out all the work required by the scientists. A beer canteen had been set up on the main Hermite island, and there was swimming over the side and sunbathing, but few other amenities except for film shows, so the stay began to pall.

The ship's company had been allowed to believe that the bomb would be unloaded at Monte Bello, but once we arrived it was made very clear that it was to be exploded aboard, hence the destoring and stripping of the ship of its contents. All First Lieutenants have a Permanent Loan List of items which all too often get lost and have to be accounted for. I was to blow mine up, so there was very rapidly a stream of visitors anxious to acquire everything from the wooden gratings over our bollards to pieces of cable gear, which we happily dispensed. The ship's company began to be thinned out with transfers to *Campania*, and was reduced to a 'Care and Maintenance' team by early September. The officers were reduced to the Captain, Engineer and myself, who took Duty Officer in turn, with 25 left in the ship's company to service the seven scientists who were now living aboard and involved in final preparations. Saturday 20th was the dress rehearsal, with everyone evacuated and me left alone on board to raise the alarm if anything suddenly went wrong. It happened to be Jewish New Year, and I spent my oddest Rosh Hashanah reading the service to myself all alone on the deck of a floating bomb. All the other ships left the lagoon the following week in preparation for the explosion, and Dr William Penney of the Ministry of Supply, who had directed the whole production effort, flew in from Perth with the priming device in his baggage. He was the son of a dockyard workman, product of Sheerness Grammar School, so naturally a source of pride not only to our Chatham crew but to the nation as a whole. A delightful unassuming man, he was rightly knighted following the successful explosion and, as Lord Penney, joined one of the *Plym* reunions over 30 years later. He came aboard to make the necessary adjustments, and D-1 was declared for 2nd October. We last few left that night for *Campania*, and *Plym* was atomised by the first British nuclear weapon at 0930 local time next morning.

All the task force gathered on the decks of their ships with their backs to the lagoon and their eyes shut against the flash, and after a safety pause we were allowed to turn round and see the famous mushroom cloud spiralling up over the islands. Dr Penney had been at Bikini for the American explosions and had seen how their expensive measuring devices had been destroyed in the blast, so he based his measurements on strategically placed empty oil drums, which at almost no cost gave most effective blast readings. We had all been issued with radiation discs to wear round our necks before we left England, and these were checked regularly to ensure that we were not exposed to excessive radiation. Only specially protected personnel were landed on the islands after the explosion to assess the damage, but apparently later tests at Woomera were controlled less carefully.

Not all the boffins were as charming as Bill Penney. There was bad feeling in *Campania* between some of them and the officers, and one evening at Monte Bello all our caps disappeared over the side from the hooks outside the wardroom as some of the boffins showed their displeasure. That seemed to clear the air for the rest of the operation. Dr Penney had come out with a collection of arming keys, similar to the one with which he primed the bomb, which he presented to a number of us chiefly involved, and mine is one of my more unusual possessions. We also had a number of the porthole wingnuts suitably engraved as souvenirs of *Plym*, and an artist in *Campania* decorated the inside of scallop shells, which were plentiful on the beaches, with paintings of the nuclear cloud. These sold in their scores as they came off the production line on the way home. The *Plym* officers and most of the ship's company were absorbed into the complement of *Campania*, the rest being distributed among the LSTs, and the squadron was able to sail by the end of the month.

We had a much more relaxed journey home with little except watchkeeping to occupy us. After a break in Fremantle as a reward for the months of isolation at Monte Bello, we sailed direct to

144

Aden, which we reached 16 days later, the longest unbroken sea voyage that I ever made in peacetime, and entirely out of sight of land except for a glimpse of Addu Atoll in the Maldives. After refuelling we proceeded up the Red Sea and through the Suez Canal for a final stop in Gibraltar. The shops there enjoyed a financial surge as we completed Christmas shopping for our families. We arrived at Portsmouth on 15th December and I left the ship next day, having only joined her for passage. I went by train direct to Esher to meet Jill at our new home in Hinchley Wood. It had been an unusual year, fitting out a frigate for a unique mission, steaming halfway round the world, blowing her up, returning in an escort carrier and now picking up family life again.

I was just in time for Christmas leave and overseas service leave before my next appointment. Jill was heavily pregnant, and on this occasion was booked into Woking hospital to have the baby as she was no longer living with her parents and I might not be around. In fact I was still on leave when David was born on 23rd January 1953. We had gone to stay with Jill's parents when the baby was due, and she was taken into hospital early that morning for his birth. The custom then was for mothers to stay in bed for several days, but she was home by the end of the month with piles of nappies to wash. In those days before disposable nappies, children were rapidly house – or rather potty – trained, and Mary at 16 months rarely caused a problem.

Jill and I were enjoying our home and little family and getting to know the neighbours and the area, when in February I was appointed to the Reserve Fleet at Harwich. This was almost the last place that I wished for, a backwater in every sense, and I made it my business to get away as soon as possible.

# 11

## *Pompey*

At that time there was a huge Reserve Fleet, larger than the Fleet in commission, made up of surplus wartime ships available to recommission and replace any damaged or due for major refit, and to deal with any Cold War crisis that arose. This vast fleet was spread around the country in naval ports, constantly being moved around according to some mysterious master plan, so I took the first opportunity to move. Personnel were accommodated in the depot ship *Mull of Kintyre*, from which ships moored nearby in the Stour were maintained. She was lying off Parkeston Quay, the railhead near Harwich, a historic but run-down little port which had just suffered that winter's terrible east coast floods. I quickly volunteered as Towing Officer for the cruiser *Phoebe* being moved to Portsmouth, and within ten days of joining I was off again with a small crew to watch over the towing wires as tugs towed us down the east coast and into Portsmouth – or Pompey as it is universally known in the Navy. Chatham was known as Chats, and Devonport as Guzz, or Oggy Land from the nickname for Cornish pasties. I promptly transferred with my ship to come under the command of Senior Officer Reserve Fleet Portsmouth. Harwich had lost a cruiser, Portsmouth gained one, so personnel had to be adjusted.

I have never since visited Harwich, and I may have misjudged it in a bleak midwinter, but Pompey had the attractions of a big town, and being only an hour and a bit by train from Hinchley Wood I could even get home overnight. It was of course the Royal Navy's premier port, and busy planning for the big Coronation

Review. As much of the active fleet was still required overseas only a small number could be spared to back up the Home Fleet for the Review, so it was decided to commission with skeleton crews a number of Reserve Fleet ships. Ships in reserve had their guns cocooned in a waterproof plastic sprayed over nets on a light frame, with a window through which to monitor instruments measuring humidity. These were not disturbed, but the engines were activated, together with the anchors and boats, as a part mobilisation exercise at minimum cost that also served to lengthen the lines of ships for the Review.

I had a comfortable cabin in *Adamant*, the depot ship which accommodated Pompey Reserve Fleet personnel. Depot ships were basically motherships for submarines and small ships like destroyers, carrying specialist staff and stores to make running repairs between major refits, and were roomy so as to accommodate, in better living conditions, the crews of ships they were repairing. Initially I helped settle *Phoebe* down alongside another reserve cruiser, *Kenya*, but was then moved around as requirements demanded and could get home most weekends.

The Navy worked on Saturday mornings, like the rest of the country, not just shops but also offices and factories, so it wasn't until after lunch that I got away at weekends, and returned late on Sunday evening, but at least I was seeing Jill and the babies nearly every weekend. I soon began staying over and walking 2 miles to Esher station on Monday for the 6.35 a.m. train to work. After Easter I had my next towing job, in charge of the frigate *Alacrity* being transferred to the Reserve Fleet at Londonderry. We had a small galley in operation during these tows but no specialised cooks, and we had more than enough of amateur meals by the time we arrived after three days. Fortunately the sea was calm and the sun warm, so it made a pleasant minicruise. After a couple of days cleaning up the ship we thankfully passed her over to the local Reserve Fleet and returned home via Belfast and Liverpool. I can only recall Londonderry as a rather sad and poverty-stricken town, where they were repainting the bridge across the Foyle a depressing shade of dark brown. I called in at home overnight on the way back, and was delighted to find that Mary at 19 months

147

had belatedly discovered her legs and begun to walk since my previous visit. She was never backward in anything again.

I was immediately transferred to *Start Bay*, the frigate we were to man and bring out of Reserve for the next month's Review. There was almost as much to do, preparing the charts and navigational equipment, radar, anchors, cables and hawsers, quite apart from the engines and boilers, for just a few weeks as for a full commission. Even though we could forget the armament, we still needed stores, food and an operating galley, all to be prepared with a skeleton crew. We soon moved aboard to live and got down to ensuring that everything worked, exercising off Portsmouth and then working up at Portland. Coronation Day, Tuesday 2nd June, was a public holiday, so not being on duty I was able to take an early morning train to Waterloo to join my parents and staff at my father's new office in Regent Street to watch the ceremonies on a specially installed television. Afterwards we filled the windows to watch the rain-sodden procession pass beneath us. From above we could hardly see the Queen in her solid-topped gilt coach, but I do remember the stout Queen of Tonga in her open carriage grinning with joy and the slim Sultan of Kelantan wilting on the opposite seat. Noel Coward reputedly referred to him as her lunch! My father had laid on champagne and smoked salmon to help us enjoy the occasion, and we roared our cheers with everyone else as the procession passed. The Coronation really caused television to take off. Jill's father was only one of thousands to buy a set to watch the ceremonies, and she and the family gathered round to watch it on a big reflecting screen, which was then a common practice. I got home by the still-running trains to join them for supper, and left at five next morning to return to my ship.

The following week ships began forming up at Spithead, the anchorage between Portsmouth and the Isle of Wight, for the Coronation Review. We anchored near the island towards the western end of Line F, the sixth line of ships in descending order from the battleship *Vanguard* to the submarines and minesweepers beyond us. At my initiative the Senior Jewish Chaplain, the Reverend Isaac 'Harry' Levy, who still conducts our annual Remembrance Service at the Cenotaph over 40 years later, had applied to hold a service for the Jewish naval men assembled there. This was held in the aircraft carrier *Illustrious*, and co-ordinated by one of her Jewish pilots called 'Legs' Diamond. It was the only naval Jewish service I ever attended, and probably the only one held since the war, as even in those days of National Service it was not easy to find enough Jews at one naval base to justify a special service.

Monday the 15th was Review Day, and though the Fleet assembled was only a shadow of that for the previous Coronation Review in 1937 it still far exceeded the total tonnage of today's Royal Navy due to the fantastic increase in the cost and firepower of modern ships. The post-war battleship *Vanguard* had cost less to build than a small frigate does today, but we then still had plenty of pre-war and wartime-built ships to put on display for the Queen to review as she sailed down the lines. My parents and father-in-law, bringing Jill and little Mary, came down that morning with thousands of other guests to be embarked and entertained before we all manned ship in our best uniforms to give three cheers for the Queen as she steamed down the lines in the Admiralty yacht *Surprise*. There was no Royal Yacht at the time, as *Britannia* was still completing and the old *Victoria and Albert* was laid up in the dockyard being stripped of her best fittings for the new yacht. We later had a chance to look over her, and were intrigued by some apparent large sauce-boats, which we were told were designed to slip under ladies' crinolines when they wished to relieve themselves. As the *V&A* only dated back to the 1890s, these were presumably transferred to her in case fashions demanded them again, but I doubt that they were passed on to *Britannia*. We landed our guests in the evening after a memorable day for us all, especially my father-in-law, who had always loved the sea but had to do his war service in the machine-gun corps. Next day the Fleet began to disperse.

The policy was to send the Fleet to visit as many ports in the country as possible as part of the Coronation celebrations, and we were to visit the hamlets of Broadhaven and Littlehaven, which lay on the shores of Saint Brides Bay 5 miles north of Milford Haven. They probably expected at the most a minesweeper, but the planning staff can't have consulted the gazetteer as our numbers almost equalled theirs. They certainly did their best for us, with excursions to see the delightful little cathedral town of Saint David's a few miles away, and a special welcome supper followed by a dance, while we opened the ship to visitors and gave a party aboard. From there we returned regretfully to Portsmouth the following week, to put *Start Bay* back into Reserve.

I soon settled into Reserve Fleet routine of maintenance work supervision, most weekends at home, and the occasional tow. I made use of my spare time to study for and pass a number of the examinations in various subjects from signals to gunnery forming part of the Destroyer Command exams which were required before obtaining a command. There were social occasions too, like the Reserve Fleet Summer Ball in *Adamant*, when David was put down to sleep in his carrycot in my cabin, as Mary had been 18 months earlier in Chatham Barracks. We had Doug and Elsie Wilson, our companions in Malta three years earlier, as our ball guests, and I kept meeting former shipmates passing through Pompey.

Late in August I was sent to Cardiff with a towing team to prepare the frigate *Tetcott* for a long tow from Penarth to Gibraltar. One of the reasons that the Reserve Fleet was so widely dispersed was to avoid the risk of most of it being knocked out in a sudden attack, and a group of ships at Gibraltar was an immediate reserve for the Mediterranean Fleet. Due to a chapter of events, ranging from rough weather unsuitable for sailing to the earmarked tugs going to the aid of a ship in difficulty off Cornwall, we did not sail for ten days and I had plenty of time to meet my father's Cardiff cousins in the evenings while the Navy put me up in hotels. The tow eventually proved to be a week's sunshine cruise in perfect weather, with me and my crew mostly sunbathing and reading on deck as we kept one eye on the towing cables, but I would have hated to do that journey in winter. Once in Gibraltar we transferred to *Rooke*, the naval barracks named after the Admiral who captured the Rock. It didn't take long to tidy up and turn over our frigate to the local Reserve Fleet, and then we enjoyed local leave while awaiting a ship to take us home. I found myself there for Yom Kippur, and made my atonement on that Day of Atonement by attending services in each of the four synagogues in my high-necked white uniform. Each synagogue served a different group of the small community, most dating back to the eighteenth century and all well maintained in splendid rivalry. Expert critics moved from one synagogue to another to assess the music and standards of their rivals. Naturally I took the opportunity for frequent swims from the then uncrowded beaches of Catalan Bay, and finally after nearly a fortnight they decided to fly us home to be shot of us.

I stopped off for a weekend at home after a month away, and we held a family party on the Sunday to celebrate Mary's second birthday. She seemed to be getting used to this Daddy man who turned up at intervals. The following weekend a number of former *Plym* officers and their wives got together for a dinner in London to mark the first anniversary of her atomisation. In October our base ship *Adamant* was prepared for her tow up to Rosyth, and we dispersed among the three cruisers *Mauritius*, *Liverpool* and *Phoebe*, berthed together as Reserve Fleet living ships, which gives some idea of the size of the group.

Life continued uneventfully during the autumn and winter, without the tows which were reduced to a minimum during the rough weather season. Routine maintenance was carried out on the dozens of ships in the group, and I got time off to do courses at the various specialist schools in the Portsmouth area to improve and update my technical knowledge. I also took driving lessons in town, in anticipation of owning a car one day, but due to lack of driving experience or confidence I failed my first test and left a further try for the future. I started a Reserve Fleet news-sheet, *The Bally Ruffian*, the old Navy nickname for HMS *Bellerophon*, which was the overall name for the Portsmouth Reserve Fleet. Although one of Nelson's line of battle ships, she was chiefly noted for taking Napoleon into exile at Saint Helena. Based on *The Chevron Chronicle* and the more recent *Plym Pudding*, it tried to build up a good spirit and togetherness, which was particularly difficult in *Bellerophon*, which never went anywhere and had a constantly changing complement including many National Servicemen just waiting for their release. I kept it going for nearly eight months on a weekly basis until I went off to sea again, and we even had a good AB cartoonist among our contributors.

My brother Michael was home on holiday from the Far East,

where he was about to spend the next nearly 30 years living in Hong Kong and working with the family company. I entertained him at a naval guest night in December before I took early winter leave, so as to be back to do duty aboard as part of the skeleton crew over the Christmas holidays. Work virtually stopped for ten days; when not on duty I could usually go home, and on New Year's Eve I joined a farewell dinner for Michael in London before he returned to Hong Kong. I certainly had no idea that I would be celebrating the next New Year with him there.

In February I had an unexpected tow, when I was sent to Cardiff again to form a towing party for the destroyer *Tuscan* being brought round from Barry to Portsmouth. Fortunately it was a fairly calm three-day journey, but in winter one always had visions of the tow parting in a gale and the ship drifting out of control, as all we could do was let go the anchors and hope it was shallow enough for them to hold, since we could not weigh them again!

During my Christmas leave I had visited the Admiralty in the hope of another appointment soon, but the forecast was not encouraging so we started to plan for Jill and the children to move down to Portsmouth for my second year there so that I could come home every evening when not on duty. One was permitted to rent accommodation up to a limited ceiling price, and after a search we found a suitable house in Burbidge Grove, not far from Southsea promenade, which we moved into at the end of March. It was a nice little semi-detached house with a small garden where the children could play safely, and as the weather warmed up we would walk along the promenade when I got home from work. At the weekends we would play on the sands, and we settled down to a pleasant family routine. The children's particular delight was the Emmett Coronation clock – a Heath Robinson type machine that the corporation had bought and erected on the promenade as a tourist attraction. Package holidays and foreign tours were still a rarity – the vast majority holidayed in Britain – and Southsea was not only a holiday resort in its own right, but provided a daily spectacle of warships sailing in and out of Portsmouth, so we began to have family down at the weekend.

In the second half of June I took part in an interesting tactical

My parents' wedding, 1 November 1921, Bill Tyler on left, Lizzie Hart on right

Our wedding, 13 December 1949, Peter Davis on left, Magnus Osborn on right

Our childhood home,
63 Exeter Road

Brother Michael and I

## DRAKE NEW ENTRY 1938/1

G.M. Ascoli    M.C. Dobbs    A.D. Jay    J.W.N. Watkins    D.W. Winterton    M.D. Millar    H.M. Clover    E.B.C. Thornton    K.P. Hardy    M.R. Todd

W.D. Bazalgette    J.F.S. Youle    P.W. Dolphin    M. Brislee    D.G.B. Cremer    C.F.T. Poynder    R.R.H. Usher    D.M. Mann    A.R. Ellis

D.S. MacKinnon    B.H. Wainwright    A.A.W. Butler    P. Anson    G.J.R. Elgar    G.B. Wilby    J.P.H. Brown    R.C. Mayne    N.M. Walker    R.C.H. Mason    G.L. Eddis

D.A. Loram    J.H. Harvey-Jones    D.E. Mayne    A.J.I. Tyler    T.H.E. Baird    P.H.C. Bastable    T.A. Wells    D.M. Scott    C.B. Ker    J.O. Roberts

First term Dartmouth Naval Cadets, Spring 1938

Battle of Sirte, 22 March 1942. Cruiser *Dido* laying smokescreen, as seen from *Hasty*

*Hasty* alongside in Beirut, April 1942

*Revenge's* 15 inch guns ready for action 1942

*Devonshire* gunroom officers, Summer 1944, I with beard

Japanese surrender ceremony, Singapore City Hall, 12 September 1945

*Chevron* entering Venice, June 1947

*Chevron* ship's company with Regatta trophies, November 1946

Irgun ship *Ben Hecht* ex *Abril* approaching Haifa, 8 March 1947

Haganah ship 29 *November* 1947 ex *Maria Giovanni*, 28 December 1947

*Plym*  en route to Monte Bello, June 1952

Britain's first atomic cloud, Monte Bello, 3 October 1952

*Birmingham* leaving Hong Kong, November 1954

Neptune and Court welcomed aboard *Birmingham*, 21 October 1954

*Lion* below our *Tamar* flat, Hong Kong, May 1963

Tyler Brothers Golden Jubilee Dinner, August 1970. Seated from left my parents, George Copplestone, Douglas Tyler. Jill, I and Michael behind my father

The family outside Old Came Rectory, Autumn 1961

The family, with the latest arrivals, January 1996

exercise at the War Office, which gave the family an opportunity to return home for a couple of weeks. On my return to Portsmouth I found an Admiralty letter waiting for me, appointing me to join the cruiser *Birmingham* eight days later for a commission in the Far East. We quickly packed our few possessions in Southsea, turned over our 'hiring' to *Bellerophon* for another's use, and attended the Summer Dance on our last evening. We then dashed home at the weekend to settle Jill and the children down before I left them for a year. Our relatively easy moves by car in these first years of marriage were thanks to Jill's parents, who shifted the family around willingly at the drop of a hat. It was pure good luck that we had not let our house and left Jill isolated in Southsea. Her parents would have taken her in, of course, but the services did not concern themselves or worry about such family welfare matters in those days.

# 12

## Brum

Apart from the sudden parting from my family and the rushed return to our home from Southsea, I was glad to be off to sea again. I had spent most of the previous 13 years at sea, which was where I expected to be, and my first shore appointment in the Reserve Fleet had not inspired me.

*Birmingham* had been serving in the Far East Fleet for the previous two years, including the later stages of the Korean War, and had returned to her home port of Chatham to recommission for a year's general service commission out there. She was one of the large light cruisers of the Town class, built in the 1930s. Several were still active, and with our sistership *Newcastle* we formed the Fifth Cruiser Squadron. The ship had been modernised in a long refit before her previous commission, so was still a formidable warship with a fine war and peacetime record.

We were commanded by Captain John Barnes, DSO, a distinguished destroyer captain during the war, and only the younger officers and ratings did not have a chestful of campaign medals from the war that had ended less than nine years previously. We had a ship's company of about 820, including more than 60 officers, so to claim to know everyone even by sight was quite a feat. I had been promoted Lieutenant Commander on 1st April 1953 after completing my eight years as a Lieutenant, and as the junior 'Two and a Half' was put in charge of the Boats and Boys. Ships were known by their boats, the smartness of their appearance and handling being noted by all other ships, so one officer was held responsible for them, their standards and their crews. Boy seamen,

'Boys', started in a shore training establishment at 15, and after a short time in the training carrier joined the Fleet as they approached 17. They lived in their own mess under strict supervision, did not qualify for a rum ration, had various restrictions on their leave and duties and looked forward to becoming Ordinary Seamen at the age of 17½.

Work started at 0645, and our days were fully occupied getting ready for sailing in a little over a fortnight. By this time the new crew had to be able to operate everything on board and work together as a team. I spent a good deal of my time hoisting our boats in and out by crane, after they had been given a quick check-over in the dockyard, and getting the Boys organised in their first fleet warship. During that time we received a visit from the Lord Mayor of Birmingham and a civic party to present us with two shields for sports competitions and to wish us well for our commission. We maintained a good liaison with our name city, which was a boost for morale, although we didn't do as well as our sister-ship *Sheffield* – 'Shiny Sheff' – which glittered with donated stainless steel handrails.

I was fortunate to have weekend leave before we sailed. We saw *Joyce Grenfell Requests the Pleasure ...*, a revue with that versatile star as our farewell outing with Jill's parents, and my parents came down for tea to say goodbye. Then early Monday morning I left my family for a year, almost certain that Jill was pregnant again and would have to cope with it on her own. Such was naval life.

That afternoon, 19th July, we sailed down river to Sheerness, where we shook down for three days before leaving the country and the Chaplain of the Fleet, the Venerable F.N. Chamberlain, who had been Chaplain at Dartmouth when I was a cadet, conducted our recommissioning dedication service. We sailed straight into a Nato exercise, and that morning I issued the first edition of BRUM, the ship's newspaper, of which I was to produce a further 161 every day at sea during the next year. 'Brum' is the affectionate slang name for Birmingham by which we were known in the fleet, and as we sailed we heard for the first time our signature tune 'The Happy Warrior',which was always played as we left port. Brum reported that Birmingham was the second city of Britain, at

1,112,346 no less that 21,791 ahead of Glasgow at that time, and most issues played up our achievements, included comic contributions from the ship's company, or gave advance reports on places to be visited or our future programme. We started off at Defence Stations and then went to Night Action stations for the Channel exercise, before abandoning it as we headed for Malta, where we were to work up. 'Working up' involved raising all our armament and equipment operation to fleet standards, since though our engines and navigation were worked up to scratch during the week's passage to Malta, our new crew had to work up everything else.

We spent almost a month in Malta, exercising at sea most days and using the various facilities of this major fleet base. Malta is a lovely place in August for those who want hot sun, but for an intense work-up it could hardly be worse, and we all welcomed the weekends when we could go swimming and then touring the bars in the evenings. When possible I would take some of the Boys away in a boat for a swim, to show them that Malta wasn't all beer and hangovers. We certainly got to know the island and its harbours, as we anchored in most of them and visited many of the smaller towns in the evenings after the day's exercises. We were fortunate that it proved the most pleasant and least humid August that Malta had experienced for 50 years, after the alarming tales that we old hands had told the new ones, but we were still glad when the work-up was over and the Commander-in-Chief, Admiral Earl Mountbatten, came aboard to wish us well before we sailed. I also used my Hebrew officially for the only time, when I accompanied the Officer of the Guard to welcome three visiting Israeli frigates.

Among other things, the bars of Malta were famous for their hangover recipe of a 'Prairie Oyster'. From its name it may have originated in America, but I noted down the Maltese recipe, which never failed: yolk only of raw egg mixed in a glass of tomato juice heavily flavoured with Worcester sauce, salt, red pepper and garnishings. Whether it seared the problem away I can't say, but it certainly made the eyes water!

We were running a month behind our sistership *Newcastle*, whom we met briefly in Malta before she sailed for Singapore, and we followed her via Port Said where we received a quick visit from our 'chummy regiment' the Royal Warwickshires before we transited the Canal. We refuelled at Aden and continued straight to Singapore, where we arrived in mid-September and entered the Naval Base at the northern end of the island. The Naval Base had been constructed between the two World Wars in the sheltered strait between Singapore island and the Malayan coast, and was now the base of the Far East Fleet. There was a fully equipped dockyard with large dry dock and a British-supervised local labour force, a barracks HMS *Terror*, and the headquarters of the Commander-in-Chief. The Fleet had been somewhat reduced with the recent ending of the Korean War, but was still a fair-sized force, with ships remaining in the Korean area and operating from our secondary base in Hong Kong, and frigates supporting the Army's battle with Chinese Communist guerrillas by bombarding areas of the Malayan jungle. Soon after our arrival Rear Admiral Gladstone, the Flag Officer Second in Command, hoisted his flag aboard, and we then welcomed the First Lord of the Admiralty – the grand old title of the Navy Minister – Mr J. Thomas, MP, who was paying an official visit. He announced the introduction of a new seagoing Local Overseas Allowance, which meant an addition to our pay to compensate for higher local living expenses. Although only a few shillings a day, it came in handy to meet local costs, which were often higher than at home. We had under a week in Singapore, and apart from the occasional excursion by bus to the city some 15 miles to the south, we mostly took advantage of the base's sporting facilities. I managed to play squash and go sailing offshore. I also took up an introduction to the Director of the fine Botanical Gardens, who told the story of how when he first applied for a fire check he was told that he was not due for one yet as the Japanese had inspected his buildings in 1945.

We sailed next to Hong Kong, where we secured alongside at the naval dockyard in the centre of the city four days later. The dockyard had been established in the early days of the colony when the city of Victoria on Hong Kong island was just a small town, and the city grew round what became its central position, so we were able to walk ashore straight into the Central district of shops, hotels and offices. We were allowed a week's relaxation there before sailing for exercises, and among ships in harbour I found the frigate *Crane* with my former *Chevron* messmate Magnus Osborn, who showed me the sights, the clubs and the best bathing beaches.

We sailed regretfully after our visit, everyone having fallen for the beauty, the cheapness and the amenities of Hong Kong, many of them also falling for the famed bar girls of Wanchai. We went straight into an exercise off Hong Kong with the light aircraft carrier *Warrior*, which was just leaving the station for home and whose farewell party we had attended the previous evening. Luckily we did not need Prairie Oysters, as we began with a full day of anti-aircraft exercises to repel attacks from her planes, then set off with an escort of CO class destroyers of the 8th Destroyer Squadron, sisters of the CHs I had served with in the Med, for Manus. None of us had heard of the place, which was the largest of the Admiralty islands to the north of Australian New Guinea, where we were to take part in joint exercises with the Royal Australian Navy. Meanwhile we exercised with the destroyers each day, towing and jackstay transfers, and fuelled at sea from the fleet oiler *Wave Premier*, which had sailed earlier from Japan to join us.

The Australian task force of *Sydney*, a sistership of *Warrior*, with two destroyers and two frigates sailed from Manus to intercept us, then joined us for joint exercises. These exercise periods could be quite exhausting. On a typical day I had the Middle Watch from midnight to 0400, then was up at 0630 for our fuelling one of the escorting destroyers until 0900, on the bridge again until 1030 during manoeuvres, then general work round the ship until tea. In the Dogs between 1600 and 2000 I typed the next day's Brum newspaper and had a short sleep before supper and taking the First Watch from 2000 until midnight, then I was able to sleep the rest of the night. All days were not that busy, but routine work still had to be fitted in and we were glad when the exercises ended with our arrival at Manus. We anchored in Seeadler harbour, so named during the German occupation before the First World War, which was an anchorage between Manus and the smaller island of Los Negros to the east of it, and a sort of tropical Scapa Flow. The Americans had built it up as a base for the reoccupation of the Philippines, then handed it over to the Australians as a forward defence base. There was little to see or do, even bathing was unsafe in most areas, but the Aussies had set up a beer canteen, and we were glad just to relax. The Australians laid on barbecues and made us welcome during our two days there, before we faced up to 'attacks' by *Sydney*'s aircraft and the RAAF while we posed as a lone raider threatening the rest of the force acting as a convoy. We came back to Manus for a final get-together with the Australians to return their hospitality at the end of the largest joint exercises since the war, and left for Hong Kong.

We had crossed the line without ceremony just north of Manus, and had probably been back and forth across it during the exercises, but a ceremonial crossing had been arranged for our return journey, and how suitable to be on Trafalgar Day. King Neptune, Queen Amphitrite and all their court boarded at 0900 and proceeded in state to the quarterdeck to be received by the Admiral and Captain, who were then summoned to the forecastle with the rest of the ship's company to be judged. A canvas bath filled with sea water had been prepared, into which all first-timers and a number of others were plunged after being lathered and 'shaved' by the barber who is always one of the chief courtiers. Old scores were settled in some of the charges levelled, and honour was satisfied. Crossing the Line certificates were soon available from the canteen, bearing the ship's silhouette and a line for the Captain's signature to certify the named individual had qualified. That evening the wardroom sat down to its Trafalgar Night dinner served on the quarterdeck under a tropical sky, and as the phosphorescent sea flowed gently past we drank to the immortal memory of that wonderful frail little hero who saved England from invasion and loved his country, his men and Lady Hamilton.

We arrived back in Hong Kong at the end of the month, and my parents and brother Michael steamed in by P&O next day from a business visit to Japan. We were happy to spend a few days together, and I entertained them on board and enjoyed myself ashore with them, including my first ride on the Peak Tram and walk on the Peak to admire the superb views. Typhoon Pamela came heading for the colony just before we were due to leave for Japan, so we left a few hours early to avoid its effects. We ducked under its tail and passed east of Taiwan, after diverting to go to the rescue of a ship in distress, which in the event was reached first by the US cruiser *Helena*. Typhoons brew up in the Pacific, mostly in the summer months, and come hurtling towards the coast of China and surrounding countries like hurricanes – usually with heavy rainfall as well as gale-force winds. November was fairly late in the season, and we had no others. In those days the US named them alphabetically after girls, but in these days of sexual equality they receive boys' and girls' names alternately.

We spent a couple of days at Sasebo, the main US base for Korean operations since it lay on the western side of the southern island of Kyushu facing the Korean Straits. It was essentially a courtesy call, in case we were to be involved in joint operations in Korea if the war revived after the previous year's armistice – which is all that exists more than 40 years later. We entertained the Americans aboard, and they us ashore, but the town, a former Japanese naval base, had little to offer that we could not find cheaper and better later on. We sailed from there across the straits to the South Korean naval base of Chinhae, tactfully arriving on their Navy Day. As at Manus the previous month, we anchored, so all our boats for which I was responsible were in full use, and as usual we hoisted them all out by our crane on arrival and hoisted them back in and stowed them in their chocks on the boat deck, apart from the few which hung on davits, before departure. Routine stuff, but important, as we also had to land and take off all our libertymen and help with Korean visitors to whom we opened the ship. As this was an official visit by the Admiral, the usual cocktail party was held on the quarterdeck with the Royal Marine band providing background music, but more colourfully Beating Retreat ashore for the benefit of our hosts. It was not the Asian Tiger Korea of today, but a poor low-key country which had only been freed from Japanese occupation nine years before and then gone through a bitter four-year civil war after the Communist North overran almost all of it. Scrip dollars could be used in the service clubs, but there was nothing to buy in the local shops even if we had Korean currency, and the local drink was reputedly lethal, so we weren't sorry to move on after two days, hoping to find Inchon, the port of the capital Seoul, more interesting. On our way we called at Paengyongdo, an important island stronghold almost on the armistice line which divided North and South Korea, and an outer defence post for the capital and its port, which lay uncomfortably close to this line. It was a major base for Korean marines and commandos, and useful for us to familiarise ourselves with a place regularly visited during the previous commission before the ceasefire.

Inchon and the whole coast experienced tremendous tidal ranges of 30 feet or more and often the quays dried out, so naturally we anchored again and relied on our boats. Even the Fleet Landing Pier was liable to dry out at low water, and the huge tidal range produced a tidal stream of up to 7 knots in the anchorage, so our midshipmen certainly gained boat-handling experience! Again we only spent two days, chiefly devoted to liaising with the British Commonwealth Division based in the area, of whom a number came aboard to be entertained and to spend the night, but those who went ashore found only a few service canteens for entertainment.

We gladly set off for Kure on the Inland Sea, base of the British Commonwealth troops in Japan, which was still under post-war Allied occupation, that had been extended to provide bases for the fighting in nearby Korea. Kure had been one of the largest and most secret dockyards of the Imperial Japanese Navy, but was badly damaged by wartime bombing. We secured alongside in the dockyard, a rest for our boats, and discovered BAFVs, British Armed Forces Vouchers which looked like Monopoly money and were used at the shore NAAFI and service canteens. Unfortunately, the base was running down with the end of the Korea War and the fleet canteen had closed, but Japanese shops and products were plentiful and cheap.

I found my friend Magnus Osborn in port, and went with him and some friends to visit Hiroshima nearby to see the atom bomb devastation and memorial. There was little destruction to see as most of the city had been rebuilt, but the disaster was commemorated in a small park surrounding a shattered building, and the photograph displays made us realise the nuclear horror. There were also excursions to the nearby beauty spot of Miyajima, a sacred island full of picturesque temples, mostly painted vermil-

161

ion and scattered among the red and yellow autumn-hued trees. The highlight for most of us was a Japanese banquet to which we were invited by the local authorities, my first Japanese-style meal, sitting in stockinged feet eating with chopsticks and drinking toasts in sake. This was followed by a cabaret and a Japanese bath before we returned aboard after midnight. Only a limited number of fortunate officers qualified for this, but the bars and canteens and pleasure houses – despite the reputed 97% infection rate – certainly gave the ship's company a good time during our longest stay in port to date. After nine days we sailed back to Hong Kong, in theory also having done plenty of practice for the forthcoming Fleet Regatta.

In Hong Kong we started training in earnest for the following week's Regatta, before our usual evenings ashore. One evening we went to the premiere of the film *The Barefoot Contessa*, and the Governor who was present drily remarked that the crowds were obviously for the appearance of its American star and not for him. Another evening I went to see the Peking Theatre, on its first visit to Hong Kong since the war, perform a traditional Chinese opera. The costumes were magnificent, the singing high-pitched wailing to Western ears, and the scenery mostly symbolic. A few high mark-time steps represented climbing a mountain, and casually dressed stage hands walked on and off with chairs as if they were invisible, but for the Chinese, including my hostess – an Australian Chinese family friend Ada Lum – it was a wonderful occasion.

The Fleet anchored in Junk Bay to the east of the harbour for the Regatta, and though we did not win due to insufficient skill and practice, we did have the satisfaction of beating our sistership *Newcastle* for the 5th Cruiser Squadron Cock. The 8th Destroyer Squadron deservedly won the Fleet Cock, and we all had the usual cheerful 'chuck-up' parties supporting our boats and the parade of the winning Cocks afterwards. The C.-in-C. was present in his despatch vessel, the converted frigate *Alert*, and conducted fleet exercises before the Regatta as well as presenting the Cocks.

We then returned to the dockyard to spend Christmas and New Year alongside, with plenty of shore leave, and for me the added attraction of my parents and brother staying at the Gloucester

Hotel while establishing the Far Eastern office of the family company, which Michael was to run. Meanwhile, all these months Jill and I had been exchanging letters every few days, keeping each other up to date with all that was going on and Jill reporting the satisfactory progress of her pregnancy. What she did not tell me until later was that she was taking driving lessons and, heavily pregnant, passed her driving test early the next year. The ship produced its own pantomime, *Sinbad the Sailor*, running for three nights over the Regatta period for our own ship's company and the Fleet in general, though some of the 'in' jokes were lost on visiting ships. In the traditional fashion ships dressed with greenery at the mastheads for Christmas, and the officers did the rounds of the messdecks to wish them all Happy Christmas. We tried to avoid too many 'sippers' of rum without giving offence, since the sailors' aim was always to make their officers drunk. We made it safely back to the wardroom for the traditional Christmas lunch, but few except the duty officer surfaced again before evening. With my parents I went next day to the Boxing Day lunch of the manager of the Repulse Bay Hotel, and celebrations continued until the New Year.

I saw in the New Year 1955 at the Yacht Club with my parents and brother Michael, and two weeks later Michael and I saw them off for home in the P&O liner *Canton*. I had probably seen more of them in Hong Kong than I had for years, and through them as old China hands met more of the colony's leading lights than I could ever have expected, but Michael had spent three months working with his father as his boss in markets where he was now more at home and up to date, so he was glad to be on his own again.

All naval officers were honorary members of the Yacht Club in recognition of the Royal Navy having restored and revived it after the Japanese Occupation, and I enjoyed some sailing there with my brother and with other officers. I also went further afield, exploring the New Territories and climbing its peak Taimoshan for its splendid views across the Territories into China, but all good things had to come to an end, and after six splendid weeks in Hong Kong at its mild winter best we sailed in mid-January with *Newcastle* for a joint official visit to Singapore. We had been in blue winter uniform since visiting Japan and Korea, and now changed back into the white summer uniforms which we were to wear until June.

This was the only long voyage that we two cruisers made together, so the opportunity was taken to carry out various exercises during the journey. We were the only two real sister ships of the Town class in service – *Belfast*, which is now moored off Tower Bridge, was rather larger. Brum noted that we were 591 feet long with a 62-foot beam and draught of 17 feet. On a standard tonnage of 9,100 – which went over 12,000 when our full 2,000 tons of oil fuel plus other stores were added – we could reach 32 knots. We had three triple 6-inch turrets, the fourth having been removed during modernisation to allow additional equipment to be fitted, four twin 4-inch anti-aircraft guns, minor weapons and six torpedo tubes, so until guided weapons entered the Fleet a few years later we were still – though nearly 17 years old – among the Fleet's most modern cruisers.

We anchored early on Saturday morning in the naval anchorage facing the city centre where I had anchored nearly ten years before for the Liberation. Once again the boats were in full use to land libertymen and bring off official guests for the cocktail party on our quarterdeck that evening. The party was for the city council and civil authorities, to recognise their year-round hosting of the Royal Navy from its base at the northern end of the island. Two days later we sailed for Saigon, on the very day of the Chinese New Year when Singapore would be too engrossed in those celebrations to pay us much attention.

We were taking our Admiral to visit Saigon for two purposes, a courtesy call on the newly independent state of Viet Nam whose capital it was, and on the French Far Eastern Fleet, whose flagship the cruiser *Montcalm* would welcome us. France had just lost the long civil war against the Viet Cong with the defeat at Dien Bien Phu the previous year, leading to independence for the separate Communist North and 'democratic' South, whose standing would be enhanced by our visit. It was a fascinating 40-mile journey up the river from Cap Saint Jacques, which must have a Vietnamese name by now. The Mekong was like a wider winding Suez Canal, and we saw merchant ships heading towards us miles away across the flat green paddy fields.

164

Saigon had a relatively small French city centre, beyond which lived some 2 million people, and prices were high due to wartime shortages and inflation, but Brum noted there were reputedly plenty of places of amusement where that popular breakfast – A Roll in Bed with Honey – could be obtained. We held the usual quarterdeck cocktail party, neatly combining the state of Viet Nam and the French Navy, and as in several other places I was able to arrange a special sightseeing bus trip for the Boys, who were my concern, though by now their numbers were dwindling as they proudly became Ordinary Seamen at 17½ and moved out of the Boys' Mess. We were also open to visitors for the afternoon, and flooded with curious and polite Vietnamese who had probably never seen a British warship before.

We returned to Singapore, entering the Naval Base on 1st February for our local refit. By doing this, as in the previous commission, the ship could pay off in England, recommission and sail again within a month as we had, while helping to keep Singapore dockyard busy. Britain was still a first-class power in those pre-Suez days, with fleets all over the world, even if they were considerably smaller than before the war, and Singapore was equipped to support a large fleet such as had been mustered for the Korean War and might be done again. We were not a superpower like the United States, but we were easily the leader of the others with a still vast Empire and interests to defend. It was fraying at the edges – India, Pakistan, Burma and Ceylon were independent now – but otherwise except for the former Middle East Mandates it was still intact, and we who had grown up with an Empire still felt its influence even if it was now called the British Commonwealth.

We had carried the flag of Rear Admiral Gladstone since our arrival in September, and now said farewell to him as he was promoted to Vice Admiral and his successor hoisted his flag in *Newcastle*. He had been a popular guest, but his departure did cut down the obligatory ceremonial caused by an Admiral's comings and goings.

We were to spend three months in Singapore, in the dockyard at the Naval Base, where our refit began immediately. We moved ashore to live in the barracks, HMS *Terror*, and I closed down

Brum with an appeal for articles for the *Birmingham Magazine*, which I was to produce during the refit as a souvenir of our commission. The Welfare Committee voted the funds for a free copy for every member of the ship's company, and rereading it reminds me of what a happy commission it was.

We worked in the ship by day, then could take a naval bus or a local one down to the city centre at the southern end of the island, or enjoy the swimming pools and sports and recreational facilities of the base. I particularly enjoyed the squash courts, where one could lose pounds in the high humidity, and then replace it with draught Tiger beer or shandy. The Officers' Club was a popular watering hole, and gathering place also for bowling matches in the evening. We had seldom had it so good. To add to my joy I received a telegram reporting the birth on 22nd February of our second son Jonathan, and that mother and baby were doing well. His was one of 52 births notified by the time the magazine went to press.

Local leave was granted to anyone who wanted it, and early in March I flew to Penang, where I was met by Bruce Wallace, an old friend of my father's whom I had been able to help following his release from Changi in 1945. He was the doctor on a rubber plantation nearby, where I stayed with him and saw the Tamil tappers gathering the latex from the rubber trees. It ran like sap from the fresh diagonal slashes which they made each morning as they scraped out the previous day's dried latex from the little cups below the slashes. We then returned to Penang, where I looked up Hugh Cohen and his wife Jane, members of our synagogue. They had only been married a couple of years, and suffered from an excess of Coronation souvenirs as wedding presents. Their sitting room was full of royal monogrammed cushions and the like, which they wisely decided to wear out as soon as possible. They made me very welcome for a couple of days and showed me the island before I flew on to Kuala Lumpur to see the Malayan capital, still a quiet colonial town, where other family friends showed me the sights. I then flew on to Malacca to see this historic former Dutch port before flying back to Singapore after an unusual ten-day break.

I have no recollection of all these flights, but they must have

166

been relatively cheap if I was able to fly instead of taking the train. It may have been just a question of time as the flight to Penang took 3 hours from Singapore compared to the train's 24 for a journey of barely 400 miles. The planes were hardly speedy, but the train barely bettered Stephenson's *Rocket* as it made its overnight or all day journey from Singapore to KL.

The refit progressed all through March and into April, while we enjoyed the colonial life of Singapore City when we wanted to get away from the Naval Base. We ate on special occasions at Raffles Hotel, which with the Adelphi was one of the only two good hotels in the city centre in those pre-mass tourism days, or at one of the few European restaurants, and went to the cinema, which was the chief evening entertainment. Despite the humidity there was little air-conditioning except in such places; otherwise the damp air was stirred around by often ineffective electric fans, though those in the Naval Barracks did their job well. Sport continued, with the Boys winning the swimming gala against all the other teams in the ship. Since they were all under 17½ and few in numbers, I was particularly delighted as their divisional officer. Certainly their leave expiring at 8 p.m. when the rest of the ship's company had all-night leave had something to do with their success.

In late April we reluctantly moved out of the barracks and back aboard ship, re-embarked ammunition, fuel, boats and supplies that had been landed for the refit, cleaned up the ship, and three months to the day after arrival sailed on 1st May for shake down exercises, followed by a three days' Admiral's Inspection. The cruiser *Newfoundland* had arrived to replace us, as our next commission was to be in the Mediterranean, and we sailed from the Naval Base, flying our paying off pennant, for a 66-day voyage home.

We called first at Mauritius, where Brum warned that 'The local rum and women are both reported to have dangerous delayed action'. By good fortune Dicky Bird, whom we had known in Jerusalem, was Manager of Barclays Bank in Port Louis, so we had a very cheerful and alcoholic reunion and he showed me something of the attractive island, which was then unknown as a holiday resort. We sailed next for Durban, exercising offshore

167

with South African and British warships before entering harbour to hoist the flag of the C.-in-C. South Atlantic Station to take him on official visits.

This was the first time I really encountered apartheid, as one of our Boys was 'coloured', of mixed blood, and I had to advise him that to avoid the humiliation of being turned out of bars where his mates drank it would be better not to go ashore at all. It did not stop the rest of us enjoying our visit, but it left a nasty taste in the mouth.

I looked up my elderly relatives who had been so hospitable to me when *Revenge* was refitting there in my Midshipman days, and had them aboard to see the Royal Marines Beat Retreat and for dinner and a film as our return for local South African hospitality. I also took our Chaplain, John Champion, who had become a good friend, to attend his first Jewish service celebrating Shavuot, or Pentecost, in the Durban Synagogue.

We sailed up to Lourenço Marques, now Maputo and still the capital of Mozambique, which was then a Portuguese colony, for the Admiral to pay his official visit. It was a modern city, growing up in the previous century to serve as the port of landlocked Transvaal, and the large Portuguese population made us very welcome. As usual we gave a cocktail party on the first evening, which also gave us an opportunity to meet the local British community, who then usually took one out for dinner or to their homes. It was unavoidable that the officers gained over the ship's company, who usually only got free tickets to cinemas or invitations to a beer tent or general reception if they were lucky.

From there we steamed up the Mozambique Channel which separates it from Madagascar, to Diego Suarez on the northern tip of that huge island. It had been the main French naval base in the Indian Ocean, but was now little used and there were no French ships to greet us. The base staff had filled the dry dock to provide a berth for us, and really put themselves out to lay on tours and excursions and make us welcome. The Governor gave an official dinner, and next day took us out to see the feeding of the crocodiles by a native tribe who regarded them as their ancestors. The 'King' of Northern Madagascar, in a grubby white uniform covered in medals, turned up at the ceremony to meet the Admiral at the Sacred Lake. In a rather sordid ceremony lumps of meat were tossed to the crocodiles. A wreath was laid on our return at the statue of Marshal Joffre, who in his earlier days had laid out the town of Antsirana that served the base and as capital of the northern province then called Diego, followed by a *Vin d'Honneur*.

Our next call was East London in Cape Province, South Africa's only river port as all the rest are bays. Nearly half the population was of British origin, but being only the fourth port it rarely received an official visit and was very glad to see us. We were given a civic reception and lunch on arrival, having gone into blue winter uniform for the first time since Korea, and gave our usual cocktail party that evening.

After a second day of socialising we sailed on to Simonstown, the base of the South Atlantic squadron and the Admiral's head-quarters, where he transferred his flag. Simonstown was a little like Gibraltar, but only 20 miles from Capetown, so most people took the train to the big city. Again I was able to entertain people who had looked after me during wartime visits – an opportunity I welcomed. We had left our Royal Marine band behind in Singapore to continue their local commission, and had embarked that of the South Atlantic Station for the C.-in-C.'s cruise. It now played us away with our 'Happy Wanderer' signature tune as we sailed for home flying our paying off pennant again.

It was a direct journey, with just a short one day fuelling stop in Freetown, where we gave our final cocktail party and had our last 'run ashore'. Mine was with the editor of the local newspaper, who took some of us home to dinner and on to a club dance from which we returned after one in the morning to be up and ready to sail soon after dawn. We lived and played hard, and this was just typical of the hospitality we met everywhere throughout the com-mission. The weather was fine, and everyone was in holiday mood with the end in sight, working up their sun tan to show off on leave. We passed through the Canary islands, sighting the 12,000 foot peak of Tenerife looming over the horizon well before the rest, and arrived in the Channel still in white uniform in an English heatwave.

Brum was publishing daily statistics of the commission, from the nearly 18,000 tons of fuel oil used at around £7 a ton – the price of 10 litres of petrol at today's tax levels – to the 16 out of 22 games of cricket won to the 132,000 tots of rum issued to the ship's company. We steamed over 40,000 miles in just under a year, equal to nearly twice round the world, and sold over 100,000 2½d stamps – forces' postal rate to England – representing nearly 140 letters each. Last but not least from my point of view, Brum had been published on all 162 of our days at sea.

I have often felt that if I had to choose my favourite period to live again it would be that summer of 1955, returning home to wife and family after a year well spent in a happy ship. World War Two had ended ten years earlier, almost the whole world was at peace, Great Britain had recovered and was prospering, Winston Churchill had just retired in a glow of appreciation, and the future looked bright indeed.

We entered Chatham on Tuesday afternoon 12th July to see a crowd of thousands, wives, children, parents and relatives waving us a welcome home. Jill was among them with my new son Jonathan in his carrycot, and my happiness was complete.

# 13

---

## *Interlude*

My future looked bright. I had a good 'Flimsy', brief report on flimsy paper, from my Captain, and my next appointment was to the Naval Intelligence Division at the Admiralty, which sounded interesting. On the Saturday after our return Jonathan was blessed at a synagogue service attended by most of the family before I returned for my last day as Duty Officer, and the following Tuesday, just a week after our arrival, the new ship's company joined and I left *Birmingham* for leave.

Mary was now approaching four years old and David over two, both very helpful to their mother in looking after five-month-old Jonathan. Jill had bought a little A30 Austin van after learning to drive, and my leave priority was a refresher course of lessons following which I passed my test. Not for the only time in our life, she led the way and I followed. It was a fine summer and we took the opportunity to visit family and friends in our new car, enjoying the mobility it gave in moving young children around without relying on public transport. Jill's parents had moved from West Byfleet to Oxshott while I was abroad, which brought them closer to us and London, and the children enjoyed their large garden and all the attention they received. My parents were still at their flat in Avenue Mansions on Finchley Road, and were equally delighted to see their grandchildren, whom we now brought up by car. I was able to tackle our garden properly for the first time, with the prospect that living at home while I worked at the Admiralty would give me the chance to see the results of my efforts.

At the end of August I joined the Naval Intelligence Division to

171

relieve an officer in the Russian section. It was a pleasure to go to work in a suit instead of uniform, to work office hours from 9.30 to 6 and then go home free of responsibilities. I didn't speak a word of Russian, though I did make an effort to read the alphabet, but this was not important as Russian press articles on the Navy were translated before passing to us, and our main concern was scanning photographs to try and judge new technical developments and to assess the threat of their ever growing modern submarine service. Among those in the Russian section I found my old termmate John Harvey-Jones, who was a Russian interpreter and had been involved in intelligence work for almost the previous ten years after wartime submarine service. He was a great help in my finding my feet and getting the feel of this quite new type of activity.

It was the time of the first thaw in the Cold War after Stalin's death, when all four wartime allies gave up their zones of Austria to create a neutral buffer state, and an exchange of visits was arranged for that autumn between our two navies. Several officers and civilians from the Russian section were carried in the British ships that visited Leningrad, to photograph all that they could in that major naval base with their concealed cameras and to try and identify all the latest equipment that we had already seen in our photographs and in Russian magazines. Most of our intelligence was of this semi-overt type, and the Russians certainly expected or knew that a naval visit would search out all the information it could. My little contribution was to lend my mess undress uniform to a civilian my size so that he would be properly dressed on formal occasions. Naturally the latest radar sets and submarines were not on view during the visit, but a number of assumptions were confirmed, and a lot of extra information acquired for our dossiers. In return the Russian cruiser *Sverdlov* paid an official visit to Portsmouth in October carrying the Russian leaders Bulganin and Krushchev, and as a lowly intelligence officer I escorted the Russian Naval Attaché and his deputy to Portsmouth from London beforehand to tie up all the naval details in advance. Embassy personnel were not allowed to travel unescorted beyond a 20-mile radius of the national capitals as part of a Cold War 'tit for tat', and honour was satisfied by my presence.

The next day I attended the funeral of my grandmother, my father's mother, who had died in her sleep at the age of nearly 94. It was not a sad occasion but led to me buying my first bowler hat, as I was so ashamed of the battered trilby I possessed for shoving in my pocket after raising it to the quarterdeck on boarding or leaving a ship.

Most of the Russian section of NID, the Naval Intelligence Division, were invited to a reception at the Russian Embassy with our wives to mark the Russian visit to Portsmouth. I presume Admiralty assumed that they knew who we were, but the situation of their entertaining our official 'spies' did strike me as rather comic. The reception was decidedly proletarian, with good solid snacks and no fancy bourgeois canapés, and sturdy waitresses lined up to dispense the alcohol. Needless to say none of us in NID had any idea of the entirely unofficial and foolhardy fatal mission of Buster Crabb to try and inspect the Russian hulls, which nearly undid all the goodwill of the visit. I was not fortunate to draw a place for the dinner with the Russian leaders in the Painted Hall at Greenwich, but decided on the Saturday to drive down to Portsmouth to walk round the *Sverdlov*, which was open to visitors, for my own interest.

It was my first long drive since passing my test in the suburbs a couple of months previously, and we were accompanied by my father-in-law, who was keen to see the ship. Approaching Milford we skidded on a damp or greasy corner, completely turned over and found ourselves facing the opposite way on the other side of the road. The Austin vans were relatively high and liable to tilt on corners, but this was so sudden that I could do nothing before we found ourselves upside down and then back on our seats on the opposite verge, shaken but unharmed. It was a nasty shock, and we were incredibly lucky that there was no car coming the opposite way. The windscreen shattered and the car had a few dents but I was able to drive it home. It certainly made me a more careful driver, realising how easily a moment's inattention can cause a crash.

That 21st October was the hundredth and fiftieth anniversary of the Battle of Trafalgar and the death of Nelson, so I took the opportunity to slip round the corner from the Admiralty into

173

Trafalgar Square to attend the memorial service headed by the Duke of Edinburgh. A week later I was a guest at the RNVR Club's Annual Dinner and found myself sitting opposite a Russian Assistant Naval Attaché, who had doubtless come along to see what gossip he could pick up. I alerted NID to this type of risk. On 9th November I again slipped out to see the Lord Mayor's Show, which was always held on that day instead of on Saturday as now. I was taking the opportunity to see London occasions for the first time, made easy as we operated a form of 'flexitime' well before it became general, so that one could make up hours out of the office.

It was a pleasant life, Jill joining me occasionally when one of her sisters babysat so that we could go out to dinner or to a theatre, but often we would spend an evening listening to the radio. We had not even considered buying a television, though ITV began that autumn and the programmes were extending to cover more of the day. Sets were still expensive, and the car had been first priority. We began to have friends to dinner, and I to feel settled in my own home. The children were a joy, as they began to develop their characters and I had the opportunity to know them properly. They rapidly accepted a routine, to the extent that most Sunday mornings they snuggled up in bed with us so that we could sleep on until about 9.30.

We went to see a Russian ballet company with tickets provided by the Embassy, who seemed to be on a charm offensive following their leaders' visit, and early in December I visited GCHQ at Cheltenham to see how their intelligence meshed in with ours. I felt that I was becoming a useful member of the team.

During my leave in the summer I had written to the Naval Attaché at the Israeli Embassy suggesting he get in touch with Captain Jessel, who had commanded the flotilla of Z class destroyers of which Israel had just purchased two, to gather some information on their ship-handling qualities and any other advice that he could give them. I forget now if he did so, but he asked me out to lunch that autumn, and sent me an invitation for Jill and myself to their Embassy Chanucah cocktail party, which I naturally took up, particularly as it happened to be the sixth anniversary of our wedding. The previous evening we had been to NID's annual dance at the Admiralty, and it all seemed to fit into the year's-end festivities. We had a pleasant time at the Embassy, where I took the opportunity to introduce Jill to my Admiral, the Director of Naval Intelligence, whom she had not yet met.

Obviously this stirred up all sorts of concerns in his head as two days later he sent for me, and questioned me on my relations with Israel and Israelis. I pointed out that as the Navy's only Hebrew interpreter and as a Jew I took a close interest in that country, but it had no other bearing on my behaviour as a naval officer. I did see the secret Middle Eastern reports as part of my general reading, but had never passed on a word of these to anyone outside the office, any more than I would with any other information. This was in fact the very first instruction we were given on joining the division. Nevertheless Rear Admiral Irving felt that in view of the uncertain situation in the Middle East – a year before Suez when no major trouble seemed imminent – it was essential for me to leave Naval Intelligence immediately. He was good enough not to accuse me of being a security risk, but felt that I might be prey to divided loyalties if Israel seemed likely to be involved in another war and be tempted to divulge secret information. I suppose that in such circumstances I might have been tempted, but a less precipitate transfer could have been arranged to avoid any such risk.

As it was, I had to leave the following evening, so my feelings can be imagined as I attended the Russian section's Christmas party that evening. John Harvey-Jones was disgusted, and said he didn't want to continue in a service that behaved in such a way. It so happened that the following year his daughter developed polio and the Admiralty's unwillingness to grant him leave to be with her or consider another shore posting led to his resignation – to the great benefit of ICI. My Captain and Commander superiors were most sympathetic, but I felt that I was leaving with a slur on my character and a black mark against my name which would scotch further promotion.

These were the most unhappy few weeks of my life, as I felt rejected by the service to which I had devoted my life and made my chosen career, and had no idea what would come next or what to expect. I mooned around the house feeling miserable and no doubt took it out on my wife. I did not want to meet people as I didn't know what to say to them, nor did I know where I was to go next or indeed if the Navy might ask me to resign, just as I had been told to leave my job. I can still picture myself laying new linoleum, and feeling utterly woebegone. By Christmas I had cheered up enough to enjoy seeing the children opening their presents and our having a family gathering including my brother home from Hong Kong. Everyone was naturally very sympathetic, and advised me to wait and see what developed but to do nothing rash. For the third year running I saw the New Year in with my brother Michael, who joined us and Jill's brother Brian and wife Vera for a charity dinner and dance at the Trocadero.

I went up to the Admiralty early in January to see the Appointments Section, and was given an indication that I could expect something interesting which made me feel a lot better. The following week we celebrated my father's seventieth birthday with a family party at Grosvenor House, and the week after I went off to Chatham to assume temporary command of the cruiser *Sheffield,* which was commencing a year's refit there. I was to start this off for two months before joining the Royal Naval College at Greenwich for the Staff Course. The Staff Course was not necessarily the path to higher things that it was in the Army, but it was most certainly not to be sneezed at and I was cheerful again for my father's party with that future in prospect.

*Sheffield* was a sistership of *Birmingham*, which I had left only six months earlier, so I was familiar with the layout and did not find it difficult to keep an eye on the seamen's side of the refit and her small naval refit crew. I had a cabin in the barracks and no watchkeeping duties, so had each weekend at home from Friday evening to Monday morning, and enjoyed mess life during the week rather than commute each evening and morning in the dark. Time passed pleasantly, and the only thing I remember is my gaffe in announcing over the broadcasting system to the refit crew one afternoon the new improved pay code that had just come in by signal, forgetting that the dockyard workmen aboard were not getting a pay rise and must have found the broadcast galling. One learns by one's mistakes. It was my second time in Chatham dockyard, having refitted *Plym* there four years earlier, so I knew my way round, which helped, as I had ten officers and a hundred men in my refit crew to supervise. A few years later the idea of the senior seaman officer being in command during refits was abandoned as he was usually junior to the Engineer Officer, who was chiefly concerned, but we certainly worked smoothly together.

I managed to attend a course at Chatham House on the Middle East for a couple of days early in March, as I thought it would be useful for the Staff Course, and heard some of the best Arab lecturers on the subject to broaden my knowledge. Soon afterwards my successor arrived to take over *Sheffield*, and I had a week's leave before joining Greenwich.

Greenwich had been started as a Naval Hospital by King Charles II, to house sick and elderly former seamen of the fleet. Its four blocks designed by Sir Christopher Wren were named the King Charles, Queen Mary, King William and Queen Anne buildings, according to the era in which they were built, and were set out in a square near the south bank of the Thames. A central vista was left towards the Queen's House, set back below Greenwich Hill, which had been built by Inigo Jones for Charles's mother Queen Henrietta Maria, It was not part of the College, which took up residence in the late 1930s after the buildings had been restored. The dining hall was the enormous Painted Hall, decorated by Sir James Thornhill with *trompe l'oeil* paintings and a magnificent painted ceiling showing the Apotheosis, or near deification, of William and Mary. They looked most ungodly and ill at ease in their heavy robes, adored and supported by Arts and Graces and associated small fry. Greenwich had resumed its position as the Royal Navy Staff College soon after the war, and ran two five-month courses each year for about 50 officers at a time, who included a few from the Dominion Navies and one Army and one RAF officer.

We joined the College on a Monday morning to settle into our coal-heated cabins – the Navy was slow to adopt central heating and the barracks also all still ran on coal – and that afternoon we were briefed on the course and the general set-up. We had been sent a recommended reading list, if one could find the books or the time to read them in advance, but there seemed no obvious explanation of how we had been selected except that we were all Lieutenant Commanders or young Commanders who had expressed an interest in the course or had completed their previous appointment at a convenient time. Our Army friends were appalled at such casual selection, as it was a major hurdle for them to achieve it, but we all seemed to acquit ourselves well and everyone appeared capable of putting in the effort and showing the ability to keep up. No one dropped out or was dropped, and there developed a tremendous camaraderie and spirit of cooperation as we all worked well into most evenings to meet our set targets.

Our very first study was of Stalin's forced collectivisation of the farms and of the terrible cruelty and loss of life with which it was achieved — an effective introduction to the brutality of Communism as enforced on a captive people. Even during the Cold War these facts were little known or publicised, but this was the only obvious indoctrination met with during the course. Normally we were formed into teams to tackle a project and come up with a staff solution, working on it for several days and then presenting our solution to the Directing Staff and comparing it with the approach of other teams. There was an approved method of approaching a problem called Appreciating the Situation, and one of the Directing Staff took it off perfectly in an article in *Punch* on how to tackle missing the boat train, ending with the perfect solution of catching the next train just as he saw it leaving another platform!

In fact the Staff Course essentially taught logical thought processes and setting out one's conclusions, after assessing all the alternatives, clearly and concisely. Our bible was a little red book, very different to Chairman Mao's version, called *B.R. 1984 Naval Staff Handbook.* It covered staff organisation, staff work and examples of the layout of service papers and orders, and it was usually at our elbow as we worked away at our given project. Painfully slow at first, we gathered speed and confidence as we got used to the procedure of writing staff paper solutions to the more complicated problems that were set as we moved ahead.

We were called at a very civilised 0730 in the morning, and took breakfast like all our meals in the Painted Hall before working from 0915 to 1300. After lunch we worked through with a tea break until dinner, and then most evenings continued if necessary until midnight, depending on pressure of work. It was never dull, and on Friday we finished at teatime to enjoy the luxury of a long weekend with our families every week. It wasn't all projects, of course; at least half the time was spent at lectures by top speakers in all walks of life, and industrial visits to places as varied as Fords at Dagenham and *The Times* in Printing House Square to learn something of the economic life of the country.

Naturally there was no Easter leave, just the weekend at the end of March before we got into our stride, but in mid-course we had a week's leave, when Jill and I took the children down to Camber Sands on the Sussex coast and I learnt that early June is not the time for an English holiday. When it did not rain the wind blew from the east, and the children not only went nowhere near the sea, but huddled among the sand dunes to try and keep out of the wind and stinging blown sand. Our guest house – we could not run to a hotel – had few amenities to amuse them, and only on the last day was it warm enough to play on the beach which we had come for.

As the course progressed, we all had to give a three-quarters of an hour talk on a subject of our choice to our fellow students and Directing Staff and then handle questions. I chose the State of Israel, describing the rise of Zionism from the end of the nineteenth century through to the establishment of the state and its consolidation after eight years. Among the questions was whether I foresaw another war with the Arabs, to which I sadly had to answer Yes, but I certainly had not foreseen how soon, as Nasser nationalised the Suez Canal just a few days later and the Suez Crisis began. Britain began to prepare for intervention at once, and a number of officers were withdrawn from our course to join the operation planning staff. Certainly no operation with the Israelis was planned initially, or I as the Navy's sole Hebrew interpreter would not have been left working away on my course at Greenwich.

We did not seriously think we would actually invade Egypt and regarded the planning, which we knew was going forward, as a mere staff exercise only to be put into action if all else failed. The Staff Course continued as usual, with regular mess guest nights when I entertained my family and friends in the splendour of the Painted Hall, and we enjoyed a families' day when Jill and the children lunched there with a steward behind every guest's chair in a style that only the Palace could manage today. Jill had been there earlier for the Summer Ball, but the children found it rather overpowering, though they enjoyed the river launch journey to Lambeth to see a display by the London Fire Brigade followed by tea. That was in mid-August, shortly before our five-month course ended and we all went on leave. There was no final examination, we had been assessed throughout, and could now add 'p.s.c.', 'Passed Staff Course', to our qualifications.

I had thoroughly enjoyed the course, and the opportunity to be lectured to by the country's top experts on a wide variety of naval, national and international subjects from the First Sea Lord, Earl Mountbatten, to the Secretary to the Cabinet, Sir Norman Brooks, and from the War in Europe by General Sir Brian Horrocks to the National Economy by a top economist. We had spent a week at the RAF Staff College at Bracknell, learnt something of our trading activities and the merchant navy, and how to present our views in debates and discussions, and generally matured our outlook.

After summer leave, I continued on to Woolwich for the Tactical Course with most of our group. We spent three weeks on lectures and taking part in tri-service tactical exercises to round off our Staff Course experience, then went on leave again to await our next appointments. I had already received mine, to fly to Singapore ten days later to join the staff, with Jill and the family to follow. We had a short time together to sort things out before I left, and arranged to let our house as an Admiralty 'hiring' so as to recover it easily and in good order on our return.

# 14

## *Singapore*

I left home on 3rd October for the long flight to Singapore. It was still early days for trooping flights. We gathered at the assembly centre in London very early, to be bussed out to Blackbushe airport, where we arrived before 8.30 to spend the entire day. Finally we embarked, some 60 RN and RAF, in a Hermes transport aircraft at 10 that evening. It was a short hop journey, landing at Brindisi, Beirut, Bahrain and Karachi. We then disembarked for supper and to spend the night in an airport hotel. We flew on in the morning via Delhi to Calcutta, where we disembarked again at Dum Dum airport – named for the suburb where the notorious soft-nosed bullets were once manufactured – and bussed into the city for a short night at a hotel. We were roused at 3.15 to return to the airport for an early flight on to Bangkok for lunch, and finally to Singapore at 6.30 on the evening of the 6th. Despite the breaks it was an exhausting journey, little improved on the old pre-war flying boat journey, which was without doubt more comfortable.

We of the naval contingent were taken from the civil airport at Payar Lebar to the Naval Base, which I knew well from my stay the previous year, and where I was met by my predecessor as Staff Officer Plans to the Flag Officer Malayan Area. FOMA, as he was known by his initials, administered the shore-based side of the southern area of the Far East command – the British territories of Singapore, Malaya, Sarawak, Brunei and North Borneo – from his offices in the Naval Base. He was Rear Admiral George Thring, the final holder of a post which was to be abolished after the forthcoming independence of Malaya. His chief task, with which I was to become deeply involved, was the transfer of the Royal Malayan Navy from Singapore to Malaya. It consisted of a few small warships with Malayan crews but mostly British officers, based at Singapore Naval Base and cooperating with the Army in attacking the Communist guerrillas in the jungle. We had gained the upper hand, but even though fighting a losing battle they remained a threat. There was a tremendous amount of administrative and political work involved in this transfer, as well as financial and other concerns with which we were less involved.

Over the next ten months I made a number of journeys with my Admiral from Singapore to Kuala Lumpur to call on the Malayan Chief Minister, Tunku Abdul Rahman, and discuss the details. One of the many disinterested achievements of Admiral Thring was to wean the Tunku away from the purchase of one of our older cruisers to serve as his flagship, and to get him to concentrate on smaller vessels more suitable for protecting the Malayan coastline. It would have been 'jobs for the boys', as almost all the officers and senior ratings would have had to be loaned from the RN, since the RMN was so small and had so few experienced personnel. Instead they were enabled to Malayanise themselves fast and effectively over the next few years.

I had of course flown out with a generous baggage allowance as I had to bring all my uniform and civilian clothes needed, leaving the rest to follow months later by sea with Jill and the family. With the Suez crisis working towards its climax it was uncertain when that would be, so I settled down to bachelor life in the naval barracks HMS *Terror*. The Commander-in-Chief's offices were at Phoenix Park in the leafy suburbs of Singapore city some 10 miles from us in the Naval Base, so frequent visits were necessary to keep in touch with Fleet policy and thinking. We worked a very gentlemanly routine of office hours from 0830 to 1245 and 1400 to 1645 followed by a game of squash or a swim or a bus into the city. On Wednesday we had the traditional 'Make and Mend' afternoon off, and we worked Saturday mornings, so it was a pleasant life. Changi was then the RAF main base in Singapore, and within a fortnight of arrival I flew up from there to Kuala Lumpur with my Admiral for my first visit to the Chief Minister, the British Commander of the Malayan Army and others, returning by the overnight sleeper two nights later. We had a Naval Liaison Officer based there, who put us up in his large official quarter on these occasions. It was a bit hard on his wife, but part of her 'duties'.

Trafalgar Night was marked by a formal dinner in the Naval Base, attended by the Governor of the Colony and the heads of the three services, but that same week there was rioting in the city over some local problem and the services became deeply involved in protecting the transport bringing in their local civilian staff. The riots were quelled within a few days, just as the Suez Crisis burst into flames. Nothing happened in Singapore, where we watched the campaign develop and the British and French forces go in, before US and UN threats halted them half way down the Canal. It was an enormous loss of face to be halted by the opposition of almost the entire world and forced to withdraw, and speeded the end of the colonial era, though we did not see the effects so much in our area where Malayan independence day had already been set and Singapore granted self-government.

On the personal side, the blocking of the Canal meant that Jill had to face a five-week journey round the Cape to reach Singapore, and could not expect to arrive until mid-December. She set off with three young children on the old P&O liner *Corfu* into a rough sea, and all four of them were prostrate in their cabin for the first two days until the weather eased. Thereafter she found herself at an uncongenial table, with the children constantly demanding attention and without anyone to help her, so the journey was a real strain rather than any sort of pleasure.

The Commander-in-Chief had loaned his despatch vessel *Alert*, a converted frigate used as a sort of miniature *Britannia*, to FOMA in November for a cruise along the west coast of Malaya with his family. This incorporated a search for a Malayan base for the Royal Malayan Navy after its transfer from Singapore. I flew up from the Seletar airbase in one of the old wartime Sunderland flying boats which the RAF still operated. It was like experiencing the pre-war Imperial Airways, as we powered down the Singapore Straits and smoothly into the air in a roomy cabin, and put down off Lumut at the mouth of the Dindings river a couple of hours later. The Dindings had been a tiny Victorian enclave at the river mouth, a small part of the old Straits Settlements. It had been returned to the state of Perak before the war, but Admiral Thring had visited it in those days and felt it might be a suitable base. Lumut had stagnated as a little town, barely more than a glorified village, but I was amused to note that the municipal offices were in Downing Street. The water was quite deep and clear offshore, beautiful for a swim from the beaches or *Alert*, but there were absolutely no facilities at this isolated fishing port and it would have cost the earth to develop them so the idea was abandoned. We went on to Port Swettenham, the port of Kuala Lumpur and the most likely base, where the Admiral held a reception for the Chief Minister and other VIPs followed by dinner and a dance. I had the opportunity for a conversation with the Tunku, or Prince, who was a prince of the royal family of the Malayan state of Kedah. He had been at Cambridge with a close friend of my wife's family, worked in the state service and then become head of the Alliance of Malay, Chinese and Indian parties which he was leading to independence. He was an intelligent and tolerant man, dedicated to uniting the Chinese and Indian descendants of immigrants into one nation with the indigenous Malays who owned the land. They held the leading administrative and military posts, but few of them were in industry or commerce due to their poor education. That there were few inter-communal disturbances and that Malaysia grew into an advanced and peaceful society owed much to his initial guidance.

Within 36 hours of our return to Singapore I was on the Saturday night sleeper to KL to stay with Commander Burfield, the Naval Liaison Officer, and work on the budget for the Royal Malayan Navy. It was a case of the blind leading the blind, as we worked out virtually on the backs of envelopes what we thought various items would cost, the manpower requirements and expenses for the next Federal Budget and what Britain could be expected to pay as part of its contribution to Independence. On my return to Singapore I went through our rough draft with the Admiral, who took it further with C.-in-C.'s staff, and the following week it was Commander Burfield's turn to come down from KL to work on the figures and discuss them with the RMN locally. The number of people involved and to be satisfied was considerable. The Defence Secretary in the Singapore Government, which was to pass over its small navy to Malaya, had to be consulted in detail on this and the basing of a 'foreign' navy, Malaya's, on its territory for some years until it moved to a new Malayan base. There was the local RNVR which would become Singapore's mini-navy based on the commercial harbour, and various others who would be affected. All very interesting, but not exactly what the Staff Course prepared me for!

Meanwhile I had been busy finding initial accommodation for the family, at a guest house in Orchard Road. It was not the canyon of offices, hotels and department stores of today, but a long straggling development leading from the city into the suburbs, with several large stretches of undeveloped land, and Silverbank was an old colonial residence near Scotts Road that had been converted into a guest house with about a dozen rooms. The site is now part of Tang's department store and Dynasty Hotel.

The family arrived on our wedding anniversary, 13th December, the best possible way to celebrate it. I met them at Keppel Harbour, the commercial harbour to the west of the city, and took them off to Silverbank for lunch and to settle in. The Naval Movements Officer Sam Manning, who organised arrivals and departures,became a good friend, as did his wife Elsie. He was one of those who kindly took me to the Naval Base until our car arrived, leaving Jill to keep the children happy and explore the Orchard Road area and the local shops. We were in the middle of the rainy season and the monsoon rains were often heavy and prolonged, which could restrict even our weekend outings. That first weekend we went to the Botanic Gardens to feed the monkeys, an ideal entertainment for young children to see them jump from the trees for nuts. Christmas was approaching with its season of parties, so on several evenings the children were put to bed and left with fellow service residents on a swap basis so that we could go out in turn. On Christmas Day the children had presents when they got up, then we drove up to the naval barracks for a children's lunch and a visit from Father Christmas with more presents, and back to Silverbank for tea and further presents from a second Father Christmas before the guests enjoyed a festive dinner and evening. Hopefully all the activities helped the children to cheer up and adjust after their long journey from home, and Mary's traumatic bus journey among children she didn't know to an Army school which took service children from our area of the city. They were tearful days for a little girl of five meeting these extraordinary changes of routine, surroundings and climate, but the boys had Mummy close at hand to look after them.

We were fortunate to have a number of friends in Singapore, notably Mrs Nissim, the doyenne of the Jewish community, who kept an open house on Friday evenings for Jewish servicemen and their families and for any Jewish visitor to Singapore. I have happy memories of these evenings and of her festive parties for the children during our stay, and of the friends we made there. Larry Sharp was a Surgeon Lieutenant with whom we became very close, and Sam Janikoun, an RAMC Colonel and nephew of my London University professor Isidore Wartski. We also met Vic Wood, my father's travelling salesman, on a business visit to the island, and other friends passed through in the next two years.

We soon found ourselves a bungalow to be taken on as a naval hiring at 25 Marigold Drive in Adelphi Park, a housing estate developed since the war just off the Thomson Road leading from the city up to the Naval Base. It had a single large living/dining room, two bedrooms and a bathroom at one end and the kitchen and amah's room at the other, with a carport at the side. A covered verandah ran along the front, and the living room had overhead electric fans. It had a front garden about 20 foot deep facing the road, which ran the full length of the house, and the back of the house was only a few feet from the fence of a rubber plantation out of which the estate had been carved. The whole island was hot and humid year round, but the rubber trees cut off much of any cooling wind that might blow, though they did provide the children with a live lesson on rubber-tapping. We engaged a very efficient but rather shy Chinese girl called Ah Siew as our amah, who stayed with us for all our time in Singapore, and a Tamil gardener who came at intervals to tidy and maintain the garden. A naval truck moved us and our possessions from Silverbank one weekend in mid-January, and we were settled at last. There were several naval families on the estate, the nearest being John Parford the Deputy Base Supply Officer and his wife Barbara, so Mary was now able to go with their daughter Sarah Jane and other naval children on the estate by naval bus to the primary school in the Naval Base.

We were about a third of the way from the city to the base, and joined the Tanglin Club in Scotts Road near Silverbank for its swimming pool and other facilities, as well as having the use of the base swimming pool and mess during family times at weekends. A favourite Sunday morning routine was a drive up to *Terror* for a swim and a drink by the pool, listening to the Royal Marine band, then to eat in the mess a fine curry with all the trimmings followed by *gula malacca*, sticky rice with golden syrup and milk. There was a shallow pool for the non-swimmers, but within a few months the children were all swimming confidently, even two-and-a-bit-year-old Jonathan, and jumping happily into the pool. The Tanglin amenities were rather similar, but more convenient for entertaining guests, for a quick swim without a longish drive, or after shopping in town. We soon made a circle of naval friends, and among those we still see regularly are John Uniacke, the Fleet Royal Marine Officer and his wife Ricky, with whom we went on a Nile cruise recently, John and Barbara Parford, our Adelphi Park neighbours, and Bill and Peggy Newman from Kranji WT Station.

Not all weekends were holidays. I was Duty Staff Officer in the base every fifth or sixth day when I could not go home, and the naval transfer planning sometimes involved weekend work, but generally I could plot out my social life ahead and lead a normal family life. We had ordered a new Austin A30, similar to the one we drove in England, before leaving home, but due to the Suez crisis and the blocking of the Canal it did not arrive until late January, when we became fully mobile and I was able to return the car lifts I had received earlier. There was a real camaraderie and helping out of others as usual in the Navy, and we in our turn helped other newcomers. The great shopping area was at Changi village outside the RAF base, where the best bargains could be obtained, although we had a smaller version outside the Naval Base gates in Sembawang village. It was at Changi that a few months later we bought our first cinecamera, and Jill made a colour film of our daily life to send home to her family for showing on their projector. We became very keen on this, and recorded the main events of our family life for many years afterwards.

Although Singapore island is about one and a half times the size of the Isle of Wight, most of its million people lived in and around the city in the south, with the rest scattered in villages across the island on the main roads or in Malay villages, called kampongs, off the beaten track. Many of the villages and small towns had grown up to serve the service bases, and we would visit these as outings and to compare the shopping facilities with Changi. A few miles north of us on the way to the Naval Base was Nee Soon, serving the Army Base there, and nearby was the attractive park surrounding the Pearce Reservoir where we often took the children to play as an alternative to the Botanic Gardens. The reservoir was like a lake in the park, and an attractive place to picnic under the trees or for children to play hide-and-seek among them, so we did not lack for varied outings. Going further afield at weekends, we sometimes crossed the mile-long causeway into Malaya to visit Johore Bahru, the capital of the state of Johore, where its elderly Sultan, who had taken tea with Queen Victoria and already celebrated his own Diamond Jubilee, had his palace. Its tower was the main feature of this rather seedy little town, but it had a pleasant esplanade along the Johore Strait and some interesting open-air market stalls. There was of course no television in Singapore at that time, and the cinema was the main evening entertainment. We would usually go to the Tanglin Club on Sunday evenings to see a film and have a meal with naval friends and sometimes go during the week to one of the 'Worlds', the pre-war pleasure parks whose names all ended in World, with their many restaurants and choices of cinemas and entertainment. I particularly recall a group Chinese dinner and evening at the Great World to see David Niven in *Around the World in 80 days*. We all left our trusty amahs to babysit without a second thought, and were never let down. The nearest exception was when we came home one evening to find Ah Siew and the children watching in fascination as our little cat had her first kittens.

We were permitted local leave, and to take an 'indulgence', or nominal fare passage, to Hong Kong in any troopship which was heading there half-empty after offloading servicemen in Malaya and Singapore. We accordingly booked passage in the *Oxfordshire* in April to stay with my brother Michael. Unfortunately the

Malayan Navy transfer plans were reaching one of their regular crises, and I had to miss the boat to sort things out with the Admiral and others involved. After a lot of string-pulling I was able to join them the following week, flying by courtesy of the RAF from Changi on a roundabout route via Labuan and Manila. Michael was living in a flat in Felix Villas on Hong Kong island, with a lovely view out over the islands off the New Territories, and fitted us all in by moving onto a camp bed. It was a wonderful opportunity for us all to meet, and to see Hong Kong at its best. Michael drove us round the island and the mainland villages, still like Old China. We swam from the beaches and were real tourists, doing all the standard things from riding the Peak Tram to see the view from above to eating at an Aberdeen floating restaurant, not forgetting the shopping. Unfortunately it only lasted for a week, as I had to be back within a fortnight and troopships rarely ran each way to suit, so I booked our passage on a Dutch merchant ship economy class. As we proved to be the only economy Europeans we found ourselves upgraded to a better cabin, much to our surprise. The Admiralty had sent my wife out to Singapore by P&O, presumably happy for her to sit at table with Chinese police officers and other Asians, but the Dutch seemed to feel differently. It was not as if we had booked steerage, and knowing their finances I suspect many officers travelled the same way. Unfortunately Jill and Jonathan had picked up a flu bug which came out during the voyage, and arrived back in Singapore feeling very weak and miserable for a couple of days. Two months later the children went down in turn with measles, which thrived in the Tropics.

Among my lesser duties was Press Officer, a form of public relations where if there was anything concerning the local area that affected the public I was the man to draw up the press release. It was a pleasant sinecure which chiefly involved attending the occasional journalists' lunch or cocktail party and getting to know the British correspondents, rather than releasing any news of interest. The BBC correspondent Brian Denney and his Malayan wife Ee Pin became our next-door neighbours in Surbiton 20 years later, when we recalled those lunches at the Cockpit. It was there that I first heard future PM Lee Kuan Yew speak, when he was regarded as an extreme left-wing threat to the moderate

Labour PM, Lim Yew Hock, who is now forgotten. Equally almost a sinecure was being Duty Staff Officer, as we only had to be on call within the Naval Base to deal with any emergency. Apart from the riots of the previous October, there were virtually none and one could play squash, swim or go bowling or to the cinema in the evening as long as one's location was known. It really was a most enjoyable life, entertaining friends to dinner and being entertained ourselves, dances at *Terror* on special occasions like the Armada Ball, when we danced to 3 a.m., and visits to other messes, such as the Royal Malayan Navy, where most of the wardroom was RN, including Mike Roden who had been one of my midshipmen at Scapa Flow.

*Merdeka* was drawing near, the Malay word for Independence, so the radio would sign off with a cry of '*Merdeka, Merdeka!*' and the attractive new National Anthem '*Negara Ku*', or 'My Country', based on an old Malay folk tune. It was all part of building up a national consciousness. The RMN transfer was still not finalised but now beyond my level, so it was decided that I should go to Penang to update the Port Plan, of which there was one for every major port to put it on a war footing, and which it would be difficult and tactless to do once Malaya became independent.

I decided to take the family and combine it with local leave, so we set off in the Austin on a Sunday morning early in August over the causeway, where an imposing Customs Building had been erected at the Malay end ready to go into action and control the entry of items that carried less tax in Singapore. Leaving Johore Bahru we met our first barrier, manned by armed Malay or British soldiers, to check that we were not carrying food or supplies for, or which could be seized by, the Communist terrorists who still lurked in the jungle. One was not allowed to stop on the road outside the towns in case of terrorist attacks from the nearby jungle, so 'comfort stops' for the children had to be planned in advance. The main roads were regarded as quite safe and we reached Seremban for lunch, as we could not carry a picnic, then Kuala Lumpur by teatime, where the Burfields in their usual generous way put us up overnight. Setting off next morning we lunched in Taiping, reached Butterworth late afternoon, took the car ferry across to Penang island and drove on to our small Golden Sands hotel on the west coast at Batu Ferringhi.

Jill and the children enjoyed a beach holiday, while each day during the week I drove into Georgetown – the port and main town – to work with the retired Commander in charge of the local RNVR. We revised the Port Plan to incorporate recent developments and to allow for the use of Penang as a minor naval base and control of shipping port in case of war. Penang was Britain's oldest possession in the Far East, obtained as a base in 1786 from the Sultan of Kedah, and the original Straits Settlement before Singapore was founded by Raffles several decades later. It had fewer people, the island was not as large, and Georgetown was a more laid-back and quiet place with a smaller but still important port. Unlike Singapore, it was a rugged island with the tall Penang Hill overlooking Georgetown which we all went up by the Hill Railway, a smaller cousin of Hong Kong's Peak Tram, to see the view and for the children to enjoy the swings and playground at the top. I usually returned in time for tea and a late swim with the family, and it was while we were sitting on the beach that two-and-a-half-year-old Jonathan uttered his first sentence. He had got by until then with words and pointing, but he was so astonished by a woman driving a water buffalo past us with a stick that he shouted 'Lady smack cow Mummy' to draw our attention.

We spent a happy family weekend on the beach, making sand-castles and playing in the sea, with the children splashing around in their rubber rings, then left with the job completed. We stayed overnight in a hotel in Kuala Lumpur, I visited Port Swettenham the following morning with Commander Burfield in our continuing efforts to finalise a base for the RMN, and then home after our first long car journey of nearly a thousand miles.

Two weeks later I returned to Kuala Lumpur with the official naval group led by my Admiral for the *Merdeka* celebrations. A senior police officer kindly put me up, and I was a junior participant in the various celebrations. These started with a searchlight tattoo on the *padang* outside the Selangor Club, followed by receptions, and on the morning of Independence Day, Saturday 31st August, we set off at 6.20 for the Merdeka Stadium a couple of miles away where the ceremony was to take place at 8.

191

Unfortunately the approach road and exit road proved too narrow for the traffic, and insufficient time had been allowed for the setting down and seating of the VIPs, so the most horrendous snarl-ups ensued. We found ourselves trapped alongside the Sultan of Pahang in his full Malay ceremonial dress and turban, physically cool in his air-conditioned Rolls Royce but obviously seething internally. Eventually the ceremony started an hour late at 9 a.m., probably the only time independence has been delayed by a traffic jam!

Thirty thousand people crowded the stadium to see and hear the Tunku, elevated from Chief to Prime Minister, proclaim the independence of Malaya in front of the Queen's representative, her uncle the Duke of Gloucester, and the heads of the 11 states making up the Federation of Malaya. The eight Malay Sultans and the Raja of Perlis had chosen one of their number as Yang di Pertuan Agong, or King, and every five years, or earlier in case of death, they elect a new one. The odd men out were the newly selected Governors of the former colonies of Penang and Malacca, who did not qualify for Kingship or to be shaded by a royal gold coloured umbrella. It was a truly colourful occasion, added to by the Tunku and his entire cabinet appearing in white tunics, striped blue trousers and plumed white helmets like a bevy of British Governors. They must have been laughed to scorn for aping colonialist dress, as they were never seen in them again.

The day ended with fireworks in the Lake Gardens, and next morning we were out early to reach our stand outside the Moorish-domed Secretariat to see the new King review the military independence parade. The celebrations ended with an historical pageant in the Lake Gardens that evening, and next day, after some naval discussions, we flew back to Singapore. It was the second independence at which I had been present, and quite a contrast to the birth of Israel nearly ten years earlier.

The justification for a Flag Officer Malayan Area ceased with the independence of Malaya, and he began to run down his activities as his staff was stripped away. I was the first, leaving that same week to take up a new appointment as Naval Member of the Joint Planning Staff on the staff of the Commander-in-Chief at Phoenix Park in the city suburbs. I already knew my direct boss

Commander Tony Bowen, the Naval Member of the Joint Planning Committee to which we reported, but I was now looking at the problems of the whole Far East instead of just the Malayan area so it took time to read myself in. One of our main concerns was SEATO, the South East Asia Treaty Organisation, which had been set up after the Korean War at Anglo-American instigation to involve the anti-Communist countries of the area in mutual defence plans. Apart from Great Britain, the United States and France, the area members were Pakistan, Thailand and the Philippines, Australia and New Zealand, and the six-monthly meeting was due to take place in Bangkok ten days later, so I had plenty of reading to do beforehand. Our team flew up from Changi on 17th September, the actual morning after a bloodless *coup d'état* which had turned out one government and installed another. All was peaceful, but embarrassingly for the Thais all the hospitality invitations were in the names of the former ministers and we did not even know the names of our hosts. Tanks were out on the streets, but no signs of any disturbances.

We stayed at the Erewan Hotel, one of the first modern hotels to be built in the city, which in those days had not developed into a tourist magnet. It was the 2,500th anniversary of the birth of Buddha, and being a Buddhist country, all the chief temples had been regilded with gold leaf and redecorated for the event. We were shown the Royal Palace and the Temple of the Emerald Buddha in the grounds, guarded by exotic mythical figures in brightly coloured costumes, housing the green jade figure of the Buddha whose dress was changed every quarter with the seasons. We also visited the Wat Arun, or Temple of the Dawn, with its pinnacles, and the Wat Po with its huge reclining Buddha over 150 feet long. Unlike today the traffic ran freely in the streets as few people could then afford cars, and the taxis were all little manoeuvrable Austins – part of our export success. The klongs, or network of canals, had not then been filled in, so Bangkok was an oriental Venice along the banks of the Chao Phraya river. Broad modern avenues had been laid out before the war inland from the river, with vistas opening to the parliament building and other landmarks. On one of these avenues stood the SEATO offices, in a modern building with a red and green Thai curlicue roof, where sessions were held. It was an unbalanced group, five white nations to three Asian, so great care was taken to give them priority since it was their countries which were threatened. SEATO was part of a worldwide ring round the Soviet Union, linking up to the West with CENTO, comprising Pakistan again, Iran and Turkey with their Western allies and linking up through Turkey with NATO, so the Russians had some justification in feeling encircled, though SEATO's planning was entirely defensive and somewhat embryonic. We worked on various papers during the meetings, which were basically devoted to improving joint planning against threats to the Asian members.

Thailand had never been a colony, so was without the anti-colonialist feeling of most countries in the area, and was pro-British because of our record in supporting its independence. They even drove on the left, like the adjacent former British territories of Burma and Malaya, rather than on the right like former French Indo-China, and the elite preferred British schools and universities for their children, possibly dating back to Anna's governess days with the King of Siam.

The Saturday after my return was Mary's sixth birthday, marked by a party in our garden for a dozen of her friends, and life continued uneventfully for the next two months. I was now in a different roster as Duty Staff Officer on the C.-in-C.'s staff, holding myself available in Phoenix Park for any emergency, but was rarely called on. We were kept busy on joint service plans for various emergencies, in particular the evacuation of British and Commonwealth nationals from parts of adjacent unstable Indonesia in the event of local riots or civil war. There was a change of Commanders-in-Chief, and the new one was Admiral Sir Gerald Gladstone, whose flag we had flown in the cruiser *Birmingham* three years earlier.

At the end of November I was sent to British Borneo to update the Port Plans, as I had done in Penang a few months earlier. The difference was that these were backward and undeveloped colonies, whose infrastructure was negligible. Most British North Borneo towns were destroyed in bitter Japanese opposition to the Australian invasion towards the end of the war, to the extent that in Jesselton, the capital, almost the only building to survive was the Victorian clock tower standing outside the town proper. Sarawak, except Kuching the capital, had suffered nearly as badly, and the White Rajah Sir Charles Vyner Brooke and the British North Borneo Company were persuaded to hand over their possessions to the Crown after the war with the argument that only Britain could find the money to rebuild them.

I took a Malayan Airways flight from Singapore via Kuching and Sibu to Labuan island, where I was picked up by a Shell aircraft and taken to Seria in the Brunei oilfields which were to make the present Sultan the richest man in the world. After a briefing on the situation the manager took me by jeep next morning, on a red earth laterite road, crossing rivers by ferry, over the border into Sarawak to their oilfields at Miri where the oil was still being extracted from the shrinking fields by 'nodding donkey' pumps. It was then pumped out to tankers offshore, though there was talk of building a harbour.

Next day Shell flew me back to Labuan to meet the District Officer and to prepare the plan for this well-placed port. It had been occupied in the 1840s when coal was discovered there, to serve as an extra base for our coal-burning ships, but the mines were worked out and the town and port tiny. I attended the opening of a new bakery, a major event in the small town, and a Saint Andrew's Night dinner at the Club when we celebrated a more major event – the birth of a son to the Scottish District Officer.

From there I flew on to Jesselton to stay with the Chief Secretary Mr Turner and his wife, who two years later as hosts to Lady Mountbatten found her dead in bed one morning. The town had been laid out on a grid plan over the destroyed original, the streets unimaginatively called *Jalan Satu*, *Dua*, Street One, Two, etc. and the buildings all in one style for speed of construction. In contrast the new Government Buildings had been designed in England with no thought of the tropical sun, and the big picture windows were papered over to reduce the heating effect. We discussed local defence all morning, then I went to lunch in the *Kampong Ayer* or Water Village, built out on stilts over the shallows, with Gordon Lum. He was an Australian-born Chinese who became a national hero by beating the Japanese in the Davis Cup tennis competition before the war, but as a Nationalist got out before the Communists took over. He and his sister Ada were friends of my parents, and it was strange to meet him in this remote place.

Back in Singapore I returned to general planning work after updating the Borneo plans, and we were soon into the Christmas season. Again, as the previous year, we were practically confined to the house several times in December by the intense rain of the north-east monsoon which reached its peak at that time. We did not suffer gales, just steady heavy rain that beat up from the pavements and soaked one in less than a minute. Taxis were snapped up or seemed to vanish with the rain, and one was marooned in doorways or any cover until the rain eased unless the car was parked near enough to make a dash for it worthwhile. It rained during most of the year, the driest period being the south-west monsoon about June, but normally just a short sharp shower or two followed by hot sun in which the fallen rain dried off the pavements as steam. Because of this, although nearly on the equator, the temperature rarely became excessive, anything over 35° centigrade, 95° Fahrenheit, being exceptional, but it never dropped below 20° even on a cool night and the humidity was high enough for a brisk walk to bring the sweat pouring out.

I took the Duty Staff Officer's job on Christmas Day, the family joining me for lunch in *Terror* mess, and in the evening I listened to the Queen's broadcast as a link with home. Next day we telephoned Jill's mother for her birthday, which was an even closer link with home and a rare and expensive event in those days when one was passed from Singapore to GPO operator and finally to Oxshott. It had been planned as a surprise, and she was thrilled to speak to her daughter and grandchildren.

We saw in the New Year 1958 at the Tanglin Club, and settled into another year in Singapore. It was probably one of the most relaxed periods of our life, with an amah to do the heavy work and babysit when required and I with light hours of work and plenty of time for family excursions. Despite the humidity, Singapore was a healthy place, the children thrived, and David now joined Mary at the naval school as he approached five, leaving only toddler Jonathan with Jill in term-time.

Early in January my parents came ashore from the *Chusan* to spend two days with us, sleeping at Raffles, on their way to Hong Kong on business and to see my brother. We gave a cocktail party for them before they left, which caused a minor sensation in quiet Adelphi Park when the C.-in-C.'s and FOMA's cars flying their flags on the bonnet parked in our little street. They flew in again from Hong Kong a month later, to spend a week at Raffles. Before the war there had been only two good hotels in Singapore, Raffles – named after the founder of both the city and the London Zoo – near the sea and favoured by my father, and the Adelphi near the Anglican cathedral, favoured by my uncle. A few more modern hotels had opened since the war, though only a handful as the island was not yet a tourist centre, and Raffles with its huge rooms – many looking onto its courtyard gardens shaded by travellers' palms – was still the most attractive. They had planned the flight so as to spend time with the family, and we were able to take them round the island and show them our favourite spots as well as entertaining them and being entertained. That week, before they caught another P&O liner, the *Canton*, for the journey home, was the longest that they were ever to spend at one time with the family and they saw their grandchildren every day.

They sailed on Chinese New Year's Eve, which always falls at New Moon in January or February. All the amahs and Chinese servants were traditionally given several days' holiday to celebrate their most important festival, and all social life stopped as the European ladies devoted themselves to running their homes. That weekend we visited my father's business associates the Wans to wish them a Happy New Year and to join them for a tea of traditional Chinese delicacies. These did not appeal to the children, and considerable skill was required to cover them spitting out those they disliked, but all went off smoothly.

Early in March I flew to Manila for the next SEATO conference, having flown up in January to Bangkok for a few days' advance planning and liaison with the resident planning staff there.

We flew from Changi to Manila in the plane of the C.-in-C. Far East Land Forces, General Sir Francis Festing, a forthright character whose hobbies included collecting Japanese samurai swords. We were put up in the Manila Hotel, and toured the cabarets in a cheerful party that ended at 1 a.m., well before closing time, so that we would be ready for duty when the conference opened next morning at the Foreign Ministry. We worked at it all day, broken by lunch and later a cocktail party at the Philippine Navy Club. In the evening I saw my first game of *hai alai*, the incredibly fast and fascinating Filipino ball game played on a floodlit court. Having been virtually an American colony for some 50 years, the Philippines had an American cultural and sporting veneer on their former Spanish culture imposed over several centuries on their original Asian Tagalog roots. It made an interesting mixture, *hai alai* being very much their own game, garishly painted *jeepneys*, a form of communal taxi transport, and pictures in colour on the front pages of the newspapers. Somewhat crude colour certainly but completely unknown in Europe at the time, and a misuse of limited foreign currency on a non- essential American luxury.

On its third day the conference concluded at noon, and in the afternoon we were given a tour of the war damaged old Spanish walled city, the impressive palace of the President, the university and then the shops to buy a *barong Tagalog* for the festive final evening. The *barong* is an embroidered shirt worn outside the trousers as male national dress, and reputedly made of banana fibre looking and washing like linen. It later proved a genuine and easy fancy dress on a number of occasions. Whether the conference achieved much was a matter of opinion, as in the time available few military plans could be made or even progressed by eight nations, but politically it showed togetherness, which was the main idea.

We returned in time for me to attend the farewell dinner in the Naval Base for Rear Admiral Thring before he hauled down his flag as the last Flag Officer Malayan Area and went into retirement. I had enjoyed my first staff job under him, though I am sure he found me somewhat inexperienced, and I found his frequent rewriting of my drafts rather trying. It was the time of the post-Suez contraction of the services when we faced up to the fact that we were no longer one of the wartime Big Three, and had neither the resources nor the will to maintain the Pax Britannica over wide areas. The abolition of FOMA was a token of this, but much more major and of personal concern was the government's offer of early retirement and the threat of compulsory retirement if not enough volunteers came forward. The end of the Cold War in the 1990s has seen a repetition of this painful slim-down. We were much concerned with our own futures that year; a number decided to quit, and the rest of us were very relieved when the redundancy lists were published without our names.

Meanwhile, our work and social life went on, and we began spending the occasional weekend in Malaya as the terrorists were driven further into the jungle and travel became easier. Our first weekend was at Mersing on the east coast of Johore, a three-hour drive, to stay in the Government Rest House and take the children to the deserted sandy beaches around the town. This gave us the taste for these visits, and for the Whitsun weekend we drove to Malacca on the west coast, where we and the Uniackes stayed at the Government Rest House. These had been set up all over the country for the use of government officials on tour, but were usually empty at the weekends and welcomed bookings. Sleepy Malacca was picturesque with its old Dutch buildings painted red and the ruins of its Portuguese church, but had been bypassed in the move to modern times. The children enjoyed the swimming club, and we explored the old town centre and shops though we did not find the antique Chinese bargains that occasionally turned up among the junk – even assuming that we would have recognised them.

To the south of Singapore and close by lay a number of small islands which formed part of the Colony, and to which we occasionally went by naval launch for family bathing trips, but one which was not included was Pulau Bukum. Bukum island was leased to the Shell oil company under an arrangement by which their manager acted as a sort of District Commissioner in charge of all the Shell personnel living and working there. We had got to know the current manager, 'Frass' Barton-Wright, who had earlier invited the family over for the day and now invited Jill and me to their Queen's Birthday celebrations. A Shell launch took the guests over to the island from Collyer Quay for a delightful evening dance and buffet, and at a suitable moment after our glasses had been filled there was a roll of drums, Frass said 'Ladies and Gentlemen – The Queen' and the band to his horror –

instead of the National Anthem – played 'Happy Birthday to You'. This on a formal occasion in a British colony was a major 'black', the naval slang for 'cock-up', which it took the poor man a long time to live down. Most of us were choking with laughter as we drank the toast. Fortunately the next day was a holiday for the Queen's Official Birthday, as we had only got to bed at 3 a.m., and we attended the Governor's garden party in honour of the occasion on the lawns of Government House. On a hot and humid afternoon we naval officers quietly dripped away inside our starched white uniforms. When one could forget this it was a delight to watch all the different races in their best national dress thronging the lawns, Chinese men in western dress with their wives and daughters in the loveliest silk brocade dresses and cheongsams, Malays in velvet songkot caps of various colours and stiff brocaded jackets and trousers, and Indians with their turbans or Gandhi caps and their wives and daughters in multicoloured sarees. This time there was no mistake with the National Anthem.

In addition to the Governor there resided in Singapore the Commissioner General for South East Asia – the British Government's resident co-ordinator. The post was created for and held for many years after the war by Malcolm MacDonald, son of the first Labour Prime Minister, and now by Lord Selkirk. We had some dealings with his staff in our planning role, and came in for his reception a few days later. Like many aristocrats he was much less formal than many government officials, and one quite often saw him in the pool or restaurant at the Tanglin Club. Of course the Governor Sir Robert Black as the Queen's representative, was not able to do this, but he was another popular Scot who was constantly on the move around the Colony meeting the people and visiting schools, community centres and the like.

After these brushes with the powers that be, life resumed its normal tempo, and the English summer months were matched by the driest and hottest months in Singapore. We decided, therefore, to plan our summer holiday in Malaya. Duty had taken me to Penang the previous year and chosen our holiday for us. This time we settled on Kuantan, halfway up the east coast in the State of Pahang, combined with a week at Fraser's Hill. We booked in advance at the Government Rest House, and the day before departure received a letter of cancellation. I decided to ignore it, pretend that it had not arrived before we left if there was any trouble, as we could not replan everything at that late stage. Although Malaya was now independent British influence was still strong as our forces were heavily involved with theirs in the jungle war, and I felt they would have to fix us up somehow, but in fact we were booked into our rooms on arrival using our initial confirmation. As nothing was said, I kept quiet, so never discovered how the 'cancellation' came about.

Kuantan was then a small fishing port and administrative centre, with miles of palm-shaded sandy beaches and little streams which the children enjoyed paddling in and damming. We had a glorious relaxed week, driving to various beaches north and south of the town, each one as deserted and attractive as the last, and all perfect for young children. A few local Malay children occasionally appeared and waved, but were too shy to join us. The Rest House served plain English food that was ideal for the children, and it was an outstanding success.

From there we drove back across Pahang on the red laterite road that had only recently been completed with funds from the Colonial Development Corporation and gave off small puffs of red dust as we passed along it, and up to Fraser's Hill. The road was winding and narrow, closed off by a gate, and only suitable for one way traffic. We had to time our arrival to join the hour of upward traffic before it was closed for the traffic to come down safely, as it lies nearly 5,000 feet up in the mountain range separating Pahang from Selangor.

Fraser's Hill and the rather larger and higher Cameron Highlands had been developed in the style of Indian hill stations for the British to get away from the tropical heat into a cooler atmosphere, and the Royal Navy maintained a large bungalow which took about three families and had to be booked months ahead. We found ourselves in a large village of mock-Tudor houses with fireplaces in use at night to take off the evening chill, and attractive walks and views across the mountain ranges. It was more to the taste of adults, but the children enjoyed the novelty of a jumper and a fire. It was so new in fact to Jonathan that he called it a 'burn', since he was little over a year old when he last saw a

201

fire. At the end of that week we caught the Down Gate on the Saturday morning, and were soon in Kuala Lumpur, where we stopped for lunch and a swim before driving on to spend the night at the Rest House in Seremban and see another town. We were back home comfortably for lunch next day after an ideal fortnight's break in Malaya and with all the children fit and well.

There were no more excursions for the rest of the year as we settled back to our regular Singapore routine. Mary and David caught the naval school bus early every weekday morning to their primary school in the Naval Base and were returned at lunchtime. I went off to my office likewise and on Saturday mornings, and Jill played with Jonathan and took him out with her. With our wide circle of friends we were entertaining or being entertained several nights a week, going to the Tanglin to swim most weekends and to a film there followed by buffet supper most Sunday evenings. We went to various beaches round the island, occasionally to the Botanical Gardens to feed the monkeys, or to the aquarium, or across to the zoo in Johore Bahru. Almost always there were friends, service or civilian, with children of similar age to share these excursions.

In July there had been a ceremony to mark the transfer – on which I had laboured so long – of the RMN from Singapore to Malaya, although it remained based in Singapore for some years. In September we had a visit from the First Lord of the Admiralty with all its ceremonial, and in October the usual Trafalgar Night Dinner.

Working on the Joint Planning Staff, we had our share of other service events, the Royal Engineers Ball, the General's and Air Marshal's receptions and so on, but also the more serious side. There was a fascinating view of the island from a Vampire fighter, inspection of the *Chichester*, the first post-war design of frigate who had just joined the Fleet, and a visit to Kranji War Cemetery on Remembrance Sunday for the children to see the long lines of white headstones marking those who fell in the disastrous retreat down Malaya and in 'impregnable' Singapore. Its impressive layout and beautiful setting hopefully provide some consolation to visiting relatives.

At the end of October my father's brother Douglas and his wife

Josie arrived in the *Chusan* for a two-day visit on their way to Hong Kong, where he was to replace my brother while he took home leave. They knew Singapore well, so we showed them the naval side, and took them to an, at the time, memorable performance of Gilbert and Sullivan's *The Yeomen of the Guard*. In those days before Britain became a multitcultural society, I was fascinated by the mixed British, Chinese, Malay and Indian yeomen singing their hearts out in English. Michael arrived by air early in December to spend a week with us, sleeping on a camp bed in the living room as our little house had no spare bedroom. We gave a party for our friends to meet him, he joined us for Jill's birthday dinner, and at the weekend we went sailing at the Yacht Club with his friends. The Janikouns had us to lunch at the RAMC mess, we went to tea with Mrs Nissim, who had entertained all our family by now, and finally I took him to a Mess Dinner in *Terror* before he flew home.

Just before Christmas we visited the Naval Base with the boys to see Mary take part in her class's excellent production of *Cinderella*, the first of a series of pantomimes. We saw *Aladdin* at the British Military Hospital with the Janikouns, and *Puss in Boots* in town on New Years' Eve, so the children did at least as well as at home. On Christmas Day they opened an array of mechanical toys and other presents – it was the era of battery-operated toys mass-produced in the Far East – and then lunched in the Naval Base where, as the previous year, I had volunteered for duty. Sixteen of us, eight couples, saw the New Year in at the Tanglin fancy dress dance as the eight nations of SEATO – Jill and I as the Filipinos – and got to bed nearly four hours into 1959.

We knew that we were due to return home within the next few months, as the normal overseas shore posting was two and a half years, so we enjoyed these final months in Singapore to the full. We bought presents for all the family, and topped up our sets of Japanese Noritake china and glass which were *the* thing to possess. We had been using our cinecamera and projector for home movies to show our families on our return, and acquired the traditional camphorwood chest which, though battered, still holds our spare bedding nearly 40 years on.

Late in January I started handing over to an Australian

Commander who was to relieve me, and we flew up to Bangkok to meet our opposite numbers, in particular Lieutenant Colonel Drake-Wilkes, with whom I had enjoyed a very friendly relationship and with whom we stayed. We had a couple of days there, including a break for sightseeing and shopping, which provided some colourful Thai stoles as ideal gifts for ladies to wear with evening dress.

We held a farewell children's party to mark David's sixth birthday, with games in the garden and a big tea, and I gave the usual farewell drinks parties in *Terror* wardroom in the Naval Base, and at the headquarters in Phoenix Park. We packed our belongings into big crates provided by the Navy, which would go home by naval stores ship while we took our clothes and presents home with us in the troopship. We spent our remaining time visiting friends in a round of farewells, and handed back our house to the Navy. The Janikouns were away on holiday in Hong Kong and invited us to spend our last couple of days in their splendid Colonel's house on a ridge overlooking Pasir Panjang – roomy and cool after our bungalow. They returned on an indulgence passage in the troopship *Empire Fowey* and we embarked in her the same morning for our voyage home.

Friends came aboard for farewell drinks at lunchtime, just like a passenger liner, and we sailed in the late afternoon. We were at the Chief Engineer's table, and I had my nearest experience in the service of a pleasure cruise. There was an entertainments committee, a properly organised school for the many children, with staff carried to run it, and everyone was in good spirits looking forward to their return home. On the way we called first at Colombo, where there was time for a morning visit to the city and the opportunity to buy Jill a moonstone ring, which was one of this jewel city's specialities. There were fancy-dress dinners and dances and a children's party as we crossed the Indian Ocean bound for Aden, where again we had time to go ashore.

We had arranged to meet Abraham Marks, the English headmaster of the Jewish school there, who took us to a camp outside town to meet a group of Yemeni Jews on their way to Israel. Jews had lived an isolated life in Yemen since long before the coming of Mahomed, cut off from the rest of the world Jewry in a sort of biblical cocoon, but had flocked to Aden when they learnt of the new State of Israel to return there. These very distant relatives had never seen a western Jewish child, and wanted assurance that these light-skinned children were really Jewish! With my interpretership Hebrew I was able to reassure these Arab-looking co-religionists that indeed they were. They knew nothing of the modern world, even electricity was new to them, yet they were prepared to trust themselves to aircraft – the 'eagle's wings' of Isaiah – to carry them back to their ancestral land. It was a humbling experience.

We continued on up the Red Sea to Suez, and after a wait at anchor there joined our convoy up the Canal to the Great Bitter Lake to anchor off Ismailia while the southbound convoy passed, then on to Port Said. There was considerable excitement as our bows sheered off to strike the canal bank, but no harm was done to either and we soon reached the Mediterranean. Next stop was Limassol to pick up some of the garrison, then Gibraltar for the final shopping-run ashore, and back to winter clothes after our long sunny cruise. Mary and David were both conscientious workers and fairly bright, but we were slightly embarrassed when they were both awarded their class prizes at the end of the voyage. Finally we arrived off the Isle of Wight on Sunday morning 15th March, and berthed at Southampton that afternoon to be met by Jill's parents and welcomed home to England. It was a happy end to nearly two and a half years away.

# 15

## Portland

We knew that I was unlikely to go abroad for my next posting, but there was no point in recovering our house from its Admiralty letting until we knew if we could live in it, so we gratefully accepted the hospitality of Jill's parents in their large house in Oxshott for my leave. We soon discovered that my next post was to be Staff Officer Plans again, this time to the Flag Officer Sea Training at Portland in Dorset, so there was no prospect of living at Hinchley Wood on the outskirts of London. By the summer, when Jill was pregnant again, it did not seem worth hanging on to the house that would be uncomfortably cramped with four children and only three bedrooms, so we put it on the market. Despite being in good repair, we had to sell it for several hundred pounds less than it had cost more than seven years earlier, which was one reason why so many service families chose to rent in those days.

Our leave was the usual round of visits to friends and relatives whom we had not seen for two and a half years, and to the theatre and restaurants in London, greatly helped by our resident babysitters in the form of Jill's parents. They also had living with them Jill's grandfather Alfred King-Hamilton, now aged 87 and confined to the house after fracturing his hip when he slipped as he left a train. The prospect of seeing his eldest granddaughter again helped him keep going until we returned, but he died peacefully a few weeks later. He was the last surviving Founder Member of the Automobile Association, and had been created a Vice President after over 50 years on the Committee. He never learnt to drive, and had probably been brought in because they needed a solicitor.

During this leave I noticed how the Underground seemed to be manned chiefly by West Indians, whom we had rarely seen before we left. It was a sign of the coming decline in the country's economic fortunes – not the immigrants themselves but the unwillingness of the Underground and industry in general to modernise. Instead they actively advertised for and sought cheap foreign labour, rather than buying modern machinery and adopting less labour-intensive methods like our competitors. It took us decades to make up for this complacency of the Macmillan era. His famous 'You've never had it so good' and sweeping election victory were to come that autumn, though we in the Forces took little interest in party policies.

Jill and I went down to Dorset for a few days in April to search for a suitable naval hiring, and were fortunate to find Old Came Rectory just outside Dorchester, which its Army owner wanted to let while he was stationed elsewhere. The rent was £7 a week and the maximum the Navy would pay was £6, so we met the extra £1 ourselves and never regretted it. It was a late-eighteenth-century thatched house with five bedrooms, grounds all round and a walled garden at the rear, less than 1½ miles from the centre of the county town and just within the maximum permitted 15 miles of the Naval Base at Portland. It had been the home of the Reverend William Barnes – the Dorset poet and senior contemporary and friend of Thomas Hardy, who lived half a mile away at Max Gate – and we used to have earnest students turning up asking if they could see the house.

Down in Dorset we were back in pre-war England, a gentle slow-moving country life where the baker and the milkman called daily and orders were delivered from the Dorset County Stores. Dorchester was a compact county town of barely 12,000 people, less than half the size of the holiday resort of Weymouth some 8 miles to the south on its sandy bay. The long narrow Chesil Bank connected it with the Isle of Portland, where a massive naval harbour had been constructed by convict labour in the middle of the nineteenth century when we were concerned about the threat from the France of Napoleon III.

A Rear Admiral as Flag Officer Sea Training had been established there a few years previously with a staff covering all specialisations, to organise and supervise the working-up of most warships when they recommissioned – wherever they were then to be stationed – and to put them through a thorough examination at the end to pass them fit to join the Fleet. Rear Admiral William Crawford was my Flag Officer, a Dorset man happy to be back in his own county, with the delightful Captain George Pound, son of the wartime First Sea Lord, as his Chief Staff Officer and Captain of the Anti-Submarine Training Establishment HMS *Osprey*. It was a small and happy staff, busy on a worthwhile job.

We had bought ourselves a car while on leave, a largish second-hand white Vanguard – our first real estate car as opposed to the previous van type – and we stuck with estate cars for the next 20 years until the children all had their own cars and we no longer needed the carrying space. I also bought soon after our arrival a 1936 Austin for £50, in which I drove to and from Portland every day. It was a sturdy little 'banger' which even coped with my nodding off on the return home from a guest night in *Osprey*, when I came to in a field after running gently off a country road in pre-breathalyser days. I took care not to mention it to my wife, so as to avoid a well-deserved reprimand. Drugs were almost unheard of in those days, but alcohol and smoking were very much part of everyday life, and the health dangers of both, let alone drunken driving, were not taken seriously. Road deaths in 1996 at under 4,000, though still too high, were the lowest ever recorded, with some four times as many cars as in 1959. There was great excitement when the first motorway, the M1 between London and Birmingham, was opened at this time, and our Staff Engineer Officer, who was a classic car enthusiast, drove his vintage Rolls-Royce there and back to enjoy the experience. One of the joys of naval life was the characters one met, and this Commander Douglas-Morris had a wide range of interests, which was later to include the world's largest collection of naval medals, on which in retirement he became the leading authority.

I had a relatively straightforward job as Staff Officer Plans, dealing with the national and NATO planning for the Portland area, which was only a sub-command under the Commander-in-Chief at Plymouth, whose offices I had to visit regularly. Road traffic was fairly light except during the summer holiday season, and I used to enjoy my drives through the West Country villages and towns. It was during the period when the country was divided into Regions for civil defence, with underground headquarters where Regional Controllers and their staffs were supposed to survive the nuclear attack and then administer their devastated region or any of it that survived. It was an unrealistic scenario, but better than failing to make any preparations, and I was involved in a small way with such planning and exercises, as well as with naval reserves brought in for Naval Control of Shipping exercises for which we had a headquarters at Portland. I made one of my better but unintentional jokes, when briefing the Wrens on security precautions, I warned them of the risk of leaving confidential papers in their (desk) drawers. Their giggles at least proved that they were paying attention.

On the Sea Training side I actually did little planning, as that was the concern of Commander Sea Training, so I was given my own little section of Disaster Relief. The Royal Navy has traditionally rushed to the site of disasters, particularly in Commonwealth countries or where the authorities needed support. An aide-mémoire was prepared setting out the sort of assistance that could be given by the various departments of a ship, from emergency power supplies to hot meals, and during the final examinations at the end of each work up I would appear in a disreputable suit and beret as the mayor of some devastated town to appeal for various sorts of naval assistance. It was all good fun, and hopefully prepared ships for earthquake, flood and other disasters they might be called on to assist with during their commission.

As in Singapore, it was normally a day job from 8.30 a.m. until 5 p.m., unless one was involved in an exercise or was Duty Staff Officer and had to be available all night in *Osprey*. I had enjoyed two months' overseas leave on return from Singapore, joining on the day after the Whit Monday Bank Holiday, which fell that year in mid-May. We had then neither the May Bank Holiday at the start of the month, that Ted Heath gave us as a reward for joining Europe, nor the late May Spring Bank Holiday which replaced Whit Monday because it came too close to the new Euro-holiday.

I spent a month in *Osprey*, taking a bus up to London on Saturday afternoons after the morning's work, and bussing back again on Sunday night, until we moved into Old Came Rectory in the middle of June. Jill came down with me in our car on the Sunday, and we spent all our spare time preparing for the arrival of her parents with our children the following Saturday. That summer of 1959 was one of the finest I can recall, and the children seemed to be in their light Singapore clothes every day until they went to their new Dorchester school in the autumn. One fine day followed another, and they played together in the grounds or with Jill explored the countryside. Water was pumped up from a well, and we used it happily until the autumn, when it was discovered to be polluted by leakage from our cesspit drainage. Thereafter as we were not on mains water we had to obtain drinking water from friends in large plastic carboys, but apart from that inconvenience and the lack of a damp course, which made our visitors complain that their toothbrushes never dried, it was an idyllic home. We looked out across the gardens to the Dorset countryside, and felt ourselves part of a real community. At weekends we would drive to various bays along the coast from Studland to Charmouth to play on the beaches and swim. During the main holiday season we rarely used the popular resort of Weymouth, whose wide sandy beach was usually packed, but which could offer donkey rides and seaside entertainment that the smaller bays lacked. Our favourite was Ringstead, a small pebbly bay with only a few houses, where we could park easily and picnic sometimes even in winter, protected by a semicircle of low hills. Mary and David joined Mrs Pellow's Dorchester Preparatory School in September, and the brown and cream school bus would stop at the end of the drive to collect them each morning and to drop them back at the end of the day, to be joined in January by Jonathan as he neared age five. It was a good old-fashioned co-ed prep school which gave them a good grounding, good manners and a sense of responsibility. Strangely, in a school of well over 100, ours was the only Mary.

Naturally with spare bedrooms and a well-placed house for holidaymakers, we had a regular stream of visitors, especially at weekends. Both my parents and Jill's came regularly to enjoy their grandchildren, as did brothers and sisters, relatives and friends. After years away in Singapore, it was an opportunity to entertain them at leisure and revive old personal and service friendships.

Naval friends would pass through Portland in ships working up, and family friends call in on their way west or to stay overnight. Jill took all this in her stride during her pregnancy, but looking ahead to another child, we decided to rent a television and in October took delivery of our first black and white set.

I remember as a boy seeing a box in the house of one of my father's friends, which I was told was a television that showed programmes for a few hours in the evening, but we only saw it at rest during the day and neither my parents nor any other of their friends had the time for such a gimmick. There were just a few thousand of these rich men's toys when the service was suspended on the outbreak of war in 1939, and it did not really become widespread until the demand to see the Coronation live. It was actually used for party political broadcasts during the 1959 election, even though it reached a smaller number of the people than the radio, but in the next decade it really took off. We would probably have had a set earlier if we had not been away in Singapore, but the cost was still high as a proportion of income and they could frequently go wrong, so hiring a set with the rental company liable for any repairs was the most economic and popular way to obtain the service. We had two programmes, BBC or the four-year-old ITV alternative with its advertising breaks, and the children were allowed an hour's daily viewing if they had done their homework, while we watched the occasional serial or evening programme and news. It made an alternative to the radio on dark evenings, but we did not foresee it wiping out the plethora of cinemas in every town and village.

Among my outdoor activities was a regular bonfire of garden rubbish, and we kept a sack of newspaper on the back porch for kindling it. Jonathan, as an intelligent four-year-old, took a keen interest in bonfires, and one day in December found the matches and decided to help by setting fire to the sack. A heavily pregnant Jill discovered the blazing sack as it began to flare upwards, and soaked and exhausted herself dousing it with buckets of water to save the thatch. The fire brigade was called to damp it down, and in the middle of this the children returned from school and with perhaps praiseworthy sang-froid proceeded upstairs to their rooms to get on with their homework! I was down at Portland in the

211

middle of an Admiral's Inspection and by the time I got home all that remained was the smell of burning and one very worried small boy.

We were expecting the baby on David's seventh birthday, and arranged for Jill's parents to arrive on the previous Saturday, 16th January, so that she could have a few restful days first, but she met her mother at the door saying that she felt it was about to come. She retired to bed, the doctor and midwife were summoned, and Simon was born that evening. It had only recently become acceptable for fathers to be in at the birth, which we were both keen on, and the doctor agreed, so I was for the first time able to experience the thrill of seeing my child born. It was a most emotional feeling as the baby slithered out, and gave its first yell. The other children were delighted with their new brother, and almost fought over their turn to push him round the garden in the pram. He was none the worse for the previous month's firefighting, and with Jonathan going off to school Jill had the baby to herself all day except at the weekends.

We had a change of Admiral, with Rear Admiral Peter Gretton becoming the new Flag Officer Sea Training. He had been my house officer at Dartmouth before the war, and a war hero with the Distinguished Service Order and two bars for his exploits in convoy escorting and attacks on U-boats. He had one of the most alert and questioning minds I ever experienced, and went on to become a member of the Board of Admiralty. He would have been an outstanding First Sea Lord if his health had not broken down, and during his tenure I believe the Board of Admiralty had a majority of Roman Catholics for the first time since the Reformation. I was particularly impressed by his attendance at the Anglican Remembrance Day Service at Portland, at a time when Catholics were strongly discouraged from attending non-Catholic services. Happily such discrimination no longer applies. Gretton could not help but keep everyone on their toes, it was his nature, and a drive with him round the Base when Duty Officer soon led one to find out the answer for him on some matter that had never occurred to one before. He expected a hundred per cent efficiency standard, which is a rarely achieved target but stimulating to work towards, and he made an already efficient organisation quite outstanding.

Many of our NATO allies sent their ships to Portland to be worked up by the British, which was a tribute to the Royal Navy's prestige and the standards of the Sea Training team.

We had transferred some furniture to the Rectory soon after we arrived when we decided to sell our home in Hinchley Wood, so with that left by the owners we had sufficient to furnish all the bedrooms to cope with visitors. We spent over two and a half years there, and fell permanently in love with Dorset. We walked regularly on the ramparts of Maiden Castle, that huge earthwork strongpoint of the ancient Britons, visited all the lovely little towns from elegant Blandford Forum to precipitous Lyme Regis, and its famous houses from Elizabethan Athelhampton to Lawrence of Arabia's Clouds Hill cottage, and when we preferred to stay at home we could enjoy our rectory grounds. Partly we could enjoy it all so much because of the agricultural decline of the nineteenth century, which led to many Dorset towns recording a lower population at the 1961 census than a century earlier. The modern city of Bournemouth, which had drawn much of its growth from Dorset and is now part of it, was over the border in Hampshire. Our nearest synagogue in Bournemouth was more than 30 miles away, so the children's introduction to communal prayer had to be restricted – to prevent them associating God with car sickness! It was all very well to break our longer journeys round Dorset for stomachs to settle, but one did like to get to services on time and it did not matter if other journeys got the car sickness blame. Dr Snowman, the *mohel* who came down from London to do Simon's circumcision, said it was the first he had done in a rectory, though he had done Prince Charles at the Palace.

We usually went back to Oxshott during our three fortnightly leaves a year, to stay with Jill's parents and visit mine and our London friends, but in the summer of 1960 when Simon was six months old we took a week's holiday in Cornwall, where Jill had regularly gone camping as a child, and where we were able to look up some of her old friends and revisit several childhood beauty spots. The following summer during one of Jill's parents' visits, they asked to take David home with them for a few days. We had already planned with Jill's sisters a secret visit to Oxshott for their Fortieth Wedding Anniversary on 1st September, so set off about

213

5 a.m. on the single-lane roads that were then the 'A' roads, to burst in on them at breakfast and take them out for a day's picnicing by the Thames at Hampton Court. They were delighted, and particularly impressed that David had managed to say nothing about it in advance. School and the weather prevented us arranging a similar type of surprise for my parents' Fortieth Anniversary on 1st November, but fortunately they had gone away for the week to Bournemouth so we were able to join them there in the evening.

Among my various duties was Staff Security Officer, making sure that the Confidential Books were correctly handled and locked away, the staff offices locked at night and so on, which was no great headache with a Duty Staff Officer available to check on everything daily. Further south on the Isle of Portland, below its great hill of Portland stone from which the blocks for Saint Paul's were quarried, lay the Admiralty Research Establishments, which were no concern of ours. At this time there unfolded the Kroger spy case, the Russian couple posing as Americans who ran a spy ring stealing secret information from the Anti-Submarine Research Establishment. A corrupt former Master At Arms and his girlfriend had been smuggling out secret documents for money, not for ideological reasons like the Krogers, to whom they were sold. It gave Portland a sudden interest to the general public, and I joked that I had tightened up our security, but we were all very embarrassed that the Senior Service had been disgraced by their activities.

My time at Portland was coming to an end, as was my time in the promotion zone, where like musical chairs too many people were jostling for the limited number of Commander's hats available. I was thus 'passed over' and visited the Admiralty to see what attractive jobs were coming up, since one might be obtainable as some compensation for loss of promotion. The First Lieutenant of *Tamar*, the Naval Base in Hong Kong, was due to be relieved in the spring of 1962, and I expressed my interest in that post as strongly as I could, calling on the support of my newly promoted Vice Admiral Peter Gretton. To my delight I received that appointment, and my successor duly arrived at Portland. A leisurely turnover of duties took place in December, before we went off to spend Christmas leave with Jill's family in Oxshott.

We came back to start packing up for our journey and preparing for our move from our much loved Rectory, before sending our furniture to join the rest in store. We did not want to miss Mary's 11-plus exams, so the children returned to Dorchester Prep School for the first half of the term. We gave up our Rectory 'hiring' on 1st March, Mary took her exams successfully next day, and two days later we all flew out to Hong Kong.

# 16

## *Hong Kong*

Air trooping had vastly improved since my journey to Singapore more than five years earlier. We arrived at Hendon air centre on Sunday afternoon, from where we were bussed to Stansted to fly at 7.30 in a Britannia. We landed at Istanbul, then Bombay and reached Hong Kong at 7 a.m. on Tuesday local time in under 28 hours. Not surprisingly in such a situation, and with our reduced forces overseas, troopships were now being phased out, but with four young children it was still exhausting. We were carried off from Kai Tak airport by naval transport to the old pre-war Repulse Bay Hotel – a long, low building with only a few dozen rooms which looked as if it had strayed from the Riviera. There were a number of good hotels, but all were quite small as tourism was only just expanding. We watched with interest that year as the first two large hotels, the Mandarin and the Hilton, rose up behind the Naval Base. As each floor was added to the Hilton a number was hung on it until it reached 25, boasting 1,000 rooms. The skyscraper era was beginning.

The new Naval Base itself was just being completed on the seaward side of the recently closed naval dockyard, through which Harcourt Road had been cut to join Wanchai directly to the Central District without detouring round the old dockyard wall. The Royal Navy got there first in the 1840s, and the growing city had to spread round it. We had been allocated the sole flat in the new base – on the sixth, top, floor of the administrative A Block which housed the offices, wardroom and cabins for the unaccompanied officers.

First, however, we could enjoy life at our seaside hotel, as the flat was still being completed, and our first day was spent on the beach in the warm spring sunshine. My brother Michael, who was still based in Hong Kong, arrived to welcome us, and having him there throughout our stay opened up a wider circle to us and added to our enjoyment. Each morning I went into town by the hotel's regular bus service, and returned by it in the evening, but within a week had bought a Ford Consul so as to be fully mobile. There were as yet no parking meters in Hong Kong, though they began to appear within the year, and one could often find somewhere to park even to go shopping, but it was already difficult, and to have a parking place in the Naval Base right by the Star Ferry was one of the Navy's most popular perks. I took over from my predecessor by the end of the week and he left a couple of days later, so I was soon extremely busy working on the transfer arrangements for the move from the old dockyard barracks to the new Naval Base which was to take place the following month.

Hong Kong was in the charge of a Commodore, a title roughly equivalent to a Brigadier given to a senior Captain with special responsibilities. Under him was his Chief Staff Officer, a Commander, with whom I worked closely as in effect the third in command and roughly the equivalent of an Army adjutant. As my father would say, the general dogsbody who made sure everything worked.

The Commodore had his offices on the first floor once we moved in, overlooking the Bulls Nose at the entrance to the Naval Basin in which the smaller ships berthed and on the outer wall of which and also under our windows berthed the cruisers and medium-sized ships. All ceremonial took place on the Bulls Nose, the reception of visiting officers and the hoisting and lowering of the colours each day, often supervised by two-year-old Simon out of the Commodore's sight and five floors above his balcony.

I had my offices on the ground floor, well placed to dash out and deal with any emergency or to receive visiting ships. We acted as 'mother ship' to all visiting naval vessels, and I made sure that each one was visited on arrival with an aide-mémoire on how to obtain every kind of assistance and to try and deal with their problems. I was also in general charge of our ship's company, both the

RN ratings who were to live in B Block further along the jetty from the officers in A, and our Chinese Locally Entered Personnel, or LEP, who all lived ashore but also had C block near the Main Gate to accommodate those on duty. There were about 30 officers, 200 men and 300 LEP, some of them manning the Hong Kong based 8th Minesweeping Squadron.

After a fortnight we moved into our new flat, and for a month we had the whole Naval Base to ourselves at night until the great Transfer Day on 17th April. The power was on, so we could ride the lift up and down to the flat, and enjoy normal electricity and water supplies, but the others were still in the old barracks. The children were collected by bus to go to the Services Primary School in GHQ up the hill behind us, and brought back each afternoon, to be welcomed by Simon. We engaged an amah, Ah Hing, who had the use of a small amah's room in the flat. We had a double bedroom with en-suite bathroom, which was a new improvement in married quarters, two other bedrooms shared by the children, and a big living room with picture windows looking out across the harbour to Kowloon and a small window over the Bulls Nose. It was lovely in winter, but devilish hot in summer without air-conditioning and we were very glad to buy his second hand air-conditioners when Michael refurbished his office. It took months of negotiation before the Commodore was able to get authorisation for air-conditioning in the new blocks, as Admiralty thinking seemed to be that they had electric fans, which should be good enough. The combined heat and humidity in summer was worse than Singapore, and all modern offices and stores were automatically air-conditioned when built, but not the new Naval Base.

The move was a frenetic day, a hundred coolies and twenty 3-ton lorries driven by Gurkhas helping the ship's company to move everything across from the old to the new in one forenoon. Every department had sighted its new offices and stores in advance, and the transfer went remarkably smoothly. The ship's company delighted in their new messes and furniture, as did the officers with their new wardroom, and the drawbacks only appeared later.

We had a few weeks to settle in and find our feet before a hectic May. As the latest in service accommodation, we were looked over by all and sundry. The Fourth Sea Lord, one of the Admiralty Board, toured the base on a visit from England and the following day we held the first Hong Kong Navy Day for years. Thirty thousand of the public flocked in to walk round the base and visit the warships alongside, which ranged from the cruiser *Tiger* to the submarine *Ambush*. The day had to be carefully planned and controlled, as thousands were waiting when the gates opened, and these had to be closed at intervals before we reached saturation point with its risk of injuries to our visitors. As always, the Chinese were good-humoured, well-dressed and cooperative, queuing under umbrellas in the hot summer sunshine, and clearly enjoying their day out.

Two days later, when we had cleared up, the Commander-in-Chief appeared for his walk around the new base, and he was shortly followed by the Governor, Sir Robert Black – who had been Governor of Singapore when we lived there – to inspect our facilities. He returned that evening with two score of the Colony's leading citizens to attend the wardroom's first Mess Dinner. The following week the Flag Officer Second in Command of the Fleet had his turn at walking round, and later the same week we held our May Fair, a charity occasion with stalls, coconut shies and other fund-raising activities, open once again to the public. Towards the end of May there were also celebratory dances held separately by the chief and petty officers and the rest of the ship's company, to which all the officers and their wives were invited, so June was looked forward to with relief as a break after all these activities. All the official ones had to be meticulously planned, and I as First Lieutenant, working closely with the Commander, had to ensure that there were no slip-ups. Fortunately I got on extremely well with Tony Armitage, a sparkling and entertaining character. He and his wife Celia lived on Stonecutters island off Kowloon, and had four children in the same age bracket as our four, so we all soon became very friendly as the children often shared the same classes, Cub packs and other activities.

One unusual feature of the new base was salt-water flushing, which soon proved a boon. Due to well below average rainfall, water supplies in the Colony were restricted to four hours a day from mid-May. We were spared having to save used water for flushing, but bathplugs were removed and only showers used, to save water. The Colony was heavily dependent on Chinese reservoirs, which rationed supplies to meet their own irrigation needs.

Swimming was our great summer recreation. The new base had been provided with an excellent swimming pool for the officers and ship's company, which was of course shared with visiting ships and naval families, so the children had a reserved time daily and at weekends when they could enjoy it during family hours. There were also naval lidos on Stonecutters island with uncrowded sandy beaches, but our favourite Sunday outing was an early morning drive to Big Wave Bay on the south side of Hong Kong island, like a large sandy Cornish bay. It was almost deserted and relatively cool at 7 in the morning, and about 9.30 when it began to really hot up and become crowded, we left for a late breakfast at home and in the afternoon swam in the base pool two minutes' walk from our flat. Swimming was not then popular with the Chinese except among the more westernised, so the limited number of island beaches was enough to serve the mostly European and American bathers. As in Cornwall, limited parking was a problem, and if one went after mid-morning on Sundays it involved a long sweaty walk to and from one's car. Saturdays, of course, the services still worked in the morning, so it was rarely worth risking the afternoon crowds, and that was our shopping time.

Among our messmates in *Tamar* whom we had known in Singapore were Lieutenant Bill Newman, his wife Peggy and family, and Commander Donald Ross, the Base Supply Officer, and his wife Elizabeth, but we soon became friendly with almost all the officers. We took it in turns to make up groups for excursions to outer island beaches in *Tamar* boats at the weekends, and entertained one another regularly as well as meeting for family parties in the wardroom. Jill made it a point to welcome all new officers' wives, to explain the local organisation and help them settle in, and she and Mary Coker, wife of Tony Armitage's successor, also visited each new rating's wife to help her adjust to her surroundings. Life might be exotic, and an amah to do the hard work very welcome, but to those young women who had never been out of England before it was all rather alarming.

220

Naval Housing Officer was among my duties, operating a roster for the next to qualify for a naval married quarter. The officers' married quarters were in blocks of flats on Mount Austen up the Peak not far from the Peak Tram terminus, with wonderful views over the surrounding islands on a fine day, less hot and humid than down in the city but at times wrapped in depressing grey cloud. The ratings were having three blocks of married quarters built for them in Happy Valley near the racecourse, again very nice, but not nearly enough. Hirings were therefore permitted, to house families until they qualified for a quarter, but this took time to arrange and many families had to live in rather spartan conditions until a quarter became available.

We had heard of typhoons and had a list of typhoon precautions for the base, but no recent experience of one striking. July was the hottest ever recorded, and though unremarkable for some tropical areas an average daily maximum of over 90°F can become very exhausting when combined with a record humidity level which made any sort of brisk exercise most unpleasant. August was very similar, and it then became apparent that Typhoon Wanda with winds of up to 250 kilometres, or over 150 miles an hour, would hit Hong Kong on 1st September. The famous hurricane which hit south-east England in October 1987 reached 115 m.p.h., so the force of the wind can be imagined.

All ships had been ordered to sea the previous day as the typhoon approached, and all moveable items like chairs round the swimming pool had been locked away or lashed down, but we were not prepared for the force of the wind. Every window leaked, every carpet in the base was soaked, as were the curtains and any loose items. The rain beat against our windows facing the harbour, as if buckets of water were thrown at them, joined by the waters of the harbour itself whipped up and flung at the buildings. Surprisingly, the windows held, and the children, in bathing costumes, delightedly mopped up the incoming water with towels and squeezed it into buckets to pour away down the bath and basins. Luckily we kept our electricity supply, but no-one dared venture out of doors for hours while the storm raged. We could see the lamp standard arms in Harcourt Road twisted into strange shapes like semaphore arms, and rubbish, collapsed scaffolding

221

and shop signs blocking the streets. At a given warning, they were numbered from the first alert at No. 1 upwards, the Star ferries stopped running and in those pre-tunnel days Hong Kong and Kowloon were then completely separated. Junks and small boats crowded into the typhoon shelters on each side of the harbour, the trams and buses stopped running and cars took refuge in garages or wherever they could. Only the radio kept going to report the situation. Many ships were driven aground, boats wrecked and houses demolished, especially the lean-to shelters on the hillsides of recent immigrants from China seeking work, but deaths were fortunately few.

After the typhoon had passed, working parties were soon busy clearing the roads and the base. The swimming pool had to be drained to clear all the debris swept into it, and for years we used in our Christmas decorations the strands of plastic holly swept up from some damaged factory or warehouse. These and an assortment of abacuses and other junk were gleefully collected by our children as they went on a scavenging tour of the jetties. The smell of damp carpets hung out to dry permeated the base for days until they were removed for dry-cleaning and reshaping, and we added a new typhoon instruction that all carpets were to be rolled up and stowed away at Typhoon Warning No.3. To add insult to injury the water supply was cut from four to three hours a day, as the annual rainfall was still below average and the dry season approached. Additionally, typhoon damage set back completion of the ratings' new married quarters by at least a month, to the disappointment of families waiting to move in.

We had our first visitors from home when the *Cathay* entered harbour on the day after the typhoon, carrying our Royal Marine friend Peter Davis and his family on their way from the USA to his new posting with the RM Commando in Malaya. The year's only other visitors were my Uncle Douglas and Aunt Josie. He came out from the London office to relieve my brother Michael for a couple of months' home leave, so we were able to take them on several outings and show them something of the Navy during their stay.

In October there were alerts for the two Chinese National Days. The 1st was the Communist National Day with red flags paraded, and the Double Tenth, 10th October, the National Day of the Kuomintang, now ruling only Taiwan. There was always a risk of their supporters clashing, so leave was restricted to daylight hours and families advised to stay at home, but fortunately there was no serious disturbance during our years.

Autumn comes late in Hong Kong, and it was not until November that we first put on a pullover in the evening before the Guy Fawkes Night bonfire outside the officers' married quarters on the Peak. Clocks were put back an hour to winter time then, but we did not go into blue winter uniform until early December and were still able to swim on Boxing Day when we made a boat trip to the beaches of Lamma island with the Armitages on a lovely sunny day.

In November the Commodore in charge was relieved by Commodore George Symonds, a more relaxed character whose wife soon made herself very popular by her involvement and interest in the naval wives and families. That same month the Commander-in-Chief Sir David Luce was relieved by Vice Admiral Sir Desmond Dreyer, who naturally in his turn came up to inspect us in January and sent us a very appreciative message, of which I thought so much that I got Mr Wu, who ran my office, to reproduce it in Chinese characters in my First Lieutenant's Daily Orders. These ran to one or two A4 sheets daily, and listed every duty man from Duty Commanding Officer to Duty Senior Steward, the routine to be worked, dress of the day, leave details, sun rise and set, high and low water and the day's events plus any relevant announcements and orders. Most of our Chinese LEP could read and understand enough English to follow the routine, or at least get a friend to explain these orders and we took it for granted that verbal orders were understood. We were never let down, and were proud of them and their loyalty. My excellent Chief Petty Officer Greenwood had under him Chinese Petty Officer Kwok Tim in charge of our Chinese barrack seamen, an absolutely loyal and reliable deputy. He continued as a friend for over 20 years, exchanging cards each year and greeting us and the children when any of us returned to the city.

Chinese New Year fell towards the end of January, and was like a second Christmas with everything coming to a halt for the three-day festival. It is the highlight of the Chinese year, when all work stops and everyone celebrates, exchanges gifts and visits. Traditionally red for good fortune predominates in the decorations of the houses, and a red packet or *ang pow* is given with money inside as a New Year gift. We visited the most fascinating open-air New Year markets, with glorious displays of flowers, lucky flowering orange trees, and special New Year foods. We enjoyed them each year for their riot of colours and crowds of busy shoppers, and one of the few Chinese phrases we still remember is *Kung Hey Fat Choy* for Happy New Year.

On our own religious side there was the Ohel Leah synagogue, built at the turn of the century by one of the Sassoons, in Robinson Road, with the Jewish Club in one corner of its grounds. It amused me that this was open for those needing a stiff drink before or after the services, and I occasionally made use of it. The children were now of Sunday school age, and joined the cross-section of Jewish children from British, European, American and Asian backgrounds who made up the classes under suitably mixed teachers. In due course I found myself on the synagogue council, which would meet monthly at lunchtime over sandwiches in the offices of the community's president – Lawrence Kadoorie. His family had moved East from Baghdad in Victorian times and prospered. He became Sir Lawrence and eventually the first and only Hong Kong peer as Lord Kadoorie, who in his eighties addressed the House of Lords on Hong Kong affairs.

The children were starting to grow up, Mary was 11 at the end of September, and David 10 in January when Simon turned 3. The two elder boys were active in the Cubs, all had their sports activities and hobbies, and for a pet we had a beautiful Siamese cat that practically lived in the flat or on the verandah, as we rarely took her down in the lift to walk the stone jetties of the base. In winter there were all the English sports, and the swimming pool on their doorstep for most of the year, with weekend outings during the winter to walk and explore in the unspoilt country of much of the New Territories beyond Kowloon.

The next big event for us was Navy Open Day on Sunday 31st March, which I was responsible for organising. This year it was to be Commonwealth Navy Day, taking advantage of the visits of the

Australian aircraft carrier *Melbourne* and her escorting destroyers and the New Zealand cruiser *Royalist*, as well as the British cruiser *Lion*, frigates and minesweepers. It was an expansion of our first Navy Day the previous May, and this time we upped the throughput to 41,000 visitors in six and a half hours without a single casualty. Apart from touring the ships, there was a large static display of weapons and equipment set out in the base by groups from the ships, while a *Tamar* boat permanently cruised around to rescue anyone who fell in. It all took some organising and was quite a fraught occasion in case anything should go wrong. A few days later we changed into white uniforms for the summer, and reopened the swimming pool for the long summer season and the four-day Easter weekend holiday.

I by now was preparing for my next special duty, to lead the Queen's Birthday Parade in Kowloon at the head of the *Tamar* contingent, for which we carried out a number of rehearsals to ensure that the Royal Navy drill was up to standard for this ceremonial march past. We were all in full dress white uniform, wearing our medals and officers with drawn swords, as we marched past the Saluting Base in Gascoigne Road, where the Governor in ceremonial dress wearing his feathered helmet stood on a covered dais to take the salute. It was glaringly obvious to us old Hong Kong hands watching the rain-soaked Governor and Prince of Wales at the Farewell Parade in 1997 that omitting the covered dais for VIPs had risked ruining the ceremony. Wives and families sat each side of the dais to observe the parade, which was a colourful sight that we had already watched the previous year, with infantry, Gurkhas, Hong Kong Regiment and RAF marching past, followed by armoured cars and an air force fly-past. Ceremonies ended with a Royal Salute fired at noon by warships and the Royal Artillery, by which time we had dispersed to shed our sweat-soaked uniforms.

The following week was May Day, the other potential riot day in addition to the National Days in October. Leave was restricted but there was no trouble, and we then relaxed for the summer. Unfortunately it proved the hottest and driest May on record, relieved by a mere ¼ inch of rain to bring the year's total to only 1½ inches against an average of 22½. Not surprisingly water rationing grew more and more severe, supplies being cut to only three hours a day at the end of April, and to four hours on alternate days from mid-May. Standpipes were set up in the streets throughout Hong Kong and Kowloon, and water supply cut to four hours every fourth day. People queued patiently in long lines with their topless petrol cans on yokes over their shoulders or with plastic containers, waiting to fill them when the water was on. Houses and blocks with cisterns were better off, as these could be filled and showers taken during the ration period, but the poorest who relied on taps had to store anything they could fill. Despite the hardships people somehow managed to look as smart as ever, and there were almost no reports of fights at the standpipes.

Our salt-water flushing in the base really proved its value. In all the married quarters, and in town, washing water had to be saved to flush the toilets, so we had a regular stream of shopping wives and families visiting the base to spend a penny. Everyone got used to the restrictions; we used to sit three-year-old Simon in the basin for an economy 'bath' when necessary, and the older children complained 'bath night *again*' when the fourth day came round with water available. True, the salt-water swimming pool was available daily, but salt water dries stickily so we tried to keep enough fresh water for a sponge-down. Everyone filled their bath with water before supplies were cut off, so as to have a reserve to ladle out during the next four days. A vast new reservoir at Shek Pik had been completed on Lantao island, designed to increase the Colony's capacity by almost half, but it lay almost empty, unable to help out, and the Canton area was equally dry. Gradually the rains came, but even by the year's end averaged only 40% of normal and the harsh rationing had to continue into 1964 in case of a further dry year.

Summer passed uneventfully, as hot and humid as usual, and at the end of September Jill's parents and her younger sister Anne arrived by air to stay with us. By squeezing four young children into one large bedroom we fitted them all in, and enjoyed showing them the city and the beaches. The three elder children were by now aquaplaning skilfully on a ski board towed behind the *Tamar* pleasure boats, and David and Jonathan excelled at double acts and crawling through each other's legs. Their grandparents were suitably impressed. They spent six weeks with us, during which we all went over by ferry to the Portuguese colony of Macao on the other side of the Pearl River estuary. It was settled in the middle of the sixteenth century and could boast many picturesque old buildings and an attractive promenade along the seafront. We stayed in the friendly Hotel Bella Vista, which lived up to its name, with a balcony overlooking a sea speckled with sailing junks. At that time Macao was a quiet backwater, whose main industries were making fireworks and mosquito coils, backed up, and soon to be overtaken, by gambling saloons.

Thanks to Michael we shared a large number of his friends, in particular the Laufers, who often invited us to their house Tolo Ridge in the New Territories beyond the town of Sha Tin, where we were welcomed to the use of their pool and to enjoy their Siamese cats and kittens. They were a popular calling place on our excursions, and they also made Jill's family very welcome. They found a job for Anne as a music teacher at the King George V High School, where Beryl worked, so Anne stayed on with us when her parents sailed home in early November on the *Chusan*. It had been a wonderful opportunity for us to return some of the hospitality we had received from them over the years of our marriage, and as my father-in-law loved the Navy he had spent many happy hours on our balcony watching the ships and their routines. I was even able to bring him to our Trafalgar Night Dinner, the highlight of the naval year, which was attended as usual by the Governor, the Commander British Forces and the rest of the top brass.

They were asked to go out one morning during the visit of the First Lord of the Admiralty Lord Carrington – many years later to be Chairman of Christies when David became its Financial Director. The personnel officer who arranged his interview was Colin Forbes, at this moment the young Flag Lieutenant to Commodore Hong Kong. Jill was asked to offer morning coffee and a view from our balcony to Lady Carrington and the Commodore's and the Commander's wives while their husbands toured the base, and enjoyed her ladies' morning.

On 17th October the maximum temperature dropped below 80° for the first time since April and we began to think about our winter parties and activities. We had a beautiful large model of the

*Victory,* which was brought out and set up by the Main Gate, floodlit at night, for all special occasions like Navy Days, Trafalgar Night and Christmas. There was the Children's Party for the Chinese staff and their families at around Chinese New Year, charity fêtes organised by the naval wives with the support of the Commodore's wife and all sorts of other activities to help the local population. Apart from her work with the naval wives, Jill helped in a local clinic weighing and monitoring Chinese children, whom their mothers brought in tied to their backs like Red Indian papooses, as well as in the Soldiers', Sailors' and Airmen's Families Association, SSAFA, clinic and taking the library trolley round weekly at the British Military Hospital.

Although rather remote from the main world events, we did keep up with them. I can certainly remember where we were when we heard of President Kennedy's death. We were asleep on Sunday morning when David, who got up early to read the papers, burst in on us with the glaring banner headlines. Special memorial services were held throughout Hong Kong, even in the synagogue.

Autumn and winter are always the best seasons in Hong Kong, with low humidity, little rain and English spring and summer temperatures, when we enjoyed walking in the New Territories or taking our turn for boat trips to the outer islands at weekends to go climbing or even have a swim on a hot day. This being our second winter, we knew what to expect, having enjoyed ourselves the previous year while Britain endured one if its bitterest winters since the war.

Christmas Day was unusual as it included the funeral of Mr Chan Tuck, the naval tailor. He was a much respected tradesman for his reliability and honesty, and many of us, including the Commodore, chose to attend. Like most Chinese he had a very tough time during the Japanese Occupation, and told me that his chief concern was to ensure that all his children had a good education since it was the one thing that nobody could steal from them. I entirely agreed. On a lighter note we saw the New Year in again at a dinner dance in the wardroom with our wives. For the only time in my life I did not have to worry about what I drank at a mess dinner, as I was unlikely to be too drunk to press the lift button for the top floor.

As 1964 was certain to be my last full year in Hong Kong, where I was having a wonderful time as well as doing a satisfying job, I now had to think about my future. I would be 40 in April, and could serve on another ten years until I was 50 for a reasonable pension. I could not expect any other post as interesting as *Tamar*, and did not fancy a succession of unstimulating appointments while I served out my time, since I was unlikely to find a good job easily at 50 with no non-naval experience. There was a smaller pension payable if I left early, arbitrarily cut by a further 7½% for doing so, and I decided to retire in 1966 as soon as the two yearly pay and pension review due then had taken effect. I sent off a letter to that effect in the spring through the Commodore, and duly had it noted by Their Lordships.

I had taken the opportunity to discuss my proposed retirement with my father, to ensure a longstop opening in the family company if nothing better offered. My parents had arrived by sea in the *Cathay* in February to visit their two sons and grandchildren, but combined pleasure with business as my 78-year-old father was still the very active managing director of the family company. He wanted to see how the Far East end of the business was operating, as it was doing more than all the other markets combined now that India and so many other former large markets were raising tariffs to protect their own industries and shut out British goods. He had known many of the leading Hong Kong customers as young men assisting their fathers before the war, and we were swept into a round of Chinese dinners in his honour. We were able to entertain them in the flat, and take them out for drives, but both my parents knew Hong Kong well and were more interested in their grandchildren than any sights we could offer. The Kadoories showed them their model farms set up to help the Chinese farmers – they said they knew everything about pigs except their taste, and had also introduced healthier new strains of pig to the Colony – and some of their industrial activities from China Light, the Hong Kong electricity company, to their carpet factories.

In March my mother's sister and brother-in-law, Lizzie and Sidney Capper, came up from Melbourne for a family reunion, and we took them all out for weekend cruises in the *Tamar* boats and for drives into the New Territories. We also visited their old friend Ada Lum, whom we had of course met earlier through Michael. She had established her own brand of Chinese dolls in traditional costume, as well as a high-class jewellery store in the luxurious new Mandarin Hotel, where my parents were staying, and was a beautiful and dynamic Australian-born Chinese. Her jewellery was well out of our price range, but she was a character worth knowing, always dressed in the finest cheongsams and jewellery. Cheongsams are a Chinese equivalent of the saree, elegant costumes for ladies, featuring high necks and skirts slit up one side, which are becoming rarer as Western dress becomes ever more common. My parents left with the Cappers to go on to Australia, arriving in time for my cousin Anne to produce her second daughter, named Fenella Louise in honour of her great-aunt Louisa.

We had a very jolly party in our flat on my fortieth birthday, proudly displaying a beautiful hand-woven carpet which we had recently bought for our intended English home at the annual sale of cancelled special orders and other special offers which was held each winter. We had also added a couple more camphorwood chests to the one we had brought home from Singapore, not to mention various ornaments, carvings and snuff bottles and other items which I bought on evening visits to the antique shops of Cat Street. Among other things which fascinated me were cash, the copper coins with a hole through the middle which had been currency for some 2,000 years in the same shape and weight. They used to be assembled on strings or wire 100 to the dollar and not separated for decades or centuries, so that one could find coins issued by the Tang Emperors well over a thousand years earlier selling for a few pence, and I gathered as full a range as possible. Snuff bottles were a more artistic item, developed in ivory, wood, glass and porcelain, and beautifully carved or painted after snuff became the rage following a gift of it by Louis XIV to the then Chin Emperor.

Confrontation with Indonesia over the amalgamation of our Borneo colonies with Malaya into the enlarged state of Malaysia had reduced fleet visits to Hong Kong except for short periods of rest and recreation. For the same reason the stepped-up American involvement in Viet Nam increased the number of American visits so that the bars of Wanchai did not suffer any downturn. One visit out of the ordinary was that of an elderly Portuguese sloop from Macao that called on her way down to Portuguese Timor, where she was supposed to resist the entire Indonesian Navy if the dispute there came to a head. Fortunately it did not, but their nonchalant gallantry in facing the likelihood of certain death, in the same way as the outgunned old Portuguese ships took on the Indian Navy in the defence of Goa, deeply impressed me.

In July we went on a local leave holiday to Japan with the four children, quite an adventure at that time before tourism there had been developed. We travelled by the French liner *Laos*, which offered cheap rates to fill up the ship on the last leg of her journey from France to Japan. There was a film every afternoon, which the children enjoyed, and dancing on deck in the evening, and we lazed around until we reached Kobe after three days. We were taken out by our company's agent Mr Ohtaki, whom we had entertained when he came down to meet my father in Hong Kong in March, to view the city from the mountain behind it and to descend by cable car. Next morning we took the train to nearby Kyoto and joined a Japanese tour of the city. We did not understand a word but certainly saw the finest temples of the unspoilt old capital. The Japanese in their polite way took these strange foreigners in their stride with smiles and bows, and we duly returned to the ship by train in time for supper.

The following day, even more adventurously we set off by train across central Japan to Atami, to spend the night in a Japanese hotel called the New Fujiya, where we slept on tatami mats laid on the floor. This was as nothing to the children compared to finding the unknown luxury of a television set in their room, on which we all watched with interest the trial run of the fast new 'bullet' train. Even more interesting was the sensible Japanese hotel custom of providing guests with loan kimonos with the hotel name on the back, both for advertising and so that any who passed out after drinking too much sake could be returned to the correct hotel!

In the morning we took the train on to Tokyo. There was then little Western lettering in Japan but all the stations had their name in English and Japanese, so providing we caught the right train we knew when to get off. We had planned our itinerary carefully in advance, and rather than stay with the ship we intended to rejoin her at Yokohama, the port of Tokyo, for our voyage back. For meals, with our lack of Japanese, we relied mostly on the very realistic and highly coloured reproductions of meals displayed in café windows on plates with a price in yen shown on them, so we could choose egg, tomato and chips or whatever looked attractive and suitable. It was extremely hot, and we stopped regularly in the towns to feed a coin into drink machines which then discharged the selected fruit juice into a plastic cup. In Tokyo we saw the walls of the Emperor's Palace compound lying behind its moat, and went on to visit the Asakusa Kanon temple and shopping area. We watched the worshippers waft incense smoke from the great braziers in their direction and sip the purification waters, and loved the little terrapins for sale in bowls of water. We then returned to the ship for supper and a quiet night. Looking back on it, I am amazed at our astonishing self-confidence in a country where we could neither read nor speak a word.

We went by train again next morning to the seaside resort of Kamakura, to see the enormous seated Buddha some 40 feet high and cast in bronze in 1292. From there we went to the seashore, to share the wide beach with thousands of Japanese. Many had never seen a European child before, and Simon had a splendid time surrounded by admiring Japanese girls. We returned by train to Yokohama in the afternoon and explored the streets, being treated to an anti-war demonstration with banners, before returning to the ship to sail back to Hong Kong. It had been a fascinating experience of Japan before the age of tourism, and good material for several future dinner parties.

The rest of the summer holidays for the children passed with the usual weekend outings to swim at Shek O and Big Wave Bay, boat trips to the outer islands, aquaplaning and swimming, and visits to the New Territories to look over the border river near Lowu into the closed land of China with its similar green paddy fields and hills. David had by now passed his 11-plus and went on to join Mary at St George's School in Kowloon, a services comprehensive of high standard which they both enjoyed. Jonathan was rising steadily up the services primary school near us at the bottom of the Peak Tram by GHQ. The Peak Tram, with its stations all the way from literally downtown to the Peak terminus at 1,300 feet was a much used travel route and tourist draw. We used it occasionally as a more exciting alternative to the car when we wanted a healthy walk round the Peak, or part of it, with stops to admire the magnificent views over the harbour and Kowloon into China, or out to sea across the outer islands in all other directions.

Fortunately weatherwise 1964 did not repeat the rainfall shortages of the previous two years, the water rationing was gradually eased, helped by a number of typhoons, and was finally abolished when the big new Shek Pik reservoir overflowed. Typhoon Viola in May deposited nearly 10 inches of rain in a day, causing landslides but not much damage otherwise, and Ruby in September pushed Shek Pik over the top. We had just seen the Olympic Flame arrive on its way to Tokyo for the Games, and be set burning overnight outside the City Hall. I am not sure if a spare flame was sheltered inside the hall, but it is hard to believe that the typhoon did not extinguish the one in the open which we saw blowing in all directions as the wind built up. Certainly several ships were driven aground by it.

As part of my job-seeking I had taken up an advertisement for recruits into the Civil Service at Executive level from the Forces and Colonial Service. I sat written exams during the summer, and was flattered to find myself among those selected for interview in London. I was given leave and flown by Caledonian early in November to Gatwick for two full days of interviews and examinations at the Civil Service Commission in London. My group included more senior officers than myself in the other services and the Attorney General of Bermuda, so it is perhaps not surprising that I was not successful. I eventually found myself spending more than a fortnight in London after this, before I was flown back again from Gatwick. This time I caught a jinxed plane, which had to land in Athens for repairs, long enough for a day and a half of sightseeing, and I finally arrived in Hong Kong after over three weeks away. Fortunately for part of the time Jill had the company of her brother Maurice, who had arrived on leave from his post in the Tanganyika education service while I was observing the early weeks in office of Harold Wilson's new Labour government.

I was back in good time for the Christmas season, whose planning as usual began weeks ahead to prepare for the Ship's Company Dance, the Children's Party and the Wardroom New Year's Eve Dance. Thousands of miles from home and relatives, families developed close friendships as they shared similar experiences and we still keep contact with a number of the friends we made more than 30 years ago. One shadow hung over the season, our bereaved Commodore. Mrs Symonds had died three months previously, a shock to those of us who did not know of her struggle with cancer, and it was impossible to comfort a bereaved senior officer.

On our personal side we had acquired a television set from an officer returning home. Hong Kong operated cable television decades ahead of this country, because with its mountainous terrain reception would otherwise have been very patchy, and as there was no set in the officers' block a special cable had to be laid to connect us. It certainly proved an attraction when Sir Winston Churchill died in January, and our flat was packed with wardroom officers to see his funeral. Our generation venerated him as the greatest Englishman of the century, and memorial services were held in the cathedrals, the synagogue and throughout the Colony to mark his passing.

In February after the Chinese New Year came the party for the children of the Chinese sailors and base staff. As for all children's Parties, the '*Tamar Belle*', a lorry disguised as an engine, towed carriages of delighted children around the base, bands played, conjurors and jugglers performed and there was plenty to eat. Added colour for the Chinese party came with stilt walkers and a dragon dance.

Chinese culture of course dominated Hong Kong, which was 99% Chinese. We were swept up in it throughout our stay. Apart from all the glamour and celebration of Chinese New Year there were many other colourful festivals and occasions. We had been out to Chung Chau for the Bun Festival with its tall poles stuck with buns like huge kebabs, and watched the exotic Dragon Boat Festival in summer when the multi-oared dragon boats with drums throbbing paddled at breakneck speed down the course, six abreast until the fastest surged ahead. We had been guests at Chinese weddings, where the bride and groom in gorgeous tra-

234

ditional robes posed in the restaurant before an impressive display of brandy bottles waiting to be drunk, and where the clack of mah-jong tiles only ceased momentarily for the actual service. Chinese love to eat and drink and entertain, and we enjoyed dozens of wonderful Chinese meals in highly coloured restaurants, for the Chinese love bright colours and mix them in startling but effective ways. It is said that the Chinese are everyone's favourite foreigner because of their good nature, and the Jews of the Far East because of their industriousness. We certainly enjoyed living with them, and regretted our coming departure.

One of the advantages of our position was that we could be in our seats in the City Hall theatre within five minutes' walk of our flat, and we saw many of the top talents from Gracie Fields to Joyce Grenfell during our stay. The theatre had been launched early in our time by Sir Malcolm Sargent and the London Symphony Orchestra on their way to Japan, and we had the benefit of leading world orchestras performing as part of their Far Eastern tours. We were fortunate also to have two excellent amateur dramatic societies, the Stage Club and the Garrison Players. Michael was a regular performer in both, so we got to know quite a few of the players, whom we also met at the Yacht Club. We saw and enjoyed almost all of their performances, both plays and musicals. Other companies also came out from England, the quatercentenary of Shakespeare's birth bringing us a dramatic company to present *The Tempest*, and that winter the newly famous Beatles on their first Far East tour gave a concert, which we vetoed the children spending all their savings to attend. We proved justified, as there was such an uproar in the hall that we heard them far better on the radio.

We worked hard at interesting jobs but also played hard. Every Sunday evening there was a buffet supper and film show in the wardroom for officers and their wives and guests, welcoming cocktail parties there for visiting ships as well as return parties aboard, and dinner parties often twice a week in our flat or return hospitality in other naval quarters. Dinners in the many excellent European and Chinese restaurants in town and weekend boat trips and excursions filled our lives, yet there was always time for quiet periods with the children.

It may sound like a constant swirl of entertainment but it did not seem so at the time, and we were very fortunate with our amah Ah Hing, with whom we could always leave the children with perfect confidence. We had the added pleasure of having my brother Michael there, to spend quiet evenings in his flat served by his efficient servant Ah Chim, and parties with him and his friends at the Yacht Club or the Eagles Nest at the top of the Hilton looking down on the city. Finally there were the old China hands whom my father had known in Hong Kong and Shanghai before the war, such as Betty Church running her advertising agency, who made the younger generation welcome for his sake.

We really had enjoyed our time, but the thought of a fourth long hot enervating summer made us glad to prepare for our return home. There was a constant change among the officers and ship's company, who had all arrived at different times, unlike in a ship commissioned as one group, so we were by now almost the oldest inhabitants, having waved off most of our friends going home. My relief had been appointed, and we began to prepare for our April departure. Fortunately this meant the children could complete their spring school term, five-year-old Simon spending his first term at Victoria Junior School, where Jonathan was nearing the top, and we could enjoy a further fine winter.

Our last major official visit was in February, by Admiral of the Fleet Earl Mountbatten of Burma, on one of his farewell tours as Chief of the Defence Staff. He was still a handsome man, though quite elderly compared to when I had last seen him 20 years before in Trincomalee. I was amused to see him in civilian clothes wearing a suit in the same check pattern and shade that I too had made up by Chan Tuck, the naval tailors. Their clientele was very wide, as one of our Chinese leading seamen appeared in a twin of the heavy Harris tweed sports jacket that I had just bought to take back to England.

As if in advance celebration of our departure, the Hong Kong and Shanghai Bank laid on a stupendous firework display one evening in March to mark its centenary. Niagaras of light poured down into the harbour and cloudbursts of stars rose over it. The large banks and public buildings were always illuminated and framed with necklaces of lights for public holidays, Christmas and

New Year, and the Bank of China with red lanterns and hangings for National Day, so we seldom wanted for colour. Ten days later Commodore Symonds was given an affectionate send-off, towed out of the naval base in a rickshaw by his officers, while we began to fill our packing cases to ship home our possessions when we flew back with a few suitcases of clothes.

Mr Lawrence Kadoorie, knowing that I was retiring from the Navy, was kind enough to offer me a position in one of his companies. If I had been a single man it might have been a very tempting offer, but it would have meant near permanent separation from our family and friends at home, school for our children in England and indeed separation from my wife, as Jill was not prepared to live permanently in Hong Kong even if I was, so we declined with thanks. Hong Kong remains a happy memory, but I never regretted that decision.

*Tamar* was a unique home for us. As the only family living in the Naval Base, its people became our friends and neighbours in a quite different way to all the other naval personnel who worked there. Mary Gash, who lucratively controlled and disposed of all naval rubbish and surplus items, Jenny Side Party whose 'girls' washed and cleaned and painted the sides of the ships in harbour, Chung Kee the watchmaker and his family, the barber and all the Chinese labourers and sailors were part of the children's naval village, whom they saw every day. As First Lieutenant I felt like the squire of the village looking down from my balcony to see that all was under control within its walls, and walking round both in working hours and outside them to check on the swimming pool or the boats in the basin or the ships alongside.

We had acquired a small skiff, which the children loved to row round the enclosed basin and which we towed behind the picnic boat at weekends. This was disposed of, the TV set was donated to the wardroom, and I received the inscribed tankard presented to all departing mess members. Jill produced her twenty-eight-consecutive monthly *Newsletter for Naval Wives*, we gave our farewell cocktail party and went to various farewell dinners, and on Tuesday afternoon 6th April we left in a *Tamar* boat for Kai Tak with the traditional explosion of firecrackers and farewell waves of our friends.

# 17

## *Civvy Street*

We arrived at Gatwick the following afternoon thanks to the eight hours' time difference, to stay for the last time with Jill's ever-willing parents.

Much of my leave was devoted to looking for a permanent home. I intended to work in London, and with Jill's parents living in Oxshott we looked inwards from there as far as the river at Kew and Richmond, which were my initial choices. We briefly looked at Wimbledon, but when an agent kindly told us that the type of five-bedroom house we wanted could not be found there for under £20,000 we turned to less expensive areas. We had the proceeds of our Hinchley Wood house sale, but I also had a windfall. My father had given us his shares in the Hong Kong company, two-thirds to Michael, who built it up, and a third to me. I had no idea what they were worth, and was delighted when Michael paid some hefty dividends, which came tax-free while I was resident abroad, but we needed to buy without a mortgage since I could not take that on as well as my other outgoings.

We found what we wanted in Surbiton, the last stop on slow trains from Portsmouth that reached Waterloo from there in 16 minutes. Unfortunately the house turned out to be under offer so we continued our search, but saw it a couple of weeks later in another agent's window. We went in and said we were looking for a house like that, and when he asked what was wrong with that one we said it was under offer. It turned out that the potential buyer had withdrawn, so we slapped down our 10% deposit subject to survey, and eventually it became ours that summer. We were able to persuade my father-in-law that after 15 years I was unlikely to abandon my wife and family, and he agreed to transfer her 'dowry' money from the trustees to Jill so that we could buy our own house directly.

While all this was going on we had taken David down to Rendcomb College near Cirencenster in Gloucestershire, to which we had been recommended when we lived in Dorset. It had been founded and endowed by the Wills tobacco family as a memorial to those lost in the First World War, and was the smallest public school in the country, with under 150 boys. The setting in the Cotswolds was beautiful, and we liked the headmaster. David settled there happily, and Jonathan joined him in the September. We looked at two schools for Mary, and gave her the choice. She chose Surbiton High and soon settled down there, though she did complain that all the girls had been on holiday to such exotic places as Spain and Italy. The fact that her last summer holiday had been in Japan apparently cut no ice.

We took delivery of our new Cortina car on arrival in England, so were immediately mobile for our house-hunting and school visits, and for our preparations for my return to Civvy Street – the services word for all life and work outside the forces.

I had spent a day or two in the Tyler Brothers office when I was in England the previous November, and a week in it during my leave, to see something of how it operated and whether I wished to work there. My uncle Douglas at 70 had decided to retire at the end of the year, and my father, who would be 80 the following month, was obviously not going on for ever but would show me the ropes. Mr Copplestone, the Company Secretary, whom I had known all my life and admired, would be around for a few years yet, and their salesman Cyril Jenn we had met and liked when he visited Hong Kong. Their second-floor offices at 91 Regent Street were conveniently placed in the West End near Piccadilly Circus and less than a hour from our Surbiton house by a three-quarter mile walk, train, Underground and short walk. I could have looked further for a job, but the family business seemed secure and interesting and I would in due course be my own boss, so I decided to join.

That settled, we could concentrate on our new home at

239

Ashcombe Avenue in Surbiton. It was part of the Southborough estate, carved out of the grounds of Southborough House, a Nash-designed house whose grounds originally ran down almost to the Thames a mile away, and which still stands in our road as a large private house. Its coach house and outbuildings had been converted into three adjacent houses, and most of the other houses in the road were erected between the wars. None were allowed to cost less than £1,000, which did not make them all that large or expensive, but ours had been well-designed by an architect for himself and had the required five bedrooms so that there would be three for the four children as they grew up plus a guest room. The house stood on a half-acre plot with a 200-foot-long back garden with fine old oak trees and yews at the far end that had been part of the drive to the big house. There was a large lawn for the children to play on, and a patio which faced south-west and received plenty of sun. For us it was ideal and cost just over £14,000. It seemed an enormous sum at the time, but we were investing all we could for the family's future. Since Jill's parents were prepared to put up with us a bit longer, we had it completely rewired, as the original wiring was nearly 40 years old, and fitted with radiators throughout and a new boiler in place of the previous partial central heating system. Redecorating was kept to a minimum, and achieved over the next few years when money permitted.

Jill and I moved in by ourselves on 13th August, our engagement anniversary. It was a Saturday night, and we hardly slept for aircraft roaring overhead. We thought we had made a terrible mistake and bought a house under the Heathrow flight path, but discovered to our relief that it was only at weekends at the height of the holiday season that planes came over, perhaps half a dozen times a year, and it has proved a delightfully quiet house. Other gardens cross at the end of ours, so that even in the suburbs we have hundreds of feet of greenery behind us.

I had been appointed to join *Bellerophon*, the Reserve Fleet at Portsmouth, in mid-June after my leave to see out my time. This considerably placed me near my home so that I could join the family each weekend, but it was never worth coming home overnight except for something special. I was pleased to discover that they worked a five-day week, so that I could go home on

Friday evening and return early Monday morning. The work was dull but not arduous, maintaining ships in reserve as I had done over ten years earlier, but one could see how it could cause alcoholism among those not locally based, as it was all too easy to get sozzled on cheap booze in the evenings when there was little else to do but watch television or make one's own amusements.

I had applied before we left Hong Kong to attend one of the Queen's garden parties that summer, reckoning that there was less chance once I retired, and we duly received our invitation. I naturally attended in uniform, with Jill in one of her finest Hong Kong-made ensembles, and we strolled the lawns trying to recognise the celebrities. One of them was Jill's uncle Alan King-Hamilton, by now a judge at the Old Bailey, and we went on with him and his wife for a meal and to see the film of the popular musical *The Sound of Music*. Jill had been down to Portsmouth the previous week for the Summer Dance, when we took the opportunity to look up some of our former Hong Kong friends now stationed in the area.

During our leave we had of course seen plenty of the family, including Jill's brother Brian and sister Ines and their young families, so that the children could get to know their cousins again after a three-year absence, and we saw more of them during the school summer holidays as we were not going away that year while preparing to move into the house. Instead at the end of August we acquired a puppy, Ruffles, who was our much loved dog for the next 17 years. We called him a Surrey Terrier because he was so handsome, white with brown markings and a cross between a spaniel and a terrier. He was my idea of a perfect dog as he exercised himself, racing at full speed after squirrels and cats trespassing in his garden, though despite his enthusiasm he never caught one, and so sure of his territory that when we had the garden fences renewed he never strayed into the garden on either side even when the fences were down. He was affectionate and the pet and friend of all the family.

We had been down to Rendcomb for David's exeats during the summer term, and found that he had rapidly settled down and was enjoying his new school, so we were not too worried when we took Jonathan back with him in September as the two would be company for each other, quite apart from the friends they made. Simon had been at the local primary school in Oxshott for the summer term, but there was no good one nearby at the time in Surbiton, so in the autumn he went to the private Woodlands school in the area, where he stayed until it was his turn too to go to Rendcomb. All the boys passed their 11-plus, but initially we felt that Rendcomb would give them a better education than the local government schools. We were probably wrong, as they might have done as well locally and we would have seen more of them. None of our grandchildren have been to boarding school, but Rendcomb was a splendid school and they all enjoyed it.

I spent the rest of the year at Portsmouth, living during the week in a cabin in the old cruiser *Sheffield* which with the depot ship *Rame Head* formed the living quarters and administrative base of *Bellerophon*. We regularly inspected the ships laid up in Fareham Creek to check on the standards of maintenance, so that they could be manned or prepared for sale to foreign countries at short notice. One dull winter's day I stepped off the ladder into the boat collecting me from one such ship and found myself up to my neck in the cold waters of Portsmouth harbour. I had somehow missed my footing, and trod water wishing I could have seen myself drop in. I had a hot bath as soon as I got back, and was none the worse for my dip.

Half-term had coincided with Guy Fawkes Night, and we had a splendid bonfire to dispose of the garden rubbish, with a family-built guy in one of my old suits topping it and burning most satisfactorily as we let off fireworks. That was a routine we kept up for quite a few years, until the children grew too old to enjoy it. At Christmas instead of a pantomime we took David and Mary to see Agatha Christie's *The Mousetrap*, already after 13 years the longest-running play ever, but in no way outstanding. Thirty-two years later we took David's children, but still could not understand its success. However they did all get a pantomime on New Year's Day, when Jill's parents took them to the new Yvonne Arnaud Theatre in Guildford to see Thackeray's *The Rose and The Ring*, which I had not seen since taking part in it as a school play in Willesden.

Returning after Christmas leave I spent my last few weeks in the Navy attending resettlement courses in the Naval Barracks. Being not very handy, I had chosen household maintenance, and endeavoured to acquire a bit of practical knowledge of how to deal with the problems of our new house. At least it got me out of mid-winter boat trips round Fareham Creek. In the middle of it I came up to London for my father's eightieth birthday on 14th January, when we were all to dine with my cousin Edward, but my father was rushed to hospital with pneumonia, which put a major damper on the occasion. He was out of action convalescing for the next two months, leaving George Copplestone to run the office with his usual efficiency.

I was dined out for the last time at the end of the month, then Jill came down for a mess cocktail party and stayed overnight at the Nuffield Club. I gave my farewell drinks party at lunchtime next day, and left that afternoon for home. I noted in my diary 'Retired from Royal Navy 042359 Feb 1966'. It was just over 28 years since I joined in January 1938.

Being unemployed, I immediately went on the dole for the one and only time in my life, as I was not due to start with Tyler Brothers until April, so I went along to the Labour Exchange twice weekly to 'sign on'. The sum received was small, but not to be sneezed at on a pension of £810 a year from the Royal Navy. I spent the two months settling into our new house and seeing what came up in the garden, though it took a full year to discover just what perennials we had.

Towards the end of February my father moved down to Bournemouth to recuperate, on his way to recovery, and we could relax on that front. Then on 31st March we drove to Braintree for the wedding of my first cousin Bill Tyler to Diana Adams as a family party, my father being back in action again. In a General Election the same day Harold Wilson was returned with an increased Labour majority.

The following week we drove up to Leeds to spend Easter with Jill's brother Brian and his family. The M1 had not yet reached there and it was a six-hour journey even in midweek. The weather was dreadful, wet and misty the whole time, and an unattractive introduction to the wonderful county of Yorkshire. It really did appear grim on that first visit, great cooling towers trailing clouds of vapour, narrow winding roads before the coming of the motor-ways, and dark gloomy moors and mills. I was soon to learn the error of my initial impressions, though the cities were far more depressing and drab than today, but that first time we were glad to return south again. We were a southern family, and all my home naval postings had been in the south of England from college at Dartmouth onwards, except for a few wartime experiences of Tyneside and Scapa Flow, so anywhere north of Watford was almost as much a closed book as civilian life. I am astonished now to realise how limited was my knowledge of my own country, compared to areas of the Mediterranean and Far East, and we are still discovering the attractions of various English counties. In recent years as Friends of the Imperial War Museum we have enjoyed their annual long weekends, usually based in a cathedral city, to explore a county from Durham to Norfolk.

I now started work with the company in Regent Street and left Jill at home on her own, as even Simon was at school all day. She was not prepared to fill her life with housework and socialising, and soon found a multitude of other activities. She began by fostering three young babies in turn until they were ready for adoption, then graduated to work on the committee of the National Adoption Society. When changed outlooks reduced babies for adoption to a trickle, she went to a closing tea with its patron Princess Alice, Queen Victoria's last surviving granddaughter, at Kensington Palace. She began parallel with this a nearly 30-year stint with Central Aid, the local Kingston charity that worked in association with SSAFA, running their office every Thursday morning. She also distributed Meals on Wheels with the Red Cross on alternate Monday mornings. She was involved in running the Home for Jewish Unmarried Mothers until the demand for that also declined, when she was recruited to support Nightingale House, the Home for Aged Jews in Wandsworth. This was the largest old age home in Europe, with over 400 beds, where she soon joined the management committee and eventually ran the shop. The Home has occupied every Wednesday and at least one other half-day most weeks as her main charitable activity for over 25 years. These were only her leisure activities, as she still had a family to care for.

# 18

## *Tyler Brothers*

Tyler Brothers (Eastern) Limited was established in 1920 by my father and his younger brothers, who obtained the agencies of mainly Yorkshire and Lancashire cloth manufacturers to sell their goods in the Far East, and built up a good business over the next two decades. The business went into suspended animation after the Japanese invasions of 1941, and was revived after the war when exports were encouraged to pay off the nation's war debts and fund needed imports. With a salesman, first Vic Wood, whom we had met in Singapore, and later Cyril Jenn, whom we had met in Hong Kong, they revived the pre-war routine of journeys out and around by P&O with trunks full of samples. Looking for new markets as old ones closed, they opened up first East Africa and then the Arabian Gulf oil states on their extended journeys. By the time I arrived they represented well over 50 British manufacturers and a handful of Continental ones in various areas from Kuwait to Tokyo and Nairobi to Bangkok.

My brother Michael covered Hong Kong and Japan and Cyril Jenn the rest. A separate company, Tyler Bros (Far Eastern) Ltd, had been established in Hong Kong under Michael in the 1950s to take advantage of the lower tax rates there and with the idea of eventually operating independently, but most of the administration was still handled in London. I found what I considered an overblown staff of my father as Chairman, George Copplestone as Company Secretary, Cyril Jenn when not travelling, Ron Smith, recruited recently as potential successor to the Secretary, an assistant and two typists, plus myself in place of my uncle. The set-up had become top-heavy, with a large administrative staff to support a limited sales staff and our resident subagents in most overseas markets. I spent the first weeks reading myself into the job, learning what all the manufacturers made and where we sold their goods, who the sub-agents were and their interests, the office routine and meeting any manufacturers or customers who called at the office.

My father had been brought up in the thorough and precise Victorian system where nothing was omitted. Every letter and envelope was addressed 'Messrs ...', usually with the full address on both, and letters concluded 'With compliments, Yours very truly, Tyler Brothers (Eastern) Ltd' followed by the signatory's name. The wasted typing time with dozens of letters going out a day was enormous. My first change was to point out that as the company's name was printed at the top of each letter, there was no need to repeat it at the bottom, then it was agreed that 'With compliments' could be taken for granted, and eventually we dropped the 'very' from 'Yours very truly'.

My uncle used to write out in his beautiful clear longhand almost every letter, and then dictate it, so within a year we were able to dispense with one typist and eventually with the other as the dictation speeded up. Within a few years we introduced small dictating machines, so that staff did not have to sit and take dictation, with further time wasted if the phone rang, but simply put the cassette on the machine and type what came through their headphones. This meant that when the assistant retired he too did not need to be replaced. Finally, when VAT was introduced in 1973, we transferred all the Far Eastern agencies to Hong Kong, to save both ourselves and the manufacturers all the work of paying it and claiming it back for export business, as commission could be paid to an overseas company free of VAT. Later that year when George Copplestone retired there was less bookkeeping to handle, so Ron Smith was able to take his place and we engaged an excellent new typist – June Pile.

Michael came over every summer to visit manufacturers and discuss the requirements of his markets, particular changes in taste and the sort of designs and colours being called for in men's cloth, which was his main business. I went with him to Yorkshire

246

that summer of 1966, and learnt to appreciate the talent of the designers, before spending a week with Towles of Loughborough learning how they knitted men's socks, knitwear and underwear, which we sold in all our markets. Design and colour were the sales key for all except underwear, where 'long johns' in wool were almost identical and sold on the perceived softness of the wool and the popularity build-up for a particular manufacturer's brand name. We had been selling Towles 'Paramount' brand since the war and established it, but there was strong competition from Wolsey and many other big companies.

Our summer holiday that year was in Elgin, where I spent two weeks at Johnstons fine wools mill. They wove cloths in luxury wools, from the rare and expensive vicuna down through cashmere and mohair to the finest quality sheep's wools. They sold cloth for fine overcoats, scarves which they wove themselves, and a variety of special fabrics. They moved with the times, adding modern looms, but still operated looms nearly 100 years old for the simple jobs. The children played on the nearby fine sands of Lossiemouth, but did not venture into the cold North Sea, and we met some old friends when we visited the Lossiemouth Naval Air Station for its Navy Day that August. During the week they were able to explore the surrounding countryside of Morayshire, the mild-climate lowlands to the east of Aberdeen known as the Garden of Scotland for their fertile soil.

I had been sent to Johnstons because they were a forward-looking company, but many companies were not, so the great British textile industry was slowly contracting and fading away. Lancashire had almost lost its cotton industry, and the government had assisted it to close down without too much hardship. Michael recalled how in the 1950s he used to visit Lancashire companies to tell them what the market wanted, and be told that he did not understand that they had always done and produced things in a certain way and were not going to change. They did not, foreign competitors took their business and most of the mills closed. Yorkshire was going the same way. Both had been spoilt by the post-war boom when they could allocate their production to customers crying out for it, as most other production had been destroyed during the war or was fully taken up in its home market.

247

Too many companies rather than modernise by buying expensive new machinery took the short cut in a labour-intensive industry of encouraging the immigration of cheap labour from the Indian sub-continent. This was the ultimate short-termism, since as the new immigrants became unionised wages were forced up, and too late mills found themselves priced out of the market and closing down. This had already begun, and some of the mills we visited that year had already closed by the next.

With three areas hit at once, 1967 was a bad year for export. The Six Day War in the Middle East upset business there and closed the Suez Canal, delaying all exports to the Far East, which had to go round the Cape; the Viet Nam War intensified, there were riots in Hong Kong which cut back business; and in Africa the Biafra civil war upset even East Africa. It all affected the national balance of trade and contributed to the sudden devaluation of the pound that autumn, which kick-started exports as prices in sterling suddenly became more competitive, though of course the cost of imported raw materials rose.

I made my first overseas sales journey that spring by flying out to Hong Kong at the end of March to study the market and look up old friends while staying with Michael. I flew to Japan with him to meet our various subagents in Osaka and Tokyo, where we stayed in Frank Lloyd Wright's famous old Imperial Hotel shortly before it was torn down and replaced by a sky-scraper block as land in central Tokyo was too valuable to continue supporting a spreading low building. Returning to Hong Kong, we flew down to Bangkok to meet up with Cyril Jenn, and after a joint assault on the Bangkok market Cyril and I flew on to Singapore to work that market. These visits gave me an opportunity to acquaint myself with our manufacturers' ranges as we displayed them to customers. Mostly goods sell themselves if the price is right and customers can afford to restock because their present stocks are selling well, so much depended on personal relationships and we were fortunate that Cyril had a friendly personality. He also spoke Hindi following war service with the Indian Army, so was able to chat with the Indian customers and also bargain if necessary.

I found it most interesting to see Singapore and Malaya from a commercial instead of a naval angle, and to appreciate the need to

248

avoid customers underselling one another on the same items as it cut their profit margin and made them look for alternative suppliers. By visiting a market regularly, one got to know which customers were financially reliable and could be given credit and supplied on Sight Draft or Cash Against Document terms, as against the less reliable who must pay in advance by Bank Draft or for larger orders by Letter of Credit. In the Far East we had our local subagents, who shared the commission, advised on creditworthiness, brought the customers in to the hotel or us to their shops and were our eyes and ears. They made life easy, but still had to be visited regularly to maintain personal contact with customers and check up on the subagent. We discovered that our wily man in Bangkok, who demanded large stocks of Silhouette bra and swimwear samples, produced few orders as they were sold in his retail shop! He was promptly sacked.

My father instructed me to leave Cyril in Kuala Lumpur as he reckoned I had got the feel of the Far East, and fly back via Beirut to investigate our subagent there and then on to Athens to assess our potential new subagent for Greece. It was the beginning of June, Nasser had forced the UN to withdraw from his Sinai territory and he had closed the Tiran Straits to Israel-bound shipping to cut off Eilat. There were mobilisations and rumours of wars, but Beirut seemed untroubled by it all as I visited customers with our salesman. Not surprisingly with war threatening, they did not rush to buy, but I spent a pleasant two days there, including watching an Arabic spy film being shot in my Alcazar Hotel, next to the top-class Saint Georges, with a microphone rising from a vase of flowers to pick up the spy's conversation.

I then flew to Nicosia for the weekend to discuss the market prospects with our local subagent, and into Athens on Monday morning the 5th just as the Six Day War began. I was a little surprised to get no reply from our potential subagent's office that afternoon, and not knowing Greek did not discover until next day that war had broken out. Our new man proved to be Jewish, and was so concerned with Israel's safety that he had gone home that day to sit by his radio. However, he was back at work next day, cheered by Israel's destruction of the enemy air forces, and we spent the rest of the week seeking local reactions to the Yorkshire cloth that I was carrying. There appeared to be reasonable prospects, but in the event we never got established in that market. Meanwhile I went to an exuberant Thanksgiving Service in the Athens synagogue on the Friday evening for the miraculously speedy defeat of Israel's enemies, and saw the Israeli ambassador cheered away as he left in his car, driving on the Sabbath because of the national emergency.

In the summer we had our first European holiday, a package tour to Canet de Mar on the Catalan coast north of Barcelona. Mary was now almost 16 and discovered boys on that holiday, having previously not been interested. There were plenty of young English fellows on the beach, and she spent most of her time with them while the rest of us played and swam together. We had held a joint confirmation service earlier that month for Mary and David at our local Wimbledon synagogue, which we had joined when we settled in Surbiton. Jill and I were both confirmed at 15, which had been adopted by Reform Jews as a more suitable and mature age than the traditional bar mitzvah at 13, but the fashion has since changed back to the traditional 13. We celebrated with a family lunch in the garden – a far cry from the lavish parties which are now almost de rigueur.

The following January I had my first full Middle Eastern tour, leaving London on the 24th and drinking a toast on the plane to my brother Michael and his bride Anne Schmitt, who were getting married that day in Hong Kong in the presence of both pairs of parents, our Aunt Lizzie from Melbourne and our Aunt Phyllis from London. I had a quick day in Cyprus with our subagent to visit Limassol and Larnaca to book some knitwear orders, then on to Beirut for just a day to visit customers, again with our subagent, and to Kuwait to join up with Cyril Jenn. I discovered at once the difference in Gulf markets. There were no reliable subagents, so one worked the markets alone. It meant that we did not have to share our commission – agents live on the commission included in the price of goods – but it all depended on regular visits and personal chemistry. Cyril had been working the markets for seven years already, so the customers knew him and awaited his annual winter visits, and were nearly all Indians or Pakistanis, as most Arab proprietors left the running to their staff, so his Hindi paid dividends.

The Arabian Gulf – never the Persian Gulf when one is on the southern Arab side – was just recovering from the shock of the Six Day War and getting used to its oil money, which had begun to flow in a small way in the 1950s and was now increasing year by year. Conditions had been primitive at that time when Vic Wood had made the first visits for us, and had to find a bed in desert forts or small Asian hotels, but were advancing fast.

Kuwait had rebuilt the main street of the city, Fahd al Salem Street, inland from the old market area, in the last few years, and we stayed in the newish but already tatty Bristol Hotel near the main Safat Square. Cyril kept cases of samples in his large room, where he received customers, first calling on them on arrival to arrange appointments which '*Insh Allah*', God willing, they would attend. Poor God was blamed if they forgot or were delayed elsewhere or thought of something better to do. The Indian staff were quite good, as were the Indian companies, but where Arabs were concerned one often had to write off a wasted hour as one dared not double-book or both took offence if they both turned up. Fortunately, apart from in Saudi Arabia, business did not stop for prayers, but every morning one was woken before dawn by the muezzins' amplified voices calling the dawn prayer from the mosque minarets. People were friendly and hospitable, always welcoming one with tea, coffee or a soft drink to lubricate the conversation, and I found it an interesting experience.

After more than a fortnight, since Kuwait was the largest and richest market, we flew on to Bahrain. Bahrain was unique, an island trading centre for over 2,000 years and the base of the British Resident, who advised those at that time dependent states. The British had been there for decades, oil had been pumped since the 1920s and was now almost exhausted, but it was the commercial centre of the Gulf as the local Arabs were experienced merchants and traders. We stayed at the Capital Hotel in Manama, the capital, a small and basic hotel of the type standard at the time and within walking distance of almost all customers in the compact business area. This was centred on the main shopping area Bab al Bahrain Street, leading up into town from the arch of Bab al Bahrain, the Gate of Bahrain. Customers were more businesslike, and we completed business in a week, but I also had a naval inter-

251

lude visiting the British Naval Base at Jufair. The government in its post-devaluation reassessment was now preparing to abandon its bases and the protection of these small states and leave them to fend for themselves, even though the oil-rich sheiks were prepared to pay for our continued presence. A lot of the future troubles in the area stemmed from this bipartisan policy of scuttle, which Heath failed to reverse when he had the chance two years later.

We then flew to Doha, the capital of the state of Qatar, which sticks out like a cucumber from the Arabian coast just to the east of Bahrain, and where we stayed in the fine modern Oasis Hotel on the seashore near the airport and a short taxi ride from town. Doha was only a small place but had been well laid out and had made a good start to modernisation, though as yet business was poor and was covered in a couple of days.

All our flights were by Gulf Air, the joint airline of the small Gulf states, still very much British-run and piloted at that time, which now took us on to Abu Dhabi for the company's first visit. It had only recently come to prominence following the British-backed removal of the reactionary old Sheik Shakbut by the modernising Sheik Zaid and the release of the oil income for development. We had an introduction there to Mohan Jashanmal, one of the family whose stores we had dealt with for years in Kuwait, Bahrain and Dubai, and his Land Rover met us at the new airport to take us into town. The new road was still being tarmaced, so we set off across the desert in a rare downpour of rain, with just one windscreen wiper working and no recognisable landmarks. We were very relieved to end up on the seafront outside a small newly built hotel, the Al Ain Palace, whose swing doors led to the bar where we could down a much needed beer.

The Sheik's large palace lay half a mile away, a few new small buildings faced the sea, including Jashanmal's store next to the Chartered Bank, and nearby was a covered souk, or market, where the rain ran off the corrugated iron roofs as we called on customers. We did not do much business, but we had got in on the ground floor with some companies that were going to grow. It seems almost inconceivable that 20 years later, after a visit on the way back from Singapore, I had to think which of my photos of

252

the skyscrapers in the business centre were of Abu Dhabi and which of Singapore.

We flew on to Dubai, the trading centre of the Lower Gulf, with its twin towns of Dubai and Deira facing each other across the Creek. The Creek is actually a fair-sized inlet from the sea, which made it a protected harbour and the town a trading centre, but the coming of oil had stepped up the volume of trade enormously. We stayed at another small Indian-run hotel, the Airlines on the Dubai side, and took the little *abra* ferries which ran constantly across the Creek when we needed to visit our customers on the Deira side. Then after five weeks away I left Cyril and flew home to prepare for my next journey.

The previous year when all our markets were having difficulties we had looked at possible new openings, and decided that we should investigate the Scandinavian countries, which were among our partners in the European Free Trade Area. Cyril Jenn and I had made a prospecting visit to Stockholm and Copenhagen that September, carrying a wide range of samples to discover what sort of British products would appeal, and now following devaluation I was going to make my first solo sales trip, hoping that the keener prices would bring in business.

I had less than a fortnight to sort out and assemble my samples before I flew off to Stockholm in mid-March, having fixed as many appointments as possible by letter in advance. I devoted a week to each of the two cities, getting to know them in more detail by foot, bus and underground, and enjoyed them though finding most items nearly twice as expensive as at home. Despite this, price alone did not sell our products, and it took time and twice-yearly visits to build up enough business to make the visits worthwhile. One personal bonus of these visits were the weekends when I could visit the sights, palaces and museums of these two attractive cities, and spend occasional weekends in Vasteras with Jill's college friend Nancy and her Swedish husband Lars Adler.

In a year or two I branched out to include Oslo and Helsinki, covering them all in a fortnight both in spring and autumn, fitting in a large provincial city like Gothenburg, Malmo, Bergen or Turku to widen our coverage. For certain products we were able to appoint a subagent, although shared commission was not enough to tempt them unless turnover was likely to be large, but a number of these agents became good friends, especially Bo Scheja in Stockholm and his English wife Kathy. Another reason we chose Scandinavia was that the business language was English, which made life much easier.

Every summer I went with Michael during his visits to our Yorkshire cloth manufacturers, and at other times of the year with Cyril Jenn to our other manufacturers in Leicestershire and elsewhere. The most popular was to Jersey, where the Channel Islands Knitwear Company with its 'Summerland' brand was growing into our best-selling item in the Middle East, and a visit with our wives combined with a weekend and hospitality from the Sangans was a welcome break. That summer of 1968 Anne came over with Michael to meet us. We clicked at once, and have enjoyed her visits ever since as she is entertaining and good company and ideal for him. She was also a great help to him on the social side, as his manufacturers visiting Hong Kong expected to be wined, dined and fussed over.

On the family side, we drove regularly to Rendcomb to see the boys at school, and went off together for our summer holidays. That year it was North and South Wales, based on Penmorfa and Amroth. The following year we spent a really warm Easter with another of Jill's college friends, Elizabeth, and her husband Stuart Whyte near Paris, and our summer holiday was one week experiencing Butlin's at Minehead before a return to Amroth.

In 1970 we had a real Tyler Brothers holiday when we flew to Pisa to join Cyril at his favourite resort on the isle of Elba. We all stayed at Franks Hotel near Porto Azzuro and were joined by Michael and Anne. The swimming and beach were ideal, boats ran to the little town across the bay, and Cyril had towed his own boat across Europe, which we could all sail in. We explored the nearby towns, but otherwise relaxed in the sun and enjoyed lazing. On our return we held a dinner at Grosvenor House to celebrate the Fiftieth Anniversary of the founding of the company, attended by two of the original brothers and their wives, the widow of the third, the rest of the staff and their wives and we two Tyler brothers with our wives carrying on the company.

The following year our parents celebrated their Golden

Weddings. Jill's parents booked a hotel at Chagford on Dartmoor for all their family, their five children, spouses and grandchildren for a week at the end of August, when we all explored the area together, including a tour of the Naval College at Dartmouth, which I had not seen since I was a Cadet, and held a big family dinner on the wedding night, 1st September.

My parents followed with their Golden Wedding dinner at Grosvenor House two months later. David and Jonathan wore dinner jackets for the first time, and Simon came in a suit. My father had finally retired from the company two years previously aged 83, but was still fit enough to turn up at the office one day having walked from Hampstead to Regent Street to see how long it took.

Mary was at Cardiff University reading Social Administration and sharing a house in Splott, and David had just gone up to Trinity Hall at Cambridge to read Economics after spending the winter cruising the Mediterranean as an assistant on the school ship *Uganda*. He had proved most useful during the six-week postal strike as we were able to send mail to him weekly by air to post at the nearest port to our overseas agents and customers. Telex was only just catching on, fax did not exist, and the postal disruption caused vast losses of business and indeed jobs.

We had reached the decade of strikes.

# 19

## *Trouble and Strife*

Great Britain had forged ahead after the Second World War in improving conditions for the whole country, with wages and living standards rising faster than productivity, and this became apparent as exporting to pay for our import needs grew more difficult in the face of global competition. Our major traditional industries, steel production, shipbuilding, textiles and others, began to wither away as their products were undersold from cheaper-wage countries and those which modernised faster.

This was accompanied by a rash of strikes in both the nationalised industries and the private sector, as workers clamoured for excessive rises to advance their living standards further. They saw a lot of the bosses resting on their laurels and granting themselves excessive pay rises, and naturally wanted their share. After debilitating strikes the management usually gave way, having denied that the desired increase was possible, depleting their reserves so that eventually they could not continue and then folding. Nationalised industries of course did not fold; they simply raised prices to their captive consumers and so precipitated further wage demands to maintain living standards.

This process became noticeable in the early 1960s, and accelerated as I settled into civilian life. When the country went decimal in 1971, changing from 240 pence to 100 new pence to the pound, the first class letter rate was raised to 2½ new pence, double 1961, but by 1981 it had reached 14 new pence, a near sixfold increase. This was more than double inflation for the period and 300% inflation was serious enough. My 1966 pension soon purchased only a fraction of its original worth, and those who had retired on a fixed pension were hit very hard.

Strikes at the docks, on the railways, in the public utilities and in private industry began to grow in the late 1960s and became a national epidemic in the 1970s when we were regarded as the Sick Man of Europe, and the British Disease was a byword for inefficiency. Exporting became more and more frustrating, as many deliveries were delayed by strikes until customers lost faith in Britain and started ordering elsewhere. To its credit the textile industry, although among the worse paid, hardly ever struck as its leaders realised sooner than most that a strike merely cost jobs in the medium to short term as the world was waiting to snatch our business. It took the country as a whole almost a generation to realise this.

I became accustomed to regular and wildcat rail strikes, when I had to drive to Wimbledon to catch the Underground to the office, or Underground strikes when it was quickest to walk from Waterloo. I had to placate customers whose urgently needed supplies for the opening of a new hotel or store were strike-bound at British docks or late due to delays in supplies reaching the factories. One could understand why Margaret Thatcher was swept into office in 1979 by the protest vote.

Most of this was in the future when my father retired in mid-1969, and George Copplestone became Chairman in recognition of his long service and experience. We carried on as before but looking for new markets, since the Hong Kong office understandably wanted to reduce our share of its commission, which had been keeping us in profit.

Cyril Jenn was building up the Middle East to take its place, and I took over his visits to Singapore and Malaysia once a year. Thailand was now almost a closed market, with a flourishing textile industry and high tariffs to protect it, so I turned to the East Malaysia territories of Sarawak and Sabah and the oil-rich state of Brunei as a substitute. The Sultan of Brunei had declined to join Malaysia and it became an oil-rich state of Middle Eastern type. Its 200,000 people found themselves living in a welfare state but without any say in it, as the Sultan ruled and still does as an autocrat. I flew over from Singapore by Brunei Airlines on an excursion ticket which cost more the longer you stayed, as if designed to discourage tourists. I stayed at Angs Hotel, a glorified but comfortable guest house in the capital, Brunei town, which had been renamed Bandar Seri Begawan. The old town was built out on stilts over the Brunei river, and the new town had grown up on the shore alongside it. The previous sultan, who had abdicated in favour of his son, was a great admirer of Winston Churchill, and had built a Churchill museum with a statue of the great man giving the 'V' sign in front of it. One of his Harrow schoolboy suits featured among the mementos on show in an impressive small display. We had been dealing for some years with a company called Glamour, whose Singh family made me very welcome. They proved to be the main department store and also a government contractor who did good business with us for many years thereafter.

With Malaysian Airways I flew through Sarawak, the former domain of the White Rajah, and enjoyed its capital Kuching, which had escaped wartime destruction and still featured his crenellated palace, the Istana, on the far side of the river from the town in case of riots. There was a handsome Georgian-style post office with the Rajah's coat of arms over it, but few other signs of its history in the pleasant little town, where I found a few customers. Its port of Pending has its name immortalised in the 'wait and see' basket of many English-speaking offices. From there I flew on to the second town of Sibu and to the centre of its declining oilfields at Miri, then via Labuan to Kota Kinabalu in Sabah. It was the former Jesselton, chief town of British North Borneo, both now renamed. Like Brunei, it had its water village, as well as the adjacent town on land which I had visited years earlier to write its Port Plan for the Navy. Neither it nor Sandakan, the other large town, proved worth a regular visit as business potential was decidedly limited, though there were more prospects on Labuan island, which was to become a duty-free port to drum up customers.

Back at home we had a bad year in 1973. My father, whose health had declined the previous year, died of pneumonia in January just before his eighty-seventh birthday. He had enjoyed a full and active life so we could not be too sad, but it was a loss all the same, and of course involved a lot of paperwork even though his affairs were in good order. My mother was deeply upset although she had seen it coming, and we had to spend quite a bit of time with her over the next few months. Far more tragic and quite without warning was the death of Jill's nephew Martin. He fell when climbing in the Alps with a school party in early September. He was not yet 15. The whole family were shattered by the tragedy, but could do little to comfort her brother Brian, Vera and their daughters living up in Yorkshire. That same month my uncle Douglas died and the first generation of Tyler brothers had all gone. Only a few weeks earlier George Copplestone retired after nearly 50 years with the company, and the last link with the past was broken.

The following month the Yom Kippur War broke out, several weeks of bitter fighting before peace was restored between Israel and the Arabs. Once again business was upset, but this time so was the whole world economy as the oil-producing states led by the Arabs sharply increased the price of oil and threw the world into recession. At home this coincided with the second all-out miners' strike, the Heath government having given way previously, but this time it stood firm with fuel rationing that caused the Three Day Week and further damage to Britain's trading position, leading to the February 1974 election when Labour just squeezed in and gave the miners what they wanted. The stock market had collapsed in the face of all these problems, inflation rapidly got out of control, rising to over 25% a year before being brought down, and companies began raising prices every few months to offset increasing costs.

Mary had by now obtained her university degree and was working for the Social Services Department in Cardiff, David was in his last year at Cambridge and Jonathan had just started reading Business Administration at Lanchester Polytechnic in Coventry, which ran one of the best business courses in the country, leaving Simon at Rendcomb as the last of the three Tyler brothers.

We had holidayed in south Devon in 1973 with Simon, and then gone over on the *Scillonian* for a week on Saint Mary's in Scilly. We enjoyed the laid-back life there, with the daily boat trips to the outer islands, so we returned for two weeks the following August to spend a week again at Tregarthens Hotel on Saint Mary's and the second week in a rented cottage on Tresco near the tropical gardens of the Abbey. Saint Mary's was Harold Wilson's favourite holiday resort; he had a cottage there, and we saw him out walking quite informally with his dog around the island lanes. We had Michael Stewart, the quiet Foreign Secretary, staying at our hotel, and some planning for winning the coming second election in October must surely have formed part of their holiday activities.

Ted Heath had achieved Britain's entry into the European Economic Community in January 1973, so after Scandinavia this was the next area we looked at. In the larger countries, France, Germany and Italy, companies would not want us as well as a resident local agent, so I tackled the Benelux countries on several visits. I found them quite different, with Belgium going for comfort and the Netherlands for value. The contrast was symbolised by the Belgian motorways lit from end to end, while across the border you had to rely on your headlights. We had only moderate success in Holland, but in Belgium soon had the good fortune to find an ideal local agent in Ignace Van de Vyvere of Tielt, who became a friend as well.

One of the 50 companies that we represented when I joined was Carlisle Woollen Mills. They sold blankets, shortly afterwards closed down and referred us to their supplier James Walker and Sons of Mirfield. Cyril Jenn and I arranged to call on them to obtain their direct agency, and met their chairman Sir Ronald Walker, who was even older than my father. It was a family company some two centuries old, though not as well known as its rival, Earlys of Witney, which was founded in Charles II's day but was no longer in the family. Sir Ronald had been left to run the company in the First World War when many of the other directors were killed, and had run it ever since, assisted by his nephews, now in their fifties, whom he still referred to as 'The Boys'. After some coaxing, we obtained their agency for all our markets and it had built up to be one of our leading products. It proved ideal for Ignace, who rapidly expanded their sales in Belgium and made this a valuable market within a few years to match the sales we were achieving for them in the Middle and Far East.

We celebrated our Silver Wedding at the end of 1974 with a

large drinks party and buffet supper at home, with all the children rallying round as staff. Jill had devised coloured name cards for the guests, with different colours to represent family, childhood and school friends, naval friends and post-naval friends. It worked well in mixing the guests without too many introductions. We were most fortunate in our fellow residents of Ashcombe Avenue, many of whom attended, and we had as our next-door neighbours for over 25 years Phyllis and Douglas Drage, who became and remain close friends. Our house began to empty as first Mary, who by now had moved to Harringey, and then David, who had started work with Unilever, set up their own flats.

In 1976 one of my Dartmouth term, Derek Bazalgette, was Admiral Superintendent of the Royal Naval College at Greenwich, and had the splendid idea of inviting all of us to a reunion dinner and evening there. The naval ones among us were either Admirals or senior Captains and Commanders, and the rest of us ranged from stockbrokers and professors to industrialists and farmers. Some I had not seen since 1941, and it was a fascinating evening of reminiscences. We have held two more reunions since then, the most recent when we all reached 70 and spent a weekend back at the Royal Naval College at Dartmouth. Over 20 turned up of the original 44, and we had our photograph taken on the college steps in the same order that we had stood as 13-year-olds in 1938.

I had been voted onto the Council of the Wimbledon Synagogue soon after I joined, and in 1976 began a three-year stint as Chairman. Judaism lacks the ecclesiastic structure of most Christian denominations; far more of the running of the synagogue affairs is in the hands of the lay membership, so apart from chairing the monthly Council and Executive meetings the Chairman broadly directs affairs in close association with the Rabbi. I had already spent the previous two years as Secretary so I was fully in the picture and found the job interesting, but time-consuming on top of my business activities.

David had taken out a number of girls, but now became friendly with and eventually engaged to Sharon Lantin. We had the pleasure of seeing them married in our synagogue, and the following year 1978 Mary was married to Clive Attard, whom she had met as a fellow social worker. David and Sharon set up home in

Wimbledon, not far away, and Mary and Clive in Ayot Saint Lawrence, within a stone's throw of George Bernard Shaw's house, now a National Trust property. Meanwhile, Jonathan on completion of his college time had become a salesman with Burroughs the computer company, and we said a fond farewell to Rendcomb after 13 years of cross-country journeys when Simon followed Jonathan to Lanchester Polytechnic to take the same Business Administration course.

Things seemed to be settling down family-wise and going along nicely in business where we achieved a record turnover in 1977 of £1.25 million, but that same summer Cyril Jenn was made an offer he could not refuse by Channel Island Knitwear to become their Export Manager. He had single-handedly raised their annual sales in the Middle East from £10,000 when I joined to nearly £300,000 and was being asked to work this and other markets on their behalf. They were entitled to give us six months' notice, and although they were not supposed to entice away our Sales Director we could not legally stop them and it meant another major problem for me to overcome. I did an autumn tour of the Gulf with Cyril to meet the customers and update myself on the markets, and was fortunate to find Charles Champion as our new salesman.

Charles knew the textile business well, having spent most of his business life in it, but not the Middle East, so I took him round the Gulf with me for the spring 1978 selling journey. Despite having lost our best-selling line, we did not do badly, slightly increasing the sales of our other leading lines of men's and ladies' wear and household textiles. Total turnover still exceeded £1 million and Charles took over the Middle East markets with some confidence.

One of our most important agencies was H. Booth of Barnsley, whose ready-made suits, jackets and trousers sold well in the Middle East, principally in the Yemen, where we had our only good Arab subagent. Abdul Aziz Ghanem was a Yemeni who had moved to Aden when it was a British Colony and Yemen was ruled by backward Imams, and had been our very satisfactory representative there. After Aden became independent as the People's Republic of South Yemen and its Marxist government proved unfriendly to private enterprise, he moved home to Sanaa in the Yemen Arab Republic, which had settled down after the civil war following the overthrow of the Imam. We were pleased to give him our representation there, where he had built up Booth into his leading agency, and I decided to visit him there in the autumn of 1979 before flying on for a quick tour of the Gulf.

Yemen was still almost *terra incognita,* with few airlines flying there. In early October I flew out to Khartoum by Sudan Airways, in a plane which had certainly seen its best days, where the seat trays dropped down at any vibration and the stewardesses seemed to regard the passengers as a necessary evil. We landed at 2 a.m. to await the flight to Sanaa due out at 6, but fortunately I did not drop asleep in the transit lounge as about 3.30 I heard the word Sanaa in a flood of Arabic and discovered the plane was leaving two hours early at 4. We landed three hours later, and I moved into the rather basic Sam City Hotel in one of the city's high-rise buildings. Sanaa was still a mediaeval city, surrounded by its mud and brick walls, and entered by the massive Bab al Yemen, where the beggars lay by the city gate just as in the Bible. Well-off Yemenis traditionally built six- or eight-storey narrow houses like towers, with the family living on the upper floors and the servants, and animals in the country, below. They were most picturesque, the windows with coloured glass upper panes and the house exteriors decorated with geometric designs. The shops were more mundane, but it was interesting to meet the customers with Mr Ghanem. The Yemenis are slim handsome people so they could often wear boys' suits or wanted the narrowest men's cuts, while 14 or 14½ was the standard shirt neck size. It was a useful visit, to be repeated in the 1980s when modern hotels made the stays more pleasant.

Unfortunately, sterling had risen following Margaret Thatcher's coming to power – an unwelcome tribute to the new government – and it quite rapidly reached a peak of over $2.40 to the pound compared to its fall to little over $1 a few years earlier. At these new levels many of our products became almost unsaleable, and companies began collapsing across the country as unemployment soared towards 3 million. It became painfully obvious that we would have to cut staff to survive, so with great regret when the spring sales figures proved barely half those of the previous year I had to make Charles redundant from the middle of 1981 and undertake all future travel myself. He set up his own company, attractively named Champion Exports, and acted as a one-man company from his home, exporting similar lines to the Middle East. We became friendly competitors, passing on possible business to one another and warnings on doubtful customers, until his early death a few years ago.

During his years I had added to our markets, starting with a package excursion to Reykjavik to appoint local subagents for Iceland, though with a total population not much larger than our Royal Borough of Kingston upon Thames it was never going to count for much. It did, however, provide an opportunity for me to see the clean city of Reykjavik with its hot springs heating, which additionally heated glasshouses to grow bananas and tropical fruit. I also visited Switzerland to appoint a subagent in Zurich, though our business there never expanded as I had hoped, but at least we kept increasing the number of eggs in our basket in the hope they would not all be addled at the same time.

# 20

*Carrying On*

In family terms 1981 was a happy year. In January Mary had her first child and our first grandchild, Katie Attard, and this was followed in October by David and Sharon's first child, Sarah. It is a most emotional moment to hold one's first grandchild and feel that the family goes on, and it was even more so for the great-grandparents to see their first great-grandchild. Both were neat and healthy little girls who have become lovely young women – though that is naturally any grandparent's opinion.

Jonathan, who had joined the Territorial SAS when he was 18, was still loving this as his main recreation apart from rugby, and about to move to a house in Surbiton, while Simon had gone into the mortgage-selling business and also had a flat nearby. Both boys still found their mother a convenient laundry for rugby kit and a useful weekend restaurant.

That spring my mother suffered a stroke which made nursing home attention essential, and we moved her to one in Wimbledon not too far from us, where she slowly faded away to die four years later. She had been wanting to go for some time as her quality of life deteriorated, although she was not in pain, and my mother-in-law was to feel the same before she died years later at 97. I do not consider that it is a kindness to fan the flame of life when it burns low, but active euthanasia is another matter.

During the summer James Walker had received an enquiry from the United Arab Emirates Armed Forces to quote for 140,000 woollen blankets, probably due to their having won an earlier but smaller contract. Negotiations dragged on towards a decision, and after a visit to Yorkshire to discuss details I flew out to Abu Dhabi in October as their representative to finalise and sign the deal on their behalf. On arrival I was contacted by a local company, which made very clear that the deal would only go through if a share of the commission was guaranteed to them. I was certain that they were representing someone more important who could make the final decision, and I could not afford to risk losing the deal as it might cost us James Walker's representation if I returned empty-handed, so I sacrificed half our commission. Once this was agreed I was called to a negotiating meeting at the Defence Ministry to thrash out the details, since Walkers could only deliver 10,000 a month without disrupting their other business, and we needed some protection against delays caused by *force majeure* such as dock strikes, but finally the contract worth almost £1.25 million – the largest I was ever to handle – was signed and I flew home to rush up to Mirfield with it. The commission was most welcome to take us out of the red, but the saving of jobs in Yorkshire was the biggest pleasure. The blankets, I suspect, ended up in Iraq as part of the Gulf States support for her war with the Ayatollah's Iran, but that was no concern of ours.

My first full year travelling our markets, 1982, began with regular rail strikes in January, making journeys to the office a pain due to the delays, then I flew out to Kuwait on Friday the 22nd. I always flew on Fridays when I could in the Middle East, this being the Moslem Sabbath when one could do little business. I now stayed at the Sheraton at the Jahra Gate end of Fahd Street, the gate being one of the gates of the former walled city now preserved in the centre of a large roundabout forming part of the inner ring road. Further ring roads spread out into the desert dividing the suburbs, and ran into the coastal road at either end. Most of our customers were in the city, within walking distance or a short bus or taxi ride from the hotel. I always stayed as near customers as possible anywhere in the world, as so often they wanted to see the samples one did not expect, and it paid to be able to fetch these quickly or whisk them back to the hotel.

I managed to complete my business in five days and fly on to Muscat at the other end of the Gulf the next Wednesday evening. There I stayed at the Ruwi Hotel in Muttrah, the large suburb that stretched inland from the walled city of Muscat. Muscat had been a Portuguese possession at the height of their sixteenth-century empire, and romantic former Portuguese fortresses crowned the peaks of the strategic hills. Unlike the rest of the Gulf the Muscat area is mountainous, and Muscat a picturesque old city. It is less so now that the old gates have been replaced by wider concrete ones in mock-Arabic style, but until the present Sultan Qaboos over-turned his reactionary father Sultan Said in 1970 the country was a backward mediaeval state. The Sultan was reputed to have kept the state's currency reserves locked up in the palace, there was no radio, let alone TV, only three elementary boys' schools and none for girls, and no paved roads, let alone hotels. The advance in ten years into a modern state was phenomenal, though the modern department stores were run by Indians who had been trading there for over a century.

I paid calls with our local subagent on Thursday, then had Friday to update my paperwork and send off orders, plus a swim and sunbathe by the pool as Muscat temperatures even at this coolest point rarely fail to top 80°F by day, though in Kuwait at night it can drop to near freezing. After two more days' business I flew back over the mountains on Sunday evening to Dubai. I had learnt from Cyril to fly first class by Gulf Air around the Gulf as the extra fare was not excessive. One received a glass of cham-pagne whatever the time or distance, the extra baggage allowance covered one's samples and so met most of the extra cost, one boarded last and disembarked first, had a first-class check-in desk and waiting room, and best of all might be downgraded to economy but never thrown off if a VIP turned up.

Dubai was already a modern city with plenty of customers to visit during a busy four days, then on Friday I flew to Abu Dhabi to stay at the Al Ain Palace. It had doubled in size since we first stayed there, and now faced the busy corniche road and seaside esplanade instead of a sandy beach. Abu Dhabi had become a modern city with large blocks of offices and flats, public gardens and government offices, but still only a shadow of what it would be ten years later as capital of the richest Gulf state. Like all good hotels, the Al Ain Palace had a pool, a huge one set behind the hotel where one could swim and sunbathe in the lull between the morning opening hours from 8 to 1 and the evening hours from 4 to 8. The following Tuesday I flew in to Doha, where I was now staying at the New Capital Hotel in the centre of town so most customers were within walking distance. I was able to cover the market in two and a half days to fly out on Friday to Bahrain, urged on by the fact that Qatar was strictly dry but Bahrain offered a civilised drink in the comfortable Delmon Hotel where I always stayed. Its pool was closed for winter overhaul but it was a bit chilly for swimming and the food was excellent, so again I updated my paperwork after enjoying the buffet. Everywhere in the Gulf one now had good Western meals with a few optional Arabic trimmings. Bahrain being so small I again only needed two and a half days to cover it, then flew on to Al Khobar in Saudi Arabia a score or two miles away as there was no other connection until the causeway linking Bahrain island to the Saudi mainland was opened a number of years later.

Al Khobar was part of the three-city complex of Dharan, Damman and Al Khobar which served the Saudi oilfields and had a combined population of well over a million. Most were immigrant workers, and our sales were chiefly of knitwear and clothing to take home to India, Pakistan and the Far East when they went on leave. The Al Khaja Hotel was basic and unattractive like the town, but worth putting up with for the business. Everything stopped for prayers at noon, mid-afternoon and sunset, when everyone was turned out into the street, Moslem or not, and shops shut for 20 or 30 minutes, so business was a bit hit-and-miss, and if you were unlucky you also caught up the final prayers at 90 minutes after sunset. Shops closed at noon for the midday break, and did not reopen until afternoon prayers had been said, so the disruptions were not too serious. I am not a great drinker, so the lack of alcohol did not bother me since they imported a pleasant non-alcoholic Dutch beer available in all the restaurants.

The Yemen had established its own airline, so that next Friday I flew on by Yemenia to Sanaa, where I stayed at the attractive new Sheba Hotel and returned home from there on Thursday 25th February after almost five weeks away. The following week was busy sending out orders and reports on the markets to manufacturers, and a quick drive to Yorkshire to see Walkers and Booths before stopping off overnight with Mary and Clive at their new home in Cambridgeshire.

I had given up the spring visit to Scandinavia years earlier, as it was no longer worth the effort, so the next event was my birthday on 2nd April when I had arranged a family dinner at the Institute of Directors. I had recently become a Life Member so as to have a London club for business meetings and entertainment, and its position, just off Trafalgar Square, was most convenient for visitors. Our meal was overshadowed by the Argentine invasion of the Falklands that morning, but we did not let it spoil our meal or our visit afterwards to *Amadeus* at Her Majesty's.

Various customers and subagents visited us during the year, often requiring to be taken to manufacturers' London showrooms to place an order, or to visit their mills or factories in the Midlands or North. We got away at the end of May for a fortnight's holiday in the West Country, looking up old naval and other friends and exploring Cornwall, including a few days at our honeymoon hotel the Tregenna Castle in Saint Ives for old times' sake. Soon after our return Michael and Anne arrived on a farewell round of visits, as he had just sold the Hong Kong company to his partner and they were moving to Victoria in British Columbia for their retirement. He had served 30 years in the Tropics, and though only 55 he had no family to support so very sensibly decided to take it easy.

At the end of June rail and Underground managed to strike together, making it just not worthwhile to struggle in to work, so I closed the office for a couple of days. Such behaviour, the Falklands victory and Michael Foot's campaign virtually assured Margaret Thatcher of a second election victory the following year. In July we had a visit from one of our more unusual subagents, Aroon Patel from Tanzania, who sold refurbished telephone equipment of the old 'Press Button B' variety to the Ministry of Communications. Not our usual textiles business, but we were prepared to deal with anything, and our other supplier for him provided meteorological equipment. It all went on without the need to visit his country.

Jill joined me in August for a week of visits to manufacturers in the North and Midlands before I flew to Copenhagen on Saturday the 21st for my Scandinavian visit. There I always flew in at the

269

weekend, and after an evening in the Tivoli Gardens caught the train up to Stockholm on Sunday to take the overnight ferry to Helsinki. I spent Monday with our local subagent Jouni Pukkila and sailed again that evening in the same ferry, where I had been able to keep my cabin, back to Stockholm. The cabins were extremely comfortable, the smorgasbords excellent and the return journey cost little more than two nights' hotel rooms so one cut down on both time and money, let alone the airfares involved. Bo Scheja, our subagent, met me off the ferry to call on customers, and I caught the evening train to Boras, where I spent the night. Boras was the base of the four main mail order companies of Sweden, whom I called on to unsuccessfully offer our blankets and other lines, then a short journey to Gothenburg to see a customer and take the evening train to Oslo, where I arrived at 10 p.m.

Next day, Thursday, I visited our Oslo customers before catching the 5 p.m. overnight ferry to Copenhagen, where I visited all my local customers on Friday and put up at the Triton Hotel near the main railway station, in which one could have one of the finest buffets in town. The Triton was a very comfortable bed and breakfast hotel to which I had been recommended years before, but to my embarrassment on my first stay, when I had Jill with me, we discovered that it was in the red light district surrounded by porn shops! Despite the surroundings it continued to flourish because of its central position. I fitted in final calls on Saturday morning before the afternoon flight to London after a hectic but effective week.

On 10th October I set off on a 'round the world' ticket with TWA and Singapore Airlines. I flew via New York to Washington for two days' sightseeing in that fine city, then across the US to San Francisco for a couple of days' sightseeing before flying via Honolulu to Hong Kong, where I had talks with Michael's partner who had bought him out, and attended a Navy Day being held in *Tamar*. I had a happy reunion with my now CPO Kwok Tim and others of the Chinese seamen and lunch with the Kadoories, but the visit was overshadowed by a phone call from Jill in London telling me of her brother Maurice's sudden death following an unsuccessful heart bypass operation at the age of 60.

270

I arrived in Singapore on the 19th to commence my main business, and stayed at the new Dynasty Hotel in Orchard Road owned by the connected store of our customer C.K. Tang. I spent a week there calling on customers, ending with a day flight to Kuala Lumpur to see customers before flying on to Colombo that evening. It was my first visit there, which the round the world ticket had made economic, and I stayed at the Mount Lavinia Hotel to the south where my parents always stayed and which I wanted to experience. It was a lovely spacious colonial relic, like Raffles in Singapore, opening onto a beautiful sandy beach, which I had little time to enjoy except on my last morning after two days calling on customers and sightseeing with our local subagent. From there I flew on to Dubai, where I checked in at the Carlton Tower overlooking the Creek. I spent three days making business calls and following up my spring visit, then on to my last port of call in Zurich before arriving home after a month on 9th November.

Naturally after a month away there were reports to write and letters to answer at the office, and then things began to ease up again as we approached Christmas, when we closed the office for a full week. January was full of preparations and assembling samples for my Middle Eastern journey, early in February, so my one-man-band salesman's life was quite a busy one. It had been quite an exceptional year, but I always had a winter visit to the Middle East, a summer one to Scandinavia and an autumn one to the Far East, and when possible a visit to Belgium and Holland, but after that first year I got into a routine and took it in my stride.

The following year, 1983, provided the additional excitement of Jonathan's wedding in Israel in July to Sara Zitcer of Haifa, whom he had met and fallen for when representing Britain at judo in the previous Maccabiah – the Jewish Olympics. Most of the family flew out for it, including Mary with Katie as a very accomplished two-and-a-half-year-old bridesmaid. Sharon, who had given birth to our first grandson Andrew in May, wisely stayed at home, but of course came to the second reception for all their English friends after they returned from their honeymoon to live here. Mary rounded off the year by giving birth to our second grandson Ian in November. Just before that I had done a short round the world flight eastabout, starting with a few days in Dubai, then Kuala Lumpur, Singapore and Brunei on business, passing through Hong Kong and Tokyo to Honolulu, crossing the Date Line to win a second Wednesday there before returning via San Francisco in three weeks. Flying eastabout non-stop from San Francisco took me several days to recover from, and I decided never to do it again.

Not to be left behind by the others, Simon was married to Rosemary Jones at Richmond Unitarian Church in April the next year, producing a full set of four weddings that have all lasted happily until today.

That August I took two days out on my Scandinavian visit for a tourist excursion to Leningrad by train from Helsinki. It was during the year's rule of the dying Chernenko, when the Iron Curtain was just beginning to bend. We had a seven-hour rail journey and put up in a characterless modern hotel overnight before a full day tour with an attractive English-speaking guide, ending with a two-hour visit to the Hermitage museum and the Winter Palace. It was a sunny warm day, and the city centre looked beautiful, but when I went out for an evening stroll I found the stores almost empty of anything worth buying, except the few little kiosks selling brooches, badges and souvenirs. Next day we made the return rail journey after contributing a significant amount to Soviet funds through our package tour fees. The year ended with a December visit to Belgium, taking the jetfoil from Dover to Ostend and visiting James Walker's main customers with our agent and friend Ignace.

At the end of March 1985 Sara and Jonathan continued the family tradition of a girl first with their daughter Danielle, and a few weeks later my mother died peacefully in her sleep just after her ninety-second birthday. My father had left his estate in trust with the income to my mother for life, so this was now divided between my brother and me, and my mother also divided her estate equally after legacies and donations. I had persuaded her to divide my half into five portions, one each to me and my children, so although I received a nice lump sum it was not enough to make any difference to our lifestyle.

Business sales were shrinking, since our agencies grew less as manufacturers closed down and it proved almost impossible to replace them. We had been selling over £100,000 a year of bri-nylon cardigans and jackets for Main of South Wigston near Leicester, whose chief market at home was the elderly, and particularly the health service and nursing homes as their robust garments were also easily washable. Indians and Pakistanis in the Middle East really liked them, both to wear and take home as gifts to their families, and as the product was unique it was a nasty shock when they decided to close down that autumn. Our lease at 91 Regent Street was running out at that time, so I decided to save the increased office rent and two hours' travel a day by moving the office into a large spare bedroom in our house. Sadly this meant parting company with our excellent typist June Pile after ten years, as it was impractical for her to reach us easily from her home in Kent, but we took on a Surbiton friend, Viv Friend, who had just retired from a secretarial job and wanted part-time work. We moved to Surbiton the week before Christmas, and ever since I have been able to go to work in my slippers!

We installed a telephone line for the office quite separate from the home number, advised everyone of the changes in advance, and business continued as previously. The only complaint was from Jill, who said that she had married me for better or worse, but not for lunch. I reckoned that in addition to the rent, I saved a day each week in travelling time, which made life easier, and I could be in central London within an hour whenever a customer wished to see me or visit a showroom.

# 21

## *Slowing Down*

I was now nearly 62 and though I was still enjoying the business, where a number of manufacturers, agents and customers had also become friends, I decided before we left Regent Street to ease up on travelling. The Far East and Scandinavia now only justified a visit every couple of years, and a once-yearly spring visit to the Gulf was sufficient in the days of fax and easy phone calls, so when Ron Smith was obliged to retire that autumn I felt confident enough to take on his administrative work. Quite a bit of it was 'belt and braces' type of confirmatory letters and paperwork left over from my father's era which I simply dispensed with.

At the end of July Rosemary and Simon had the joy of a fine son James after losing a stillborn girl, and at the end of August we celebrated the sixty-fifth wedding anniversary of Jill's parents. For their Diamond Wedding five years earlier they had held an anniversary lunch that included their best man and bridesmaids as well as the family. This was held near their home in Epsom, where they had moved into a smaller house soon after they knew they were free from the threat of our family descending again. This time Jill's brother Brian and his family hosted the party at their new home at Graffham in Sussex to which they had moved from Yorkshire.

The Great Storm of 1987 prevented Brian and Vera from returning home after a holiday abroad as all the road approaches were blocked, so they put up temporarily with their parents, while we saw our lawn completely covered with debris blown down from our trees and were fortunate to suffer no worse damage. That was on Friday 16th October, and on the Sunday Jill and I took off on a long-planned round the world flight, landing first at Seattle to visit Michael and Anne across the bay in Victoria. We had seen photographs of their architect-designed new home under construction, but were bowled over by its luxury and good taste. We spent almost a week with them, taking a day off to ferry over to Saltspring Island to stay with Sanchia and Denis Seward, who had been our neighbours in Hinchley Wood after our marriage. Victoria is the Bournemouth of Canada, a beautiful green city of lovely homes and suburbs, and Saltspring a quiet offshore island. It was good to find both couples so happily settled, though the news of the Black Monday stock market crash that week was slightly unsettling.

We flew on via Honolulu, losing the Sunday as we crossed the Date Line westward, to Fiji to visit my cousin Anne and her husband Helge Bendix, who had retired to its Pacific Harbour resort from their previous home in Melbourne. We were told to join a local flight from the main Nandi airport, and we were the only passengers on a fascinating flight along the coast where we could see the coral showing up clearly below the shoreline. We landed in a field, where Anne and Helge met us and other passengers boarded, and we were driven off to their bungalow in this relaxed holiday resort. Unfortunately General Rambuka had just launched his coup against the Indian-led government, to protect the rights of the native Fijians against the almost equal number of Indians, and though there had been no bloodshed there was a curfew from 6 p.m. This cramped our style and had hit the tourist trade, so the resort was nearly empty. We spent a very relaxed six days with them, as we already knew them well from their visits to England and stays with us, and we particularly enjoyed our pre-breakfast swims with Helge on a mile-long palm-shaded sandy beach which we had entirely to ourselves. The sea was clear, the sand unspoilt, and it was like having one's own desert island with all mod cons, including papayas fresh from the garden for breakfast.

We flew on to Auckland to stay with Mirabelle and John Sievers, our dental officer in *Tamar* whom we still keep up with, and were able to meet their children and spouses during our 36-hour stay, as well as receiving a conducted tour of Auckland with all its wonderful recreational facilities. From there we flew to Melbourne, to be met by Anne and Helge's son Axel, with whom we spent two nights and met his sisters Vivienne and Fenella and their husbands. The next day we watched the Melbourne Cup, the racing social event of the year, on TV, and took them all out for a Chinese dinner before we flew on in the morning to Sydney. There I did my first business, meeting our potential subagent to discuss prospects, which proved small due to import quotas, and took a bus tour in the afternoon to see something of the fine suburbs. In the evening we went to the famous opera house, to see that evening's only performance – an Alan Ayckbourn play *Women in Mind* presented in perfect English accents.

We flew the following morning to Perth, to stay with Alison Owen, née Hole, who had been Mary's best friend at school in Hong Kong, and her husband. They showed us Kings Park and the fine city of Perth, which was rapidly being ruined by inappropriate high-rise office blocks like jagged fangs. We looked up my distant cousin Neville Joel who had brought his family to see me aboard *Plym* on our way to Monte Bello 35 years earlier, and one of my Dartmouth term Chich Thornton, whom I had not seen for well over 40 years but who claimed to recognise me at once. We took the Owens and Alison's sister Cathy out that evening, had a swim next morning at Cottismore beach, and flew on to Singapore that afternoon. There we were put up in an executive room on the top floor of the Marina Mandarin, a newly built hotel to which we had supplied James Walker's blankets through our subagent Wong Kum Hong, whom I had come to visit. We were waited on hand and foot in this luxury hotel, to the extent of even our breakfast tea being poured for us.

Arriving on Saturday evening, we had Sunday to relax and recover before an excellent Chinese dinner with the Wongs, and a day of calls on Monday. I flew up to Kuala Lumpur on Tuesday morning by the half-hourly shuttle service for a day's visits, and back to rejoin Jill in the evening. The next day after further calls we lunched at the Tanglin Club with Sally Meyer, the sister-in-law of Mrs Nissim who used to entertain us when we had lived there, and the following day took off for Abu Dhabi, which I had intended to show Jill. I only realised just in time that she had an

Israeli stamp in her passport from Jonathan's wedding four years earlier – something I took care to avoid – and so would not be admitted under the petty Arab boycott. I therefore left her in the plane to carry on to London while I taxied on to my usual Al Ain Palace. Getting out my swimming trunks to use the pool, I discovered Jill's costume, as we had put them in plastic bags after our final swim in Singapore and somehow switched them. Fortunately I pulled them out in my room without going public! I got in a quick day's calls, then followed Jill home, to arrive on Sunday the 15th having been round the world in 28 days. The following Friday we held our Dartmouth term reunion in the Painted Hall at Greenwich, and I brought my term-mates greetings from Chich Thornton. We had cabins for the night so there were no drink-and-drive problems, and after breakfast I spent an interesting morning at the Maritime Museum on the College's doorstep. It had been a wonderful holiday, and the travel not at all tiring although we flew economy. It was the last such excursion and the only one for Jill. We were lucky to have been able to do it.

The next year we picked an October holiday out of our local free newspaper. We flew to New York for two days, followed by four days at Orlando with tickets to Disney World and the Epcot Centre, where we were much impressed by the cleanliness and the crowd control as well, of course, by the Epcot pavilions and displays. We felt ourselves a bit old for Disney World. We then flew on to Nassau for a week, but were summoned home because Jill's father, who had developed cancer, had suddenly gone downhill. We got back in time for him to recognise us before he lost consciousness. He had just passed his eighty-ninth birthday and sixty-seventh wedding anniversary, and had seen his latest great-grandchild, Rosemary and Simon's Sophie, who was born that September. The following year Sara and Jonathan followed with their son Guy, so that all four children now had a girl and a boy. Guy was born on an especially memorable day, 11th November, just as the Berlin Wall came down and the Iron Curtain crumbled.

Textile companies rarely, if ever, paid high salaries nor indeed high commission but I endeavoured to keep my salary at least level with the pay of a senior lieutenant commander, with the others in proportion, until we left Regent Street, and I ceased to draw a salary from my sixty-fifth birthday. I transferred my shares to my children and grandchildren, and gradually paid out the company reserves in dividends as a tax-efficient way of passing on these accumulated savings to my family, while I was able to enjoy my naval, government and company pensions and work as an unpaid hobby. It meant that I did not have to rely on the company for my salary, and could cut commission or otherwise adjust prices to obtain orders without having to worry how it would affect me.

We celebrated our Ruby Wedding by going on a Mediterranean cruise in the *Canberra*, boarding our floating hotel at Southampton. She took us in comfort to Port Said, where we joined the overnight excursion to Cairo to stay at the Marriott. It was the former palace built for the Empress Eugenie when she came to open the Suez Canal, and now provided the restaurants and private rooms between the two added tower bedroom blocks. I had been taken for drinks there a few years previously, when I stopped off in Cairo on my way back from Yemen to investigate business prospects with a delightful potential subagent who referred to his president as 'His Nibs'. Sadly duty was too high to do business. This time we saw *son et lumière* at the Pyramids and paid a return visit to these massive monuments next day, after an early morning visit to the Egyptian Museum to see the relics of King Tutankhamoun at our leisure. It was our first cruise, and whetted our appetite for the further cruises which we have taken.

I ruthlessly cut unnecessary travel, not visiting the Far East after our round-the-world journey until the end of 1991. Jill then joined me on a short package tour of four days in Dubai, where with her new passport she was able to see one of the more colourful Gulf cities, followed by four days in Singapore. There we saw the impressive mass transit underground system, whose perspex platform screens stop anyone falling onto the line and open exactly opposite the train doors as it comes to a halt. I saw the Wongs again, but as their good hotel business for James Walker was now our only connection they did not need regular visits from me.

I had reduced my Scandinavian visit to every third year and could still get round in a week, as having been going there since the late 1960s I knew the city centres almost as well as London. I was also now able to complete my spring Gulf visit in just ten days and finally a week, since by then everyone knew me and tended to order throughout the year, with my visit serving just to sort out problems and accept any orders they had ready.

In 1992 James Walker decided to give us a year's notice and take over their export selling themselves, for which I could not blame them, as so much of it had become tendering for government contracts where we could not usually assist and where even a small commission included for us on a £1 million quote might be enough to lose it to a rival. Just the same, we were still doing well over £100,000 a year for them and the loss of this would be a major blow. As part of the separation terms they were to pay for my spring Gulf journey the following year, when I was to take their director James Walker round the markets with me. I had known and liked him for a number of years, so this was no burden, and I had hopes, which were not fulfilled, that they might leave us with our retail customers.

I decided it was time to pass on the rest of our business while there was still a viable total to offer, and in due course reached an agreement with Andrew Watson, who had his own clothing exporting company in north London, to take over our agencies and to do the travelling and share the commission for a period as a way of buying me out. We had worked together on a few deals, having originally met through Ghanem of Yemen, with whom we both dealt, and I made my last Gulf journey in the spring of 1995.

I continued ticking over for a few hours a week, working with Andrew to explain our agencies' and customers' attitudes and requirements, but now felt that I could put 'Retired' against my profession on forms, and look forward to enjoying my retirement, my family and my interests. That family had expanded by two as first Sara and Jonathan came up with an afterthought, Tom, in mid-1995, then Rosemary and Simon with Alice at the beginning of the following year, so all the toys were brought out for another airing.

# 22

## Communal Affairs

There is a well-known Army saying about never volunteering; from the Navy I inherited the reverse. One always seemed to be doing voluntarily something beyond the letter of the job, extra instruction for someone, watching one's part of ship sporting events or even taking on an unofficial job like running a ship's newspaper or training for regattas.

It carried over into Civvy Street, and I have been involved in well over a dozen voluntary organisations since I settled in Surbiton. Probably the first was membership of the Wimbledon branch of AJEX, the Association of Jewish Exservicemen and women, which I joined as the Jewish equivalent of the Royal British Legion. It was set up after the First World War to prove that Jews had done their bit despite slanders to the contrary, and had continued after the Second for the same reason. I soon found myself on the committee, then Chairman for a number of years with an ailing Secretary, so that it involved me in quite a bit of work that I could gladly have done without.

The branch was based on Wimbledon Synagogue, of which I became a member as soon as we settled in Surbiton, since distance, travel and parking problems made it impractical to continue membership of the West London Synagogue near Marble Arch, of which I had been a member all my life. We left before Rabbi Hugo Gryn became its senior minister, but had the good fortune to have him and his wife Jacky as family friends. Both it and Wimbledon are Reform synagogues, the middle-of-the-road group which broke away from the Orthodox generations ago. Apart from our theological and ritual differences, we allow men and women to sit together and, since the 1970s have accepted female rabbis as well as male.

Our Rabbi Charles Berg as a boy in Prussia had gone to school with Bismarck's grandsons, studied in Berlin to become a rabbi, been thrown into a concentration camp and reached England as a refugee just before the war. After Army service he became a rabbi and had served the congregation for more than a dozen years. I attended one service, decided that I liked his lucid sensible sermon, and we joined. I do feel that a minister must command one's respect or one cannot fully participate, and I have been fortunate in all my rabbis despite their failings. Charles was very intelligent – his first choice had been law until the Nazis banned Jewish lawyers – broad-minded and kind. At the AGM I was asked to stand for the Synagogue Council, and found myself on it for the next 20 years. Apart from a monthly meeting, this involved attending a reasonable number of services and taking on a particular job. I acted as youth officer, before following my good friend Leslie Lawrence as Secretary and then Chairman of the Synagogue, having already succeeded him as Chairman of our AJEX branch.

I was later persuaded to join the National Council of AJEX, which worked hard but seemed to take itself rather too seriously, and from which I eventually resigned after a year and a half as Joint National Secretary over its opposition to Reform rabbinical participation in the annual remembrance service.

One other committee onto which Charles Berg lured me was the Wimbledon branch of the Council of Christians and Jews. This very worthy body was started by Archbishop William Temple during the Second World War, to counteract anti-Semitism and help Christians and Jews to recognise their common interests and morality and learn to appreciate each other's views. Recently I became the branch Chairman.

I have always been proud of and happy with my religion, where a Jew speaks to his God without any intermediary, and the fact that it has survived nearly 4,000 years in the face of hostility and persecution demonstrates its strength and appeal. However, I recognise that there are many ways to God, and have never had the arrogance to claim that it is the only true way. I am not an ultra-religious person and deplore those fundamentalists in our own and other religions who insist that theirs is the only true faith, that everything is laid down for them and that nothing can be queried or altered. I enjoy my religion, and while remembering many of its tragedies, of which the most terrible was the Holocaust, I come before my God with gladness, as the psalm says. I recognise a tendency to treat the synagogue as my religious wardroom, a social gathering of the like-minded, and was surprised when my Dartmouth term last met to learn that at least a third of them were or had been churchwardens, which I think shows a similar attitude. The cynics might call it a religious golf club syndrome, but none the worse for that, and most of the Jewish friends we have made have been through the synagogue.

Charles Berg retired just as I became Secretary so I never had the pleasure of working closely with him, only with his successor Hillel Avidan. He had been born Atkins and adopted a Hebrew name to symbolise his return to active Judaism. He had been trained at our own Progressive Leo Baeck rabbinical college in London, 'Progressive' covering both the Reform and the more radical Liberal movement. Rabbis move fairly freely between the two movements, as each congregation is autonomous and can if it wishes shift its allegiance to the other movement, or modify its services within reason. Hillel was a much younger man with wide interests and knowledge, who introduced a number of attractive new ideas such as the blessing of children on their birthdays and some modern melodies. He was also very active in the Merton Inter-Faith Group, of which I also became a member, and worked for closer understanding between the various faiths in the area.

He was rather more traditional than Charles, who just before he retired had confirmed our youngest son Simon when the custom was being phased out in favour of the traditional bar mitzvah at 13. Charles used to say, with his gentle smile, that if we conformed to the instruction to be bar mitzvah at 13, what were we going to do about the instruction to marry at 18? When David and Sharon were married in the synagogue, we had the pleasure of Charles as Rabbi Emeritus giving the address while Hillel conducted the service. The other event of my chairmanship was the

Civic Service that we arranged when the Mayor of Merton with his macebearer and the council in their robes attended our special service of thanksgiving for the Queen's Silver Jubilee.

By this time I had taken on another communal duty as one of our deputies at the Board of Deputies of British Jews. This organisation, a cross between the House of Commons and the Church Assembly except that it has no religious role, had become the community's voice to the government. It had sprung from the deputies of the two geographical branches of Jewry, the Mediterranean Sephardim and the Central European Ashkenazim, presenting a joint declaration of loyalty to King George III at his coronation, and was now made up of deputies elected by every synagogue and communal body which wished to have its voice heard. It met monthly in central London to discuss home and overseas issues affecting Jews worldwide. Every three years it dissolved for elections, after which the Deputies voted for a new President, Honorary Officers and members of committees covering a wide range of subjects from foreign affairs through education to *shechita* – the Jewish method of killing animals for food in a humane and kosher fashion. After three years I joined the Foreign Affairs Committee, and in later years the Public Relations and then the Defence – against anti-Semitism – Committee. Most committees met every month or two to keep an eye on the situation and recommend any necessary action, and their reports were considered and adopted, or occasionally amended, at the monthly meetings. One heard some excellent speakers, the best in my time being Lord Mischon of the famous solicitors, but there were many others, including Greville Janner and Ivan Lawrence, from opposing parties in the House of Commons, who worked together to fight anti-Semitism in whatever guise it appeared and to put the case for Israel in good times and bad. I spoke seldom and briefly, as I noted that many of those who spoke regularly and at length often defeated their purpose.

The organisations of the various sections of the community were represented by their own deputies at the Board, but its strength was that there were no parties as such and it spoke for the community as a whole when any religious or Jewish interest was threatened or when Israel was unfairly criticised and needed the community's support.

The Board was indomitably pro-Israel, right or wrong, when I joined, and as one who could see both sides of the question and was a stickler for accuracy, my very first speech was to point out the error in their map showing how small Israel was compared to all the Arab states in the Middle East. It was before the Yom Kippur War and showed the entire Sinai peninsula as part of Israel, when it was Egyptian territory under Israel occupation, which even the right-wing Begin gave back a few years later. A threat to the survival of the state brought all of us together whatever our religious or political views, and I was one of the thousands to give blood for Israel when the Board organised blood donors during the Yom Kippur War.

I subsequently became one of a group of deputies who published a letter in the *Jewish Chronicle* deploring the attacks on Beirut during the Israeli invasion of Lebanon, which had been launched purely to stop the attacks on Israel's northern towns. I also became the treasurer of the British Friends of Peace Now, a support group for those Israelis pressing for action to make peace with the Arabs while recognising the needs of Israel's security. In my final speech at the Board before I retired from it at the end of 1995 I emphasised that Israel would have to recognise a Palestinian state, something which has been anathema to Israel for decades but must be accepted if peace is to be achieved. By then quite a number of deputies shared my view, though we all recognised that, after half a century of mutual fear and hatred, peace would only come by slow degrees.

As a Reform Jew I was also at times involved as a Wimbledon representative in meetings of the council of the Reform Synagogues of Great Britain, and at its annual conference, which included the AGM as well as Sabbath religious services, a keynote lecture and discussion on this and the movement's future. These quasi-religious discussions with our rabbis involved were very much in the Jewish tradition of lay people and rabbis together discussing matters of concern to the whole community.

Because the Progressive communities were such a minority in Europe and Israel, as opposed to the United States, where they are the great majority, and in Britain, where they can fend for themselves, we had formed with the Americans the Friends of

Progressive Judaism in Europe and Israel to press for equal treatment for them and to provide funds to assist them with their development. Again I was lured into serving on its committee and taking my turn as its Chairman, which I was pleased to do though again it bought up time. Naturally I could not cope with all these communal activities at the same time and they were spaced out over the last three decades, as were my other non-religious activities.

I found myself eased into the chairmanship of our section of Neighbourhood Watch for several years, taking the opportunity to pass it on when I was asked to take the chair of the local Residents Association. These worthwhile jobs did not involve many meetings, but contributed to helping maintain the pleasant character of the area in which we lived. I had become a life member of the National Trust on leaving the Navy, and have enjoyed visiting their properties all over the country, so when in the early 1990s the nearby Ham House appealed for more stewards, I volunteered and have since worked there as a steward and guide about twice a month during the open season from April to October. The former home of the Duke of Lauderdale, one of Charles II's Cabal, and his Duchess, who owned it in her own right, it is probable the best-preserved Stuart house in England and a pleasure to work in with an enthusiastic group of fellow volunteers.

I suppose it is partly my interest in history which also made me a coin collector, and I became a member of the London Numismatic Club, whose meetings at Saint Brides Institute in the City I was usually able to attend each month on my way home from the office. My collection was of no great value nor ever fit to exhibit, but I enjoyed very erudite talks and interesting displays by knowledgeable members of the club and visiting experts. My interest was not sufficient to keep up my membership once I left Regent Street, when instead I joined the Kingston Philatelic Society, whose evening meetings I now had more time to attend and to enjoy their talks and displays. I had collected stamps ever since I was a boy, but without any serious specialisation or detailed knowledge until the 1970s. This developed further after I joined the society and began to display and study a few countries more seriously. I was soon persuaded to join the

285

committee and have had the pleasure recently to serve twice as their President.

On top of all these activities I enjoy keeping our garden in order, a job greatly eased by a motor mower and a large lawn on which our children and then our grandchildren loved to play. It provides me with the exercise and fresh air which others get from golf or tennis, as my talent and enthusiasm for ball games has always been more limited than that of my sons.

About ten years ago we bought a timeshare at Brantridge Park in Sussex, which serves as our country club. We can use its facilities all the year round, and in early September we relax for a week in our apartment and explore the countryside and local villages. We also take holidays and cruises abroad regularly, so do not lack interests to keep us occupied well into the future.

# 23

---

## *Cheerful and Contented*

My Dartmouth House Officer described me as 'A cheerful and contented boy' when I was 14, while his successor noted when I was 16 'He has kept cheerful and contented'.

Maybe these were and have continued to be my main characteristics, though I was considered very young for my age, which nowadays I regard as a great advantage. Thank heavens I have always remained cheerful, as though occasionally I do feel depressed it is never long-lasting. It is also difficult not to feel contented with my life when I consider how much worse it could have been, but as a corollary I recognise that my failings have been limited ambition and initiative.

I have always been a hard worker and never shirked my responsibilities, but must admit that I can be impractical and lack imagination. I have been too easygoing to be more successful either in the Navy or in business, due to a distaste for naked ambition, which is so often needed for ultimate success in the absence of genius.

However, in its place I have been blessed with tremendous luck and pleasure in my life. I do not believe in miracles, but I have come physically unscathed through war and peacetime incidents where a small difference could have snuffed me out. If the land-mine next door or *Scharnhorst*'s shells had exploded or my overturned car had not landed safely I would probably not be writing this. For an immature young man I made a most fortunate and successful marriage with a wonderful, compassionate and intelligent wife whom I have grown to love and appreciate more every year.

We have four fine healthy children of whose character and progress we can be proud, who have all achieved happy marriages, and have produced ten delightful grandchildren in whom we can see glimpses of our parents, who gave us so much love and support in earlier years.

Most of all we have been spared the undeserved tragedies which have struck a number of our friends, so as I enter retirement still cheerful and contented I can claim good reason for being so, and thank all my family and friends who have made this possible.